THE CREATIVE DISCIPLINE

THE CREATIVE DISCIPLINE

Mastering the Art and Science of Innovation

Nancy K. Napier and Mikael Nilsson

Westport, Connecticut
London

Library of Congress Cataloging-in-Publication Data

Napier, Nancy K., 1952–
    The creative discipline : mastering the art and science of innovation /
Nancy K. Napier and Mikael Nilsson.
        p. cm.
    Includes bibliographical references and index.
    ISBN 978–0–275–99884–4 (alk. paper)
    1. Creative ability in business. 2. Technological innovations. I. Nilsson,
Mikael, 1967– II. Title.
    HD53.N365 2008
    658.4′063—dc22   2008009960

British Library Cataloguing in Publication Data is available.

Library of Congress Catalog Card Number: 2008009960
ISBN: 978–0–275–99884–4

First published in 2008

Praeger Publishers, 88 Post Road West, Westport, CT 06881
An imprint of Greenwood Publishing Group, Inc.
www.praeger.com

Printed in the United States of America

∞™

The paper used in this book complies with the
Permanent Paper Standard issued by the National
Information Standards Organization (Z39.48–1984).

10   9   8   7   6   5   4   3   2   1

For Chase and Quinn, who are creating their own worlds

—NKN

For Bea and Malin, my patient darlings

—MN

For Stephan Zinser (1964–2006), our coauthor in spirit

In September 2006, Stephan Zinser died, along with his wife Gabriele and two young sons, Maximilien and Paul. In addition to this book project, which he helped design, he had several other projects in the works—ranging from an edited book of corporate experiences with workplace flexibility, to a residency program for masters students in Dresden to study abroad, to joint cross-border academic courses. With his tragic death, we assumed those projects would dissolve.

But Stephan has a strong spirit. His projects have been completed or continue to thrive, perhaps not in the same shape he would have imagined, but we hope in a form that would make him proud.

We dedicate this book to him.

—NKN and MN

CONTENTS

Acknowledgments

I continue to be amazed and grateful for people who help books come to life. Thanks to so many of you.

First, I appreciate very much the willingness of the organizations I visited to allow me to learn from them. So many people—from those in the theatre to high tech, health information to football—provided their time and insights. I still can't explain what a running back does or what "going zone" means, but at least now I know something about how football coaches and players think creatively!

My ever upbeat graduate assistants, Serena Bergonzi, Larissa Lee, and Kengo Usui, played detective, found great streams of ideas, and allowed me to pick their brains about creativity and innovation for long hours.

Patti Fredericksen, John Gardner, Jim Munger, Julie Oxford, and Jack Pelton, colleagues at Boise State University, humored me through patient explanations of their disciplines, from biology and geophysics to political science and mechanical engineering.

Jana Kemp, Cheryl Larabee, and Suzie Lindberg helped me wrestle through metaphors that made no sense, and then did.

Caroline Blakeslee generated scores of ideas on our morning runs. The members of St. Ogg's and MHC-Boise accepted with grace my curious connections between literature and creativity.

Alma Fisk has put up with my absentminded-professor life for more years than either of us would admit, and always has the right comment to bring me back to earth.

My father continues to exude more ideas in a year than most of us will hope to achieve in a lifetime. He and my brother, Bill Napier, put meat on the "disciplines" and the "aces" long before it was clear what they were.

Thanks again and always to my husband, Tony Olbrich, who once more "made it" through another period of creative slogging! Bewildered, but always encouraging, maybe one day he'll write his own book and understand "why."

Nancy Napier

You, readers of all kinds and shapes, have been a constant reminder of what we have been searching for and trying to communicate. Creativity and innovation are inspiring topics and many have been spurring us on, asking questions and inquiring as to what we say and do—all inspiring.

Now I am happy you have picked up this book and started to think about creativity and innovation. I think it will be a great experience for you, as it has been writing this book. Enjoy! And, thank you.

This book would have been nothing without the organizations we have met. For me, Cirkus Cirkör gave everything. You let me in on the experiences, the knowledge, and the hard-earned truths you have. I really appreciate all the good and inspiring discussions we have had, and will have, around creativity and how to develop it. Thank you so much.

This book would never have seen the light if it were not for my coauthor who has driven this idea all along and who has been a great coauthor, on this and many other pieces. Thank you, Nancy. Jeff Olson patiently guided us through this book. This has been a difficult process, and never a harsh word. The book is so much better for it too.

The book has evolved through a number of discussions with researchers battling with the same issues: the Oxford Space group, the people at Vinnova, and the individuals in the advisory groups that have given me perspective on this area in Sweden and globally, and numerous others at conferences and meetings in the fields of creativity. Colleagues at the Knowledge Foundation that have especially contributed to the thinking in this book and the connection to development of knowledge, competence, and competitive advantage are Carin Daal, Stina Algotson, Olle Vogel, and Daniel Holmberg. I am happy for everything you've shared. Thank you to the Knowledge Foundation for funding a portion of my time and travel in this project.

My family has been with me all along. You are always there. Uncomprehending (for most of the time) as to why I do this, you have still supported me along the way. Thank you also to my great friends—Henrik, Fredrik, Jonas, and Daniel. It is a gift to have people like you with whom I can discuss complex issues.

Finally, thank you to Malin and Bea, who have given me the time and always patiently waited for me to finish. This time it was harder, and you've given more than ever. Thank you!

Mikael Nilsson

Introduction: Quarterbacks, Play Actors, and Engineers

If you can dream it, you can do it.

Walt Disney

Football Magic

For fans at the Fiesta Bowl in Phoenix, Arizona, on New Year's Day, January 2007, it was a day of nail biting and magic. A crowd of over 70,000 fans watched as David beat Goliath in what some reporters have called one of the greatest American football games in U.S. history. A team known more for its wacky blue football turf than for its undefeated record and high-scoring receiver, Boise State University surprised football fans with its smashing, overtime victory against a long-winning and powerful University of Oklahoma. The much smaller, little-known team gained much of its notoriety with plays that many commentators thought were unusual, wildly difficult to achieve, and risky—in a word, creative.

Boise State University's football program has historically been known as an underdog compared to other Division I programs, lagging in funding and resources. Its players are often less sought after and smaller in size and weight. The coaches have had to find creative ways to gain competitive advantage in training, inspiring players, and generating effective plays.

They must have found something that works.

In 2006, the Boise State team finished ranked fifth in the country after the stunning 43 to 42 overtime victory against Oklahoma, one of the most successful college football programs in history. Foxsports.com's Michael Rosenberg captured the Idaho team's spirit: "Creative play calling dominates bowl season ... [as] Boise State used everything in their playbook, including the game winning Statue of Liberty play."[1]

Yet to make that creativity work, the coaches have to mix it with something that seems just the opposite: hard work and discipline—creative discipline.

Cheeky Circus

In 1995 a group of independent circus artists in Sweden had the bold self-confidence and cheekiness to set about changing the world. As they expressed it: "Tired of dreaming big and living on a small scale, we decided to go for broke and make the dream a reality." From that time, the group has expanded rapidly to have an impact far beyond Sweden. Cirkus Cirkör has taken on challenges at places and in directions the initial group never could have imagined. Today, Cirkus Cirkör is focused on creative performances, playing in Sweden and abroad. In addition, it offers training courses for corporations and schools, tours in Sweden and abroad, and is internationally recognized as a leader in contemporary circus education. The group even trains ski acrobats!

In the show "99% Unknown," Cirkus Cirkör brought together world-renowned brain researchers, neurosurgeons, and circus artists to create a show that blends the magic of the human body and the elements—both scientific and artistic—that make it work. Finally, the group has had a dramatic impact on the physical environment in which it works. Cirkus Cirkör's main office, training ground, and staging area have transformed its local environment, one that went from being filled with troubled youth and crime to a place where opportunities are increasingly possible.

Cirkör works with a mentor from the famed Cirque du Soleil, a company that employs over 3,000 people, stages five shows in Las Vegas, and contributes to what has become an important export industry for Canada. From its humble beginnings, Cirkör today employs 300 people who work in an industry that was unheard of ten years ago. It is on the verge of its next stage. The group is reaching dreams it imagined years ago, because of effort and discipline—creative discipline.

Software "Throat Grabbers"

When you rent a movie, how long do you watch it at home before you decide to stop watching because you don't like it? Ten minutes? Fifteen? "Testing out" a film is similar to "testing out" a piece of software. When the typical software user tries out a new piece of software, how long does she give it before deciding to learn it or return it?

At least one software CEO, whose firm produces very complex business-analysis software, knows the answers. The movie industry figures that viewers will stay with a film for 10 percent of the total length of the film, typically from 10 to 12 minutes. A potential software user may give it just 1 to 2 minutes.

So how, wondered Bob Lokken, CEO of ProClarity (now a part of Microsoft), could his firm learn to grab users by the throat just like a great movie does, and hold them captive for 100 or 120 minutes?

The CEO found some answers when he mixed research with discipline—creative discipline.

Automated Parking ... in Vietnam?

A young entrepreneur in Hanoi, Vietnam, has become one of the country's first builders of automated parking garages. Cars? Automated garages? In Vietnam?

In the years following "the American War," which ended in April 1975, Vietnam faced yet another crisis. The Soviet Union, its major trading partner, collapsed, and Vietnam struggled to survive, as regional neighbors like Thailand and China became stronger. But during the early 1990s, the government adopted market-based economic policies, began to train managers in business practices to compete globally, and unleashed entrepreneurs to pursue business opportunities.[2]

One entrepreneur runs a small firm that carries out specialized construction projects. Over the years, the founder's knowledge of soil conditions and how to build foundations in Vietnam has given him a competitive advantage that foreigners cannot replicate. He watched Hanoi's many traffic changes and anticipated the potential need for garages. In the early 1990s, there were few automobiles, only bicycles and a few motorbikes. By 2008, the vehicle mix reached at least 40 percent automobiles. Many of the autos were taxis, but, increasingly, private cars now barrel through the streets. However, Hanoi's streets are narrow, motorbikes zip in and out of them, and auto drivers are often inexperienced. People need space to park cars. Many drivers are still unfamiliar with the idea of parking in tight spots, however, and the entrepreneur saw the potential need for automated parking long before others did, as a way to reduce fender benders and solve a space problem.

The CEO recognized that an idea more common in other countries (automatic, robot parking) could be useful in Vietnam. He figured out a way to build automated garages given the poor infrastructure and limited space availability in Vietnamese cities. The firm has now built several garages, adapted to Vietnam's conditions.

How did the entrepreneur anticipate and then participate in such changes? In part, because he mixed knowledge with discipline—creative discipline.

Disciplines and More

Despite the quite different industry sectors they inhabit, these organizations are winners in their fields, in part because of similar and dedicated approaches and attitudes affecting creativity and innovation. These organizations represent what we have found as we have studied and worked to understand *how creative organizations work.*

First, the organizations blend and exploit the critical links between creativity and innovation and three types of discipline. Second, such creative organizations also appear to systematically mesh the three disciplines with other factors—people, locations, and catalytic efforts. These factors, which we call faces, places, and traces, enhance their ability to be effective at creativity and innovation, at a given time.

Interestingly enough, each of the organizations also seems to be "on the fringe," geographically, as well as in their attitudes. Most are outside what many would call creative hotbeds. Yet, these organizations find that "being on the fringe" can force an attitude of seeking creative ways to stand apart. In such an environment, they fight harder to prove they can succeed against stronger or better known competitors. Being on the "edge" of most action also allows for much experimenting and progress before others, especially competitors, realize what innovation is going on.

Creativity and discipline are two terms we will be returning to often in this book. We define creativity as "the development of new or novel ideas, appropriate for their context, that have value."[3] This definition seems to resonate with the people in organizations we have worked with. Discipline is the other recurring theme in this book. First, it refers to an area of knowledge and competence, a discipline, that members of an organization need and develop over time (within-discipline expertise). Second, it embraces the openness to ideas that members need to foster creativity (out-of-discipline thinking). Finally, it includes a systematic approach, or disciplined process, to generating, testing, and using ideas. Together, they comprise creative discipline.

Are these organizations unusual? Not in obvious ways. They are in industries that have experienced successes and failures, and the organizations themselves have had their ups and downs. They are mid-sized; they have generally limited budgets compared with many of their competitors. On closer examination, however, the organizations are unusual in subtle and important ways that are hard to recognize and often more difficult to replicate.

WHY THIS BOOK?

The biggest threat to the U.S. economy is lack of creativity … it's really a question of innovate or die.

Ray Bingham, CEO, Cadence Design Systems

Bingham is not alone in calling for organizations to "innovate or die." From consultant Tom Peters to Google's "innovate or die" contest for a new pedal machine, innovation is in the news. In addition, the shrillness of recent discussions about flat and spiky worlds forces us to turn our heads, partly to move away from the sharp sounds and partly to move toward things that appear to make organizations creative and innovative.

Our Creative Work Needs to Start

So why another book on creativity and innovation? One reason is that some people seem more ready to listen and learn about how to enhance creativity and innovation. Some people argue that "creativity is for children," or only for certain types of fields, like art or music. We think it can happen—and should happen—just about anywhere, even in unexpected places and sectors. So, this book is for those people ready to listen and start moving.

The current hype and general consensus on the importance of creativity is not transformed into action as much as one would hope for, and certainly seldom with the zeal of successful creative organizations. This is partly because many have not understood the profound impact creativity will have on their organizations, which chapter 1 describes. It is also partly because the step between knowing something is wrong and starting to address it is sometimes very long and hard.[4] Using a variety of examples, this book strives to show how to transform "knowing" into "doing," in your organization. It is not easy, but it's worth it.

The Creative Art and Discipline

When we started our investigation of organizations, we chose ones that seemed to be at opposite ends of a continuum of art and science: theatre and software engineering. How could they be more different: actors who talk about "creating a character"; engineers who focus on logic and analysis. And yet, we were surprised to learn how much they had in common about approaches to creativity and innovation.

Then came sports.

A couple of years ago, Nancy learned that one of her students was a kicker for the Boise State football team. To support the student, she started watching the games. During several games, the ESPN and CNN reporters made comments like "What a risky move!" and "Did you see that creative play? We just don't see things like that!"

Her reaction: "Creativity, in sports? In *football*?"

So, rather than focus on a single sector like business or the arts, we examined organizations in what appear to be widely differing fields—from the arts to engineering, from sports to consumer services. We looked at organizations in the public, not-for-profit and profit-making sectors. We talked with people from the Nordic countries of Sweden and Finland, to people in Germany and Austria, and in England and Ireland. We talked to people in Asia and the United States. In all, we spoke with more than 250 people, in over fifty organizations, and enjoyed learning from all of them.

Part of our surprise and delight has been uncovering systematic approaches to nurture creativity and innovation, whether from circus directors or gas utility managers, special teams football coaches or software engineers. But it's one thing to say that creativity can exist in a variety of sectors; it's another to find that systematic and consistent focus on finding ways to enhance such endeavors. And that appears to be part of what separates some of the stronger and more creative organizations.

As we came to know several organizations, we realized one of their common themes was "discipline," which emerged in a variety of ways. In contrast to people who think creativity is chaotic, has no rational approach, and thus is hard to manage or control, members of the organizations we looked at insist that at least three types of discipline are critical for success. For them, those disciplines become fundamental to how they create and develop new ideas that thrive. They are *within-discipline expertise, out-of-discipline thinking,* and having a *disciplined process* for creativity and innovation. The organizations also showed a common thread in the environment, what we call the "aces"—*faces, places,* and *traces*—that support creative and innovative endeavors.

In addition, during our discussions, we found a mix of "art and science" in the execution of activities. Members within organizations talked of the art and science of both the disciplines and the "aces": there was logic and structure to the creative and innovative activities, but within each organization, members acknowledged a less tangible, more artful aspect. A football coach who often receives requests from reporters, other team coaches, and fans who want to know "what makes the team work" is happy for them to observe and learn all about the "pieces." He doesn't fear that the "secrets" will be taken, because he knows that it is the art of putting them all together, designing and delivering them, that makes the entire organization work. And that comes from having a fully operating system of disciplines and "aces." Management scholar Gary Hamel puts it another way: "It's also tough for rivals to replicate advantages that are *systemic,* that encompass a web of individual innovations spanning multiple management processes."[5]

Finally, we realized that being "on the fringe" also seemed to matter. While many wonderful examples of creativity exist in some larger organizations, like Apple or Nokia or Sony, we were intrigued with the organizations and locations that are on the fringes, out of the way and perhaps not as well known, places like Boise, Idaho, Stockholm, Sweden, and Hanoi, Vietnam. Indeed, several leaders of the organizations we worked with commented that being on the fringe was a factor in their ability to be creative. Because they were small and out of the mainstream, some competitors did not really take them seriously. One CEO felt his firm could operate "behind the mountain," out of the way of prying competitors, before they had any idea of what new products his company had coming onto the market. Likewise, following the Boise State football Fiesta Bowl win, numerous people called or wrote asking, "where did this team come from, out of the blue?"[6]

So why this book?

For its focus on the *disciplines* and "*aces*" or environment critical for creativity and innovation.

For its focus on *unexpected organizations*—from business to circus to sports—as hotspots for creativity and innovation.

For its focus on *art and science*—in sectors—and art and science in how the organizations approached their creativity and innovation activities.

And, finally, for its focus on *the fringe*—locations and organizations—as fodder for creative and innovative endeavors.

LAYOUT OF THE BOOK

We've divided the book into three major sections: The Context, Disciplines, and "Aces." The Context in part I, chapters 1 and 2, sets the stage for the importance of creativity and innovation and lays out the key concepts of the book. Chapter 2 provides an overview of the six factors that we found in the organizations we investigated.

In part II, the 3D's or three Disciplines are the focus for each chapter. Chapter 3 examines within-discipline expertise and mastery and its benefits to enhancing creative and innovative efforts. Chapter 4 focuses on out-of-discipline thinking: the ability to bridge, blend, or transfer ideas from one field or discipline to another to generate ideas or solve problems. Chapter 5 looks at the disciplined processes that organizations use to come up with ideas, experiment and test them, and carry them out. The basic processes are remarkably similar across types of organizations, yet the amount of time they devote to various stages and the ways groups collaborate within organizations do appear to vary.

Part III covers the three "Aces," the factors in organizations that create an environment or surroundings that can enhance or inhibit creativity and innovation. Chapter 6 discusses three "faces" or roles critical to such activities: the creative entrepreneur, the creative leader, and the creative team. Chapter 7 covers the spaces: the organizational and physical infrastructures that come into play, from the layout of buildings and office space, to the organizational arrangements that support interaction among groups in and out of organizations. We also look at some of the ways creative regions and communities on the fringe are seeking to build their capacities to allow and promote flourishing creative and innovative activity. Chapter 8 focuses on what we call *traces*, as in trace elements. Trace elements, like their biochemical counterparts, represent the catalysts in an organization that enhance and support creativity and innovation. Sometimes they are quite subtle, nearly microscopic, or invisible; and sometimes they are artifacts. We talk about three types of catalysts or trace elements: (1) trace elements for environment (culture); (2) trace elements for practice (human resource policies); and (3) trace elements for connection (networks in and out of organizations).

Finally, we conclude with chapter 9, which brings up the big picture again: focusing on creativity and innovation as a competitive advantage for organizations, communities, and countries.

Now let us move on to discuss the creative myopia that is holding back our development.

NOTES

1. See, for example, articles about the rankings and the game: 2006 College Football Rankings—Week 17 AP Top 25 Ranking, http://sports.espn.go.com/ncf/rankingsindex; Fox Sports on MSN, http://msn.foxsports.com/cfb/story/6350780.

2. Vietnam initiated policies of *doi moi*, or market renovation, in 1986, but they really took hold starting in the early 1990s. The challenges facing managers, both local and foreign, in such transition economies are documented in several books and articles. See, for example, Nancy K. Napier and David C. Thomas. 2004. *Managing Relationships in Transition Economies.* Westport, CT: Praeger.

3. The three-part definition—novel idea, fits context, and has value—has been around for many years. Several scholars have used it repeatedly, most recently and perhaps most emphatically Robert Sternberg, former Yale professor, now Dean of Arts and Sciences at Tufts University. For example, Robert J. Sternberg (Ed.). 1999. *Handbook of Creativity.* Cambridge: Cambridge University Press; others include Herbert Simon, "Understanding Creativity and Creative Management," in Robert L. Kuhn (Ed.). 1988. *Handbook for Creative and Innovative Managers.* New York: McGraw-Hill: 11–24; Teresa M. Amabile. 1996. *Creativity in Context.* Boulder, CO: Westview.

4. An interesting argument on this dilemma and ways to address it is made in Jeffrey Pfeffer and Robert I. Sutton. 2000. *The Knowing-Doing Gap: How Smart Companies Turn Knowledge into Action.* Boston: Harvard Business School Press.

5. Gary Hamel's latest book argues for innovation as a fundamental approach to the discipline of management itself. See Gary Hamel. 2007. *The Future of Management.* Boston: Harvard Business School Press. A similar argument is made by Jan Rivkin and Nicolaj Siggelkow, who have addressed this question using a combination of complexity theory and longitudinal case studies. See, for example, Nicolaj Siggelkow. 2001. "Change in the Presence of Fit: The Rise, the Fall, and the Renaissance of Liz Claiborne." *Academy of Management Journal* 44:838–857; Jan W. Rivkin and Nicolaj Siggelkow. 2003. "Balancing Search and Stability: Interdependencies among Elements of Organizational Design." *Management Science* 49:290–311.

6. In fact, a documentary called "Out of the Blue," about the Boise State team and its surprising season, was released in September 2007.

Part I

THE CONTEXT FOR CREATIVITY AND INNOVATION

Underlying the seeming differences between science and magic are more similarities than you might imagine. Both disciplines rely on a process sparked by mystery and nurtured by curiosity.

Albert Einstein

Some people hear "creativity" and think of artists or chaos or wild ideas that appear by chance. We once mentioned the possible value of creativity to a German professor, who shrugged and said, "Kinderspiel (child's play). Creativity is for children. Why should companies worry about creativity?"

But as Einstein suggested, science and magic are similar mysteries, nurtured by curiosity. Good for artists, maybe for scientists, but what about organizations? Why should they be concerned about creativity and innovation?

In fact, organizations that ignore creativity and innovation may do so at their own risk. Throughout this book, we'll talk about reasons why it's important for organizations to make creative and innovative thinking and activity part of their culture. Some quite successful organizations from wildly different sectors are doing just that.

In the introduction we gave examples of organizations that pursue creativity and innovation in ways that some see as odd, but they are remarkably disciplined in the ways they approach it.

Chapter 1 outlines trends and factors that we hope convince you that something needs to be done. The aim is to set the stage for the subsequent chapters, and urge thoughtful leaders and successful managers in organizations, communities, and countries to boost their creativity and innovation efforts.

Chapter 2 gives an overview of the basic framework that we have developed to understand what factors creative organizations have in common. In addition, creativity and discipline are defined and described, as key concepts throughout the book.

Chapter 1

CREATIVITY MYOPIA

The level of [a country's] dynamism is a matter of how fertile the country is in coming up with innovative ideas having prospects of profitability, how adept it is at identifying and nourishing the ideas with the best prospects, and how prepared it is in evaluating and trying out the new products and methods that are launched onto the market.

Edmund S. Phelps, 2006 Nobel Laureate

During an executive MBA session, we once presented the arguments that Edmund Phelps makes regarding links between creativity and economic dynamism.[1] Heads nodded, and people slumped back in their chairs. Yes, of course, said their body language. That's what the United States does, better than any other country in the world. What's the big deal about that?

The instructor then presented data that challenged the assumption that the United States dominates in creativity and innovation. The twenty-eight participants in the room sat forward, wrinkled their brows, and shook their heads. They were bright individuals, each with over ten years of managerial experience. Many had traveled and worked globally, in high-tech firms, as well as at companies in energy production, bioscience and agriculture, and in fields like insurance, construction and housing, and environmental consulting. No one worked in an industry unaffected by global influences. But they just didn't buy the notion that the United States could be declining in its creative powers. Their comments were similar to others that come up in discussions like this one.

"How can the U.S. be in trouble? We have more patents and Nobel prize winners than anyone."

"Just about all of the world's biggest companies are here."

"Look at Apple. Look at the entertainment business. We're slamming the world."

"We still start a lot of companies. Maybe more than lots of other countries."

Finally, Ben Slaughter, a reserved young lawyer, spoke up from the back of the room. "You know, if *we* aren't willing to question whether we need to do anything differently for our companies or this country, who will?"

Silence.

Are we being shortsighted?

Could we be facing creativity myopia?

In recent years, while other countries systematically have built more creativity and innovation into their education systems, their organizations, and their communities, many in the United States are less alarmed. Bob Lokken, CEO of software firm ProClarity (purchased by Microsoft) calls it the "fish in water syndrome." Because the United States has always led the world in creativity and innovation, because American culture celebrates new startups and entrepreneurs, because risk taking and failure are part of the norm, the United States has been less aggressive about explicitly addressing the need to focus on creativity and innovation. It's part of the built-in assumption about who and what the United States has been and is, as a country. As Lokken puts it, "Americans may not see what's changing around us, just like a fish in water"—just like some of those smart executive MBA participants. But is there a drought coming?

Edmund Phelps pinpoints key factors that affect a country's willingness and ability to engage the attitudes and activities that can exploit the benefits of original ideas. He is optimistic about the United States because we still encourage creative thinking and consumers still seem willing to try new products. But as other countries change, where will we be then? Can we react fast enough?

Such watershed books as Thomas Friedman's *The World Is Flat*, Shoshana Zuboff's *The Support Economy*, and Richard Florida's *The Flight of the Creative Class* dramatically illustrate and track the way the fish's water and centers of gravity are shifting.[2] Economic principles that we thought were fixed are in flux: the centers of economic gravity have changed from primarily agriculture to manufacturing, to service, and to knowledge-based economies, with a recent twist toward idea-based creativity and innovation. For countries, communities, and organizations worldwide, this means a gradual shift in resource bases from more tangible resources, like land, labor, capital, or technology, to less tangible ones, such as knowledge, creativity, and innovative capabilities.[3]

The shift means that some regions that were considered slow to develop economically may move faster in the future and even become powerhouses themselves, perhaps even before the rest of the world is aware of what is taking place. In some cases, their heritage means that the infrastructural and cultural changes needed are less drastic, giving them the opportunity to start a new trajectory. We're seeing inklings from China, South Korea, and India. Other countries are likely not far behind. On the first trip Nancy made to Vietnam in the early 1990s, a Vietnamese colleague greeted her with an astounding statement: "We conquered the Americans in the war. Now we will conquer the Americans in business." At the time, the man owned a bicycle, two changes of clothing, and his belt was wrapped one-and-a-half times around his waist, to the middle of his back, because he was so slender. He knew nothing of business, management, marketing, or any other "Western" business concepts. Indeed, the Vietnamese language has few words for those terms. The university of 20,000 students had one flush toilet, for the foreigners who worked there, and a single fax machine. Yet, fifteen years later, the same man—and many of his counterparts—owns a house, is a leader in his university, travels, and has received his doctoral degree. The courage, determination, and moxie the Vietnamese showed even when they were very poor goes to the heart of the concern for the United States' leadership in creativity today.

Avoiding creativity myopia also means recognizing creativity and innovation as contributors to competitive advantage for both developed and developing countries, the role that creative talent plays in building that advantage, and the threats to building and retaining such talent. For the United States, long considered a creative juggernaut, such shifts represent a silent but growing threat to its strength in creativity and innovation worldwide. And the transition might not come easily. Richard Florida, speaking in Stockholm, even suggests that the perceived width between the industrial society and the emerging "knowledge-based" society is creating such a frightening perspective that the pull towards the *status quo* is all the more violent. That is one reason we see a resurgence of strong traditional values, extreme religious expressions, and the excessive use of military and police power in some nations.[4]

SHIFTING CENTERS OF GRAVITY: WHY WORRY?

Recent reports have raised a clarion call about the shifting positions of countries' and regions' levels of innovation and what this might mean for economic development. The president of the Council on Competitiveness, Deborah Wince-Smith, comments that while the United States faced almost no competition in innovation during the 1980s, it should no longer expect to hold the lead indefinitely. The United States has only 5 percent of the world's population, but employs almost one third of all science and engineering researchers, and its researchers publish 35 percent of scientific articles worldwide. But, she warns, "our lead is narrowing."[5]

Disparate, yet increasingly visible, trends confirm that shifting centers of gravity are likely. A single factor is perhaps insignificant; taken together they are a wake-up call. Other countries have responded proactively, yet there is much more to be done. A few of the trends follow.

The "Quiet Crisis"

Shirley A. Jackson, president of Rensselaer Polytechnic Institute and former president of the American Academy for the Advancement of Science, has spoken repeatedly of an impending "quiet crisis" in the United States.[6] She fears that the United States' leadership position in science, engineering, and innovation will erode, if not addressed. The "quiet nature" of the crisis suggests that the environment is changing slowly enough that few may notice or react to it in time, like the familiar story about the frog who won't jump out of a pot of water that is slowly coming to a boil.[7] Jackson likewise has said that the quiet crisis she fears is evolving so slowly that many policy makers, business people, and educators have not picked up on it. She predicts that, without action, the United States will face a crisis of education, numbers, and ambition within the decade.

A basis for this argument is that science and technology are key drivers of creativity, innovation, and competitiveness in an economy. While the overall message—that there is a quiet crisis stifling creative action—holds true, we will also argue that it is equally, if not more, important to energize other types of innovation and creativity.

The Crisis of Education

Jackson's "crisis of education" stems from poor performance in math and science by American students at the secondary school level, compared to other high school students worldwide.[8] Furthermore, fewer American students are choosing to study math and science, particularly at the more advanced levels, in both high school and college.

Chief executive officers of companies in many U.S. states have recognized the need for skilled and educated workers for their firms' future performance. In fact, in nearly all U.S. states, CEOs have formed groups to advocate for improvements in education. For example, one area that CEOs in the Idaho Business Coalition for Educational Excellence focus on is improving the quantity and rigor of math and science at the high school level. This is especially important given the number of high-tech firms, such as Hewlett-Packard and Micron, that have major facilities or headquarters in Idaho.

In addition to formal education, an increasing need is emerging for on-the-job training and other ways to guarantee that countries have access to a skilled workforce for long-term economic vitality in all sizes and types of organizations. Sweden, for example, has begun to formally encourage young people to enter skilled employment jobs that were previously perceived as having less value or interest.[9]

Convincing some legislators, especially in the United States, of the value of education, however, can sometimes be an uphill struggle. One (shocked) CEO encountered a legislator who claimed that the education he received in high school, in the 1950s, was good enough for him, and should be good enough for his kids. Why change?

The CEO's response to the legislator, who was from a rural area of the state, was to use an analogy with agriculture, since the legislator was also a farmer. The CEO argued that what water is for agriculture, education is for the economic vitality of a state. The same CEO, originally from a rural state himself, commented that his grandfather's eighth-grade education enabled him to be a successful farmer and fix farm equipment; his father's high school education allowed him to become an auto mechanic. And the CEO's engineering degree gave him the opportunity to work for a global high-tech firm and eventually to build his own company. If the CEO's grandfather had the attitude of the legislator, the CEO would still be fixing farm equipment, not building a firm that today competes globally and employs many people. It is also unlikely he would have received the several patents he holds.

The Crisis of Numbers

Jackson argues throughout her many speeches that engineering and science are the lifeblood professions of innovations in technology and science, where the United States has long excelled. But she predicts that without more attention, the country simply will lack the numbers of scientists and engineers that an innovative economy demands.

Three factors come into play. First, as baby boomer engineers and scientists retire in the next ten to fifteen years, who will replace them? With fewer students studying math and science and, of those who do, fewer able to perform well, Jackson anticipates a lack of capable people to conduct future innovation, research, and development efforts.

Second, the discrepancy in numbers may be covered (and has been in the past) through immigrants—short and long term. The United States continues to excel in graduate programs worldwide, in certain research areas, and as a result has attracted top candidates from developing countries as graduate students for years. So far, many have stayed. This "brain drain" to the United States, however, may be reversing. Today, these trained and experienced engineers and scientists from developing and emerging countries increasingly return to their home countries to exploit opportunities there, whether in academic institutions or the private sector.[10] Others never leave. Countries such as India are providing stronger educational opportunities, reducing the need to seek education abroad.

Third, visa and immigration policies in America since September 2001 now confuse and frustrate employers and potential immigrants. This may also contribute to the "numbers crisis." Some argue that availability and difficulty of obtaining visas for foreigners makes the United States less attractive as a place to study and work. For a country built by immigrants over the last 250 years, the year following September 2001 marked a dramatic change in attitude toward and number of immigrants entering the United States. The administration reacted with a zeal that has had lasting impacts. In the year following September 11, 2001, alone, the number of science and technology-related visas issued by the United States was less than half—falling from 166,000 in 2001 to 74,000 in 2002.[11]

Visa restrictions have become a problem even in the mild world of academics. Many American professors have encountered difficulties in securing visas for Chinese colleagues to attend meetings or conferences. European and Australian colleagues have boycotted conferences in the United States rather than face the unpleasant entry requirements of finger printing and photographing. Even though visa restrictions have eased somewhat since 2006, they remain a sore spot and contributor to the "numbers crisis."

The Crisis of Ambition

Finally, Jackson's most damning challenge—and hardest to solve—is the "crisis of ambition." One of us experienced firsthand what Jackson fears, during several years spent working in Vietnam.[12]

One day one of us went alone to lunch at the university's canteen. The seating was wooden stools, low enough that any Westerner's knees would come to chest level. The rickety table's plastic tablecloth was speckled with rice from earlier eaters.

That day a third-year student stopped by the table. "May I sit? To practice English?"

"Of course. What are you studying?"

"I learn accounting, to be a teacher. To teach at the university."

In the early 1990s, university teachers made $40/month; foreign firms, hungry for well-trained, English-speaking Vietnamese accounting graduates, paid $500/month. Why teach when an accountant could earn more than 10 times that much in Vietnam?

"I want to be a teacher," he said again. "I will help students learn about market economics. That is good for my country. I can help Vietnam become strong if I am a teacher. If I work for a foreign firm, I help myself only."

Most professors in the United States would be hard pressed to remember the last time American students had talked of pursuing careers that would help anyone beyond themselves or their families. But this young Vietnamese man, who was not unique, sought a career that would pay little but had a bigger payoff.

A year later, another student in an MBA program had bigger dreams, as he explained at a party one night:

> We must change our country [Vietnam]. We must learn how to compete. We are the generation to bring capitalism to Vietnam. I work for a European bank, so I can learn from foreigners. I get training and make money. After my MBA, I want to work some time more for a foreign firm. Later, I will start my own company so I can hire other Vietnamese

people. I know I must work hard, even harder and more than I work at the bank. Also, I want to get a Ph.D. and a position at a university. Then, I can still do my company work on the side.

He has almost fulfilled his dream. He got his MBA, worked for another global bank, and received his Ph.D. from a European university. But, he did not just start a company; he has built not one, but four companies.

No crisis of ambition there.

The ambition issue is a great task to take on as a nation: "How can we create motivated and ambitious people?" For a region or community an equally challenging question can be, "How do we attract people with ambition, so they stay to work and live in the community?"

In contrast, Jackson fears that many young Americans do just enough to get by in school and work, and expect to live a good life. She is not alone. In business and even in sports, the concern comes up on a regular basis now. The venerable John Young, founder of the Council on Competitiveness and former Hewlett Packard CEO, has also commented, "Our standard of living is not a birthright. We have to earn it in the marketplace every day."[13] Even tennis star Chris Evert, winner of 18 Grand Slam singles titles, laments the lack of young U.S. players' ambition and ability to make it big in current tournaments. Part of the reason, she claims, is that young American "players' lives are too cushy compared with young athletes in other countries. '[The Americans] aren't hungry.'"[14]

FLAT LINE IN THE UNITED STATES?

Even if you are on the right track, you will get run over if you just sit there.

Will Rogers

Demotion is a frightening word to most managers and employees.[15] Perhaps it should be for countries, regions, and communities as well. We might think that demotion means a drop or fall in a person's title, status, or compensation, but typically none of those actions happen. Instead, demotion comes from standing still. As counterparts move up, the one standing still goes down. As Wince-Smith's comments at the beginning of this section imply, other trends may be suggesting a type of demotion or shift in innovation centers of gravity. First, as a producer and publisher of scientific research, the United States has "flat lined." Second, in annual competitiveness rankings, the United States is slipping, relative to other countries.

In a startling headline, *Science* magazine, the top scientific research publication in the United States, commented in 2004 that American scientists were "flat lining" in their numbers of scholarly publications.[16] The United States has remained constant, as other countries' output increases.

The National Science Foundation's (NSF) annual report, *Science and Engineering Indicators,* describes statistics and reports on the status of science and engineering in the United States and elsewhere in the world. In absolute terms, the U.S. government and industry spent more on research and development than any other country surveyed in the NSF report. Even so, the number of scientific publications coming out of the United States remained essentially flat from 1988 to 2006, averaging about a 1 percent increase per year. In contrast, the volume of peer-reviewed, scientific publications from researchers in Western Europe and East Asia has soared. Starting in 1995, the number of publications out of Western European universities and companies surpassed those from the United States; they have remained higher ever since. And Western European output is not alone in the growth trend; since 2004, scientific publications from Latin America and Asia have also risen dramatically.

A final indicator that new economic and innovative centers of gravity are developing and growing stronger is the worldwide competitiveness rankings. Michael Porter's annual Global Competitiveness report offers a benchmark for how countries rank on nine factors relating to innovation and business competitiveness over the last several years. The United States does look positive on many dimensions, including innovation, but its poor economic indicators, such as public debt and fiscal deficits, hurt it overall in the most recent ranking; the United States fell from first to sixth place between the 2005–2006 and 2006–2007 reports.[17] Countries such as the Nordic countries, Singapore, and Switzerland have instead risen towards the top of the rankings.

Further, in the 2007 Innovation Output Index, compiled by the Economist Intelligence Unit, nearly 500 senior executives surveyed worldwide rated Japan as the world's most innovative nation with regard to business practices and output, with Switzerland and Sweden just behind. Interestingly, India and the United States were neck and neck in the rankings, with several other Asian nations coming in strong. The survey was commissioned by Cisco's Roger W. Farnsworth, director of the firm's Executive Thought Leadership unit. His conclusion from the survey: For a country to remain competitive, "innovation must become a priority at both the national and business level. Understanding the contributors to, and enablers of, innovation is critical to success in today's interactions-based economy."[18]

WHAT'S HAPPENING?

Alone, none of these indicators—Jackson's "Quiet Crisis," statistics on scientific publications, or competitiveness rankings—may be alarming. Together, however, they form "wake-up calls" for any country, region, or organization to consider how to push forward to remain competitive.

If you are now starting to hear the alarms go off, please keep in mind that creative sparks are flying elsewhere. In some ways, the landscape organizations are entering is different. So, let us look at some developments and what they may mean for future ways of operating. Management scholar and consultant Richard Florida has helped shake up and inspire leaders by pointing to the shifts in creative class centers.[19] He and others argue that high-talent, creative-class workers cluster in cities that have common attributes: other highly talented people, strong technology-based firms, tolerance for different people and ideas, and some territorial advantage or uniqueness. His book, *The Flight of the Creative Class*, argues that because brains and talent are mobile, the creative class cannot be counted on to be loyal to a country, region, or city. Instead, some members of the creative class will migrate to locations with the most interesting opportunities.

Germany has a long history of citizens remaining in their home towns and villages, refusing any sort of relocation for jobs. Yet, even it is changing, becoming one of the countries where Florida's predictions about "creative class flight" are beginning to play out. In the last several years, students in universities, as well as professionals, have begun looking outside the country for job opportunities. In 2005 alone, some 50,000 Germans left and do not intend to return.[20] Most were highly educated, in research, science, medicine, and management. Their frustrations with logjams in institutions, unions, and a "wait until your turn" mentality relating to career paths, make the country less appealing to them.

Spiky Creativity

So where do those dissatisfied Germans and others who epitomize a creative class go?

Richard Florida refers to "spiky" creativity—certain spots around the world where the creative class clusters. Many cities and regions are trying to attract them. Some countries have begun systematically to pursue key industries that build and draw upon the creative and innovative talents of their indigenous population and attract other creative talent. By now the story of remote Finland as a world leader in mobile telephone technology is legend. But such stories and statistics go far beyond Finland. Ireland, in twenty-five years, went from having a poor, agriculturally based economy, losing its young people to other countries, to being one of the fastest growing economies and one of the highest recipients of foreign direct investment in Europe, with a net increase in the numbers of young people immigrating for employment.

An assessment of creativity in Europe in 2004 identified fast-growing, creative class clusters in the Nordic countries, Northern Europe (e.g., the Netherlands) and Ireland.[21] In fact, Finland, Sweden, and Ireland boasted the fastest growing creative classes, with technical capabilities to grow high-tech, knowledge-intensive industries, and the willingness to invest in developing creative and technical talent.

In addition, the European Union (EU) has several objectives to become dominant in research and development worldwide by the year 2010. Its goals include creating centers of excellence that support collaboration by university labs and industry that focus on initiatives in energy, aeronautical transportation, mobile communication, and nanotechnology. An interesting recent development is that the EU, through its framework programs, is making a conscious effort to broaden the scope of research and development activities. Humanities, social sciences, and other areas are attracting increasing attention, which, given the long focus on technology, is interesting. Is there a growing awareness of other factors that drive competitiveness?

The United Kingdom is one of the few countries to document the long-term impact of a "creative economy" over time. From 1990 through 2002, creative industries, particularly those in the cultural fields of music, theatre, film, advertising, and design, represented a major portion of the United Kingdom's economic growth. They represented 5 percent of the gross domestic product, 8 percent of employment, and grew twice as fast as the service industries and four times as fast as the manufacturing sector. Further, Gordon Brown, now prime minister, developed a "10-year plan" to make Britain "the best and most attractive location for science and innovation in the coming years" by putting significant funding into research and development. Stem cell researchers, for instance, frustrated by American regulation and restrictions, have decamped to the United Kingdom, which is selling itself as the world center for such research.

Even tiny Croatia has an effort to stimulate research in knowledge-intensive industries like biosciences. Biologist Miroslav Radman has started a new laboratory for world-class young scholars. The Mediterranean Institute for Life Sciences (MedILS) was formed as an independent, international, English-language "factory of ideas," where he anticipates a mix of disciplines, perspectives, and ideas will generate solutions to some of the world's hottest science problems.[22]

This will be a challenge for many places: What can we do to find and develop a niche in an innovation landscape in which so many are running in similar directions? Certain areas such as biosciences or nanotechnology are attracting more attention. Similarly, most, if not all regions and universities, have established technology transfer offices, incubators, and science parks. But, as Anthony Townsend of the Institute of the Future noted recently, the R&D forms, locations, and areas are shifting, and to be a frontrunner requires answers to some tough questions.[23]

New Spikes? Creativity in Unexpected Places

Creativity and innovation also seem to be surfacing in places many might consider "unexpected," such as poorer developing and emerging economies.

Recent reports show at least two ways developing countries have begun exploiting creativity and innovation: to enhance economic performance and attractiveness for investors; and to serve indigenous consumer populations.

For emerging economies, creativity and innovation can help firms improve their practices and ultimately help stimulate international export performance.[24] Since many firms in developing economies provide products or services suitable for international markets, those revenues ultimately benefit the country's export performance and economy. In addition, managers who think creatively may generate more cost-efficient approaches for producing exportable manufactured goods, especially in high-tech industries. So as its business organizations improve performance and export products, the country may also become more competitive as a desirable location for investors both within and outside of the region.

The Fortune at the Bottom of the Pyramid, a ground-breaking book about the world's poorest countries, argues that emerging economies may in fact have different approaches to creativity and innovation than their richer, developed country neighbors.[25] In the so-called "base of the pyramid" (BoP) countries, with their estimated four billion inhabitants, the average citizen lives on less than US$2–3 per day. They include, for example, China, India, Brazil, several countries of South and Southeast Asia, and large parts of Africa. Such countries have wide disparities between the rural and inner city poor and a very thin wealthy upper class, but their mega-cities will dominate the world's population centers in the coming decade, suggesting huge potential consumer groups and distribution access.[26]

In fact, in case study after case study, University of Michigan professor C. K. Prahalad and others find an undercurrent of creativity and innovation that bubbles up, both in multinational firms that operate in such countries and, even more so, from locally based organizations.[27] Indeed, firms profit by consumer desire for the same brand-name goods and services that developed country customers want. Successful firms have tapped this consumer desire, taken advantage of localized distribution in highly populated areas, such as bicycle taxis, and sell high volumes of their products for low unit prices. For instance, as global toothpaste manufacturers recognized that consumers wanted name-brand toothpaste but could not afford a full tube, small, single-serving tubes appeared; large volume, low price still allowed for profits. And, as consumers move up the economic ladder, which toothpaste will they likely purchase when they can afford a larger tube?

In India, the Aravind Eye Care System has become legendary for its ability to perform over 200,000 top-quality cataract surgeries annually, for a fraction of the cost that consumers in developed countries pay.[28] And it makes a profit. Aravind's price per surgery is $50–300, including a patient's hospital stay. But more than 60 percent of its patients pay nothing. Aravind's approach uses "standardized protocols" with trained paramedics conducting some of the routine tasks (e.g., measurements, diagnostic tests, preparing patients), ophthalmologists continually operating (switching between two tables), and top notch equipment.[29]

Part of the success may rest upon the notion that if a country is resource-less, its people become resource-full, finding ways to achieve their desires for goods and services but in ways that would not be considered in more developed countries. Perhaps it's the latest version of "necessity being the mother of invention," with developing countries sparking the change. But there could be more. In 2006 the Boston Consulting Group studied companies from rapidly developing economies in Asia, South America, and Eastern Europe. They are growing at a staggering 24 percent annually and rapidly expanding into mature markets, buying companies, and ensuring their positions as partners, customers, and coproducers. One reason behind their growth is their large domestic markets and access to low-cost resources. But, other factors make them more resilient when entering the world market. For example, the difficulties of navigating immature and complex home markets, and in competing there with global incumbents, allow them to understand how these firms work. This makes them stronger as they enter the global market.[30]

As people in other countries gain confidence and recognize that creativity and innovation are resources not limited to certain groups or regions, they will increasingly become sources for competitive advantage worldwide.

The Changing Managerial Landscape

> But thanks to corporate subservience to shareholder value, which means driving up the price of a company's shares as quickly as possible, CEOs have been finding all kinds of other ways to cash in the goodwill that accountants and economists have trouble measuring.... What is to be done? All we need do is change our concept of the world.
>
> Henry Mintzberg

In the last few years, debates have emerged on education, organizational management, and structures for collaboration. Is management education really giving us the managers we want? Is there a connection between organizational and management research and the day-to-day work in organizations, or is there a widening gap? What forms of collaboration would improve management and performance? Can we really continue managing the same way that we have been, or are we on the verge of a period of management innovation?

Several strong voices in the field of management and information technology argue for an overhaul of managerial and organizational practices and processes. Gary Hamel, John Seely Brown, John Hagel III, and Henry Mintzberg[31] are just some of those voices. They have taken a hard look at organizations that are winning in the global markets. These include the stars you've heard about, like Google and Whole Foods, but also a number of Indian and Chinese organizations. Their analysis is not a kind one. They are finding a few interesting examples in the United States and Europe. But, it is when they hit the emerging markets that they see a flurry of new ways of interacting, of developing value, of strategizing, of being creative and innovative. Part of this comes back to the previous issue—these new economies provide great testing grounds for innovation. Part of it comes back to novel ways of looking for how we create value and innovative products and interactions with our customers, partners, and other organizations.

Their suggestion: Focus much more effort on innovating management and organizational practices—it will pay off much more than product and technology development. Look at organizations on the edges or fringes—they are early indicators and testing grounds, and they allow for creative testing.[32]

An example: In many organizations, especially large behemoth structures focused on developing products, services are attracting increasing attention. Services are considered a source of future growth, since the core business is stalling. Ericsson has seen this happening and is today increasingly selling services. When managers look in their own organizations, they need to ask how many persons are dedicated to developing this new area? What is the annual budget for service development? If they compare this number to the number of people and funds employed for product R&D, often funding is heavily skewed towards products. Should it be?

Another factor shifting the managerial landscape is technology, which enables connections, information exchanges, and social interaction in ways we did not consider before. Its omnipresence is so recognized that, for example, Japan and South Korea are working towards strategies for "ubiquitous technology"—that is, technology that is ever-present across society and in many facets of daily life. This affects how they do business, learn both in and out of school, store and retrieve health information, and more. They are working hard to understand how the technologies and their infrastructures should be managed and built into the national strategy for these and other areas.[33]

As managers start looking at the creative and innovative management processes as well as the areas they are likely to affect, a sound knowledge of technology's current reach should be part of the equation.

New Structures as Drivers for Creativity and Innovation

Structures, whether within organizations, communities, or regions, are beginning to emerge and change in ways that individual company managers may miss. We have mentioned, for instance, the ability of emerging-market companies to compete globally. This generates what might be called "new geographies" or power bases in areas of the world that are different from the traditional industrialized regions. Another such change, especially outside the

United States, is the creation of structures that blend strengths from public- and private-sector organizations and ways of operating, to generate new types of organizations.

Recently, one of us spoke with a professor in political science regarding what makes regions, organizations, and countries competitive. The professor described what he termed the "Third Sector" as one important approach for mixing public and private sectors' goals and approaches to handle vital societal functions. In his view, the Third Sector combined elements, goals, and methods from the traditional private (industry-based) and public (government-based) sectors to address goals that failed to fit neatly within either.

Emerging new organizational arrangements and structures include groups involved in social entrepreneurship, Public Private Partnerships (PPP), and Third Sector organizations. The notion of creating new structures for organizations that seek solutions to societal problems that may fall between the cracks seems more prevalent in some European countries than in the United States at present. Elder care is one such example. In Sweden, as in many developed countries, there is a growing concern for how to manage the increasing numbers of people entering their elder years. Several initiatives, especially in terms of financing retirement centers and health care, are emerging between private sector providers and public sector funders.[34]

Likewise, in the creative industries, new structures are appearing. Often, because the industries—such as music, media, and design—typically include small companies or freelancers, with hard-to-describe jobs drawing upon knowledge or creativity as their base, they develop different types of structures. These include collaborations and networks that are not easy to define or understand in traditional ways. To better understand the new types of organizations and structures evolving in creative industries, the Knowledge Foundation, a Swedish funding organization, started a program in 2000 both to examine and better understand the experience industry, which produces "experiences"—films or live concert entertainment, sports, or new media, rather than products—and to encourage growth in the industry. One of the program's initial tasks was to develop metrics, provide statistics, and help creative organizations and people find each other and form networks. Since the organizations that provide experiences sometimes blend public sector and profit-making groups, an objective of the program was to offer means for interaction between policy makers and this thriving and already very profitable entertainment sector.[35] In a similar fashion, people working in the circus industry have formed an association in Canada to foster creativity and collaboration industry-wide, not just within specific organizations.[36]

In 2007, Demos, a British think tank, published a report called "So, what do you do? A new question for policy in the creative age." The message was that countries, regions, and communities need to recognize that finding solutions to societal problems will take different types of entities and organizational structures, as well as different types of people, who may not fit well within the traditional organizational frameworks.[37]

Our intention in giving these examples is to show the fluid organizational changes and interaction among public sector policy makers, researchers, and small and large companies that are beginning to emerge and take form. The different sectors are collaborating more in educational settings as well. In April 2007, Harvard's Business School and Kennedy School of Government began a joint program, combining approaches from each perspective to solve problems that fall completely within neither.

So Where Do We Go Now?

Our intention in this chapter has been to set the stage for two ideas: (1) Creativity is a resource that is increasingly important, and yet sometimes does not receive its due recognition; and (2) some organizations and some places are very creative, and they are likely to become winners in the next stage.

Keep in mind:

- *Creativity is serious play.* It is not the result of chance and inspiration. Successful innovative organizations show the opposite: Hard work, effort, and creative discipline are the elements that make them thrive in spite of the heightened level of worldwide competition.
- *How do you avoid creativity myopia?* Creativity can be a resource helping organizations in facing the changes in the world today. Creativity and innovation may contribute to competitive advantage, or for both developed and developing countries; the United States will remain cutting edge in the future as it is today only if it engages in a continuous process fostering excellence.
- *Centers of gravity are shifting.* The United States' lead in innovation is narrowing; other countries are increasing their levels of innovation. The "quiet crisis" affecting the United States embraces education, demographics, and individual ambition. (Americans aren't as hungry as they once were.)
- *Spiky creativity, creativity in unexpected places, management innovation, and new structures are among hotbeds for creativity.* Clusters of creativity are present throughout the world. In particular, being on the fringe forces individuals and companies to think of new, creative ways to solve problems that in some cases rely on using fewer, not more, resources.
- *Innovate or die!* The arena expands and becomes more challenging day after day. Being creative is crucial for establishing and redefining each actor's competitive advantage.

This takes us to chapter 2, where our framework will start to emerge.

NOTES

1. Edmund Phelps's editorial in the *Wall Street Journal* focused on entrepreneurial thinking and innovation as critical for national economic success. Edmund S. Phelps. 2007. "Entrepreneurial Culture," *Wall Street Journal,* February 12: A15.

2. Several recent books make similar points about the growing interdependence of economies, organizations, and even individuals. Each of these provides good overview of the changes that have occurred in the last 20–100 years, including the nature of economic and political links, changing demographics, and factors that demand organizations take more active approaches in the competitive marketplace. See: Thomas L. Friedman. 2005. *The World Is Flat.* New York: Farrar, Straus and Giroux; Shoshana Zuboff. 2002. *The Support Economy: Why Corporations are Failing Individuals and the Next Episode of Capitalism.* New York: Viking Penguin; Richard L. Florida. 2005. *The Flight of the Creative Class.* New York: HarperCollins.

3. An indication is that in 2007 the Royal Swedish Academy of Engineering Sciences chose to create a new classification of companies in the Swedish economy. The underlying reason was to both capture all sectors of the economy and to understand the overall development of the economy, including specific sectors. In previously used categories the companies were not of similar kind, which made it difficult to analyze their combined development. Read more in their final report (in Swedish): Royal Swedish Academy of Engineering Sciences. 2007. IVA-M 358 "Framtidens näringsliv: Om de Nya Förutsättningarna för Näringslivets Utveckling" (The future industries: On the new conditions for industrial development).

4. Richard Florida spoke in Stockholm at the conference "About Folkhemmet 2.0: The Creative Class, Growth and Sweden's Role in a New Global Order," March 9, 2006.

5. The president of the Council on Competitiveness's comments join others in the need for more focus on competitiveness. See Deborah L. Wince-Smith. 2006. "The Creativity Imperative: A National Perspective," *Peer Review* 8 (2, Spring): 12–14.

6. Shirley Jackson has spoken for several years about the factors she sees on the horizon that will negatively affect the United States' (and other developed countries') ability to compete on creativity and innovation. A collection of those speeches is on the Web. See examples at http://www.rpi.edu/homepage/quietcrisis/speeches.html.

7. The story about the frog has been used numerous times; one of the earliest was by Senge. See Peter Senge. 1990. *The Fifth Discipline: The Art and Practice of the Learning Organization.* New York: Doubleday.

8. While comparisons may be skewed because some countries allow only more elite students to pursue a university track and higher-level math, Jackson's point is nevertheless worth considering. To avoid recognizing possible problems in education keeps the notion of innovation myopia alive and well. Furthermore, the United States (as well as several other countries) has opted out of conducting tests of international comparison, which some claim is because of fear that students will continue to perform poorly. See Jeffrey Mervis. 2007. "U.S. Says No to Next Global Test of Advanced Math, Science Students." *Science* 317 (5846, September 28): 1851.

9. In a recent speech, Swedish Prime Minister Fredrik Reinfeldt said that both on-the-job training and upgrading of workers' skills are important to ensure that the right people in adequate numbers are available for Swedish firms and public

organizations. In many cases, he said, where there are preconceived perceptions of what it means to work in basic industries, young people may not seek employment there; as a result, the country needs to show the value and benefits of working in skilled occupations. The forum for his speech was "Industridagen 2007" (The Swedish Industrial Committee's annual meeting) on November 14, 2007.

In the 2006–2007 report from the World Economic Forum, Augusto Lopez-Claros also notes that "Education and training have emerged as key drivers of competitiveness, ensuring that the labor force has access to new knowledge and is trained in new processes and the latest technologies." p. xiii, http://www.weforum.org/pdf/ Global_Competitiveness_Reports/Reports/gcr_2006/gcr2006_summary.pdf.

10. For a story with both the big picture and examples of how this works, read Annalee Saxenian. 2006. *The New Argonauts: Regional Advantage in a Global Economy.* Cambridge, MA: Harvard University Press. See also "On Their Way Back: The Overseas Chinese Are Returning to Become Entrepreneurs in the Motherland," *The Economist* (U.S. Ed.) November 8: 59–60.

11. Richard Florida. 2004. "America's Looming Creativity Crisis," *Harvard Business Review* (October): 122–123. Richard Florida. 2005. "The World Is Spiky," *Atlantic Monthly* (October): 48–49.

12. During nine years' working in Vietnam, Nancy had many similar experiences. This was just one of the first, from spring 1994. Adapted from Napier and Thomas. 2004. *Managing Relationships in Transition Economies*: 41–43.

13. John Young's comments were in Wince-Smith, "The Creativity Imperative: A National Perspective."

14. Throughout 2007, tennis commentators lamented the lack of American-born players who made it to the final rounds of competition. Evert's comments reflect many of those sentiments. See Lynn Zinser. 2007. "A Lifeboat for American Tennis," *New York Times,* August 27.

15. In the early 1980s, Nancy and a colleague studied demotion. They found that rather than meaning an individual's job title, salary, or position was actually reduced, demotion was a relative term. Instead, they found that a person felt demoted if others around her moved up. Thus, an employee could continue to perform as she had in previous years, but if others performed better and moved up the organization, she felt she'd been demoted. See Nancy K. Napier and Jeremiah Sullivan. 1983. "Demotion— Conceptualizing and Suggesting Directions for Research," paper presented at the National Academy of Management Dallas, TX.

16. *Science* magazine has a summary of the NSF report results. For that article, see Jeffrey Mervis. 2004. "State Profiles Join Global Review of Science," *Science* 304 (5672, May 7): 808. [DOI: 10.1126/science.304.5672.808] (in "News of the Week"); for the full report, go to the National Science Foundation Web site. The report's title is "Science and Engineering Indicators," and it appears annually.

17. Porter's global competitiveness report is published annually and is a major topic at the World Economic Forum. "The Global Competitiveness Report, 2006–2007," is available at: http://www.weforum.org/en/initiatives/gcp/Global%20 Competitiveness%20Report/index.htm.

18. Innovation output index, see: http://www.atimes.com/atimes/Asian_Economy/ IE22Dk01.html.

19. Richard Florida was an initial definer of the demographic "creative class." He's examined cities in the United States and abroad for insights on the factors that attract and keep key people who can help build them. See, for example, Florida. 2005. *The Flight of the Creative Class.*

20. See Mark Landler. 2007. "Germany Agonizes over a Brain Drain," *New York Times*, February 6.

21. Richard Florida and Irene Tinagli. 2004. *Europe in the Creative Age.* London: Demos.

22. Several reports and articles have come out of Europe in the last few years. See, for example, "Science and Technology, the Key to Europe's Future—Guidelines for Future European Union Policy to Support Research," June 16, 2004, COM(2004) 353 final. Brussels: Commission of the European Communities. ftp://ftp.cordis.europa. eu/pub/era/docs/com2004_353_en.pdf; Geoffrey Brown and Greg Baeker. 2003. "Creative Industries and Cultural Development: Views from Canada and the United Kingdom." May 1, SRA-755-e. Presentation to the Department of Canadian Heritage, in Hull, Québec, Canada; Daniel Clery. 2004. "U.K. Government promises to shore up Britain's Science Base," *Science* 305(5682, July 16): 318. Radman's laboratory was in discussion at the time of the *Science* article about it: Peter Follette. 2004. "Miroslav Radman Profile: Bringing Biology Back to Croatia," *Science* 304(5674, May 21): 1103–1104 or on the Web DOI: 10.1126/science.304.5674.1103.

23. Anthony Townsend, Institute for the Future, "*Tectonic Shifts in the Geography of R&D—The Next Fifty Years.*" speech at the International Association of Science Parks, Barcelona, Spain, July 2–4, 2007. The presentation can be downloaded at the IFTF blog: future.iftf.org.

24. See William R. DiPietro and Emmanuel Anoruo. 2006. "Creativity, innovation, and export performance," *Journal of Policy Modeling* 28 (2): 133–139.

25. *The Fortune at the Bottom of the Pyramid* has been instrumental in sparking interest in and research on countries that are emerging and poor. C. K. Prahalad. 2005. *The Fortune at the Bottom of the Pyramid.* Upper Saddle River, NJ : Wharton School Publishing.

26. For a fascinating visual display of how data about these countries can be broken down, please see Hans Rosling's presentations at Technology, Entertainment, Design (TED), an annual conference and online community whose mission is to spread innovative ideas. It is a major mistake to perceive and take action in these countries as if they were homogeneous. To better understand for example, the complex mix of wealth distribution, health care, and development in these markets, you need to disaggregate data, which is possible using publicly available information. Rosling's presentations are available at: http://www.ted.com/talks/view/id/92 and http://www.ted.com/index.php/talks/view/id/140.

27. See, for example, Stuart L. Hart. 2005. *Capitalism at the Crossroads: The Unlimited Business Opportunities in Solving the World's Most Difficult Problems.* Upper Saddle River, NJ: Wharton School Publishing.

28. Prahalad. 2005. *The Fortune at the Bottom of the Pyramid*: 29.

29. See R. D. Ravindran and R. D. Thulasiraj. 2006. "Aravind Eye Care System," *Cataract & Refractive Surgery Today* (March): 45–47.

30. Boston Consulting Group. 2006. *The New Global Challengers.* www.bcg.com/impact_expertise/publications/files/New_Global_Challengers_May06.pdf.

31. The quotation is from Henry Mintzberg. 2007. "Productivity Is Killing American Enterprise," *Harvard Business Review* (July–August): 25.

32. There is a large volume of interesting material here. Examples include John Seely Brown and John Hagel III. 2005. *The Only Sustainable Edge: Why Business Strategy Depends on Productive Friction and Dynamic Specialization.* Boston: Harvard Business School Press; Gary Hamel. 2007. *The Future of Management*; Warren G. Bennis and James O'Toole. 2005. "How Business Schools Lost Their Way," *Harvard Business Review* (May-June): 96–104.

33. Andreas Göthenberg at the Swedish Institute for Growth Policy Studies in Tokyo and their ICT reference group ITPS gave us a deeper understanding of this development. For more information, see, for example, Japan's IT Strategic Headquarters (2006) New IT Reform Strategy or MIC (2006b) Policy Framework for Ubiquitous Network Society in Japan, Ministry of Internal Affairs and Communications, Japan, March 2006.

34. Peter Majanen, Lotta Mellberg, and Dag Norén, in collaboration with Carin Daal and Håkan Eriksson. 2007. *Äldrelivsbranschen—En Framtidsbransch* [The industry for elderly care—an industry with a prospect for the future]. Stockholm: The Knowledge Foundation. The Boston Consulting Group. 2007. "Health Care Regulation Across Europe."

35. The term *experience industry* corresponds to what other countries call creative or cultural industries. Thank you, Stina Algotson and Carin Daal, for describing it to us and in their book: 2007. *Mötesplatser för Upplevelseindustrin: Metoder för Samproduktion av Kunskaps—och Kompetensutveckling* [Cross-boundary arenas for the experience industry: Methods for coproduction of knowledge and competence development]. Stockholm: The Knowledge Foundation.

36. Jan Rok at Cirkus Cirkör in September 2007.

37. Charlie Tims and Shelagh Wright. 2007. "So, What Do You Do? A New Question for Policy in the Creative Age," Demos:12.

Chapter 2

THREE DISCIPLINES AND THREE "ACES": RIGHT NOW, RIGHT FOR NOW

The relative strengths of the leading nations in world affairs never remain constant because of ... uneven growth ... technological and organizational breakthroughs which bring greater advantage to one [group] over another.

Paul Kennedy

Wise managers know that business is about finding ways to improve the odds of success—but never imagine that success is certain.

Phil Rosenzweig

Two observers on what makes nations or business organizations succeed reach similar conclusions: that nations and organizations will not likely be successful indefinitely. But those that figure out how to deal with conditions within a given timeframe and context may have a greater chance to survive.[1]

Paul Kennedy, in *The Rise and Fall of the Great Powers*, refers to world economic and political powers during the 1500s. Portugal, the Inca and Ottoman Empires, and the Mongols—these were the powers of their day. Geographically, economically, and politically, their might stretched across much of the populated world.

But which of these do we hear about today?

In *The Halo Effect*, Phil Rosenzweig argues that much of the popular and academic press about organizational performance is flawed because of wrong assumptions and poor research approaches. Books like *From Good to Great* and *In Search of Excellence*, according to Rosenzweig, suffer from the notion that what "worked" for organizations or leaders when the discussion occurred, will always work.

Writing twenty years apart about nations and business firms, about economic power and financial performance, Kennedy and Rosenzweig make a similar point: that success for nations or organizations is not certain. They rise and fall; some never rise again. In some cases, nations or organizations let hubris cloud their focus. In other cases, the external environment simply surprised or overwhelmed them into slipping from a top rung.[2] The organizations and nations that seem to survive and thrive are ones that have adjusted to changes within their environments or their own boundaries—organizational or geographical.

As Rosenzweig says, "The answer to the question '*What really works?*' is simple: *Nothing* really works, at least not all the time."[3]

Likewise, organizations that perform well today in creative endeavors may not always do so. Organizations, like Zenith, Enron and Tyco, as well as industries, like the 1990s dot.coms and the 2000s U.S. housing markets, fly high and then crash. Yet, some organizations do perform well in innovation and creativity, at least for a while. Those that continue to perform well seem to accept and build into their daily organizational life the notion of innovation and change, renewal, or adaptation to stay ahead.[4] And many seek to build the notions of being creative and innovative into the spirit of their organizations.

CREATIVITY AND INNOVATION: DEFINITIONS AND CASES

Many of us use the terms *creativity* and *innovation* almost interchangeably. Although they can overlap, we should distinguish them. An often-used definition of creativity is "the development of new or novel ideas, appropriate for their context, that have value."[5] Leonardo da Vinci's idea for a flying machine was novel, but inappropriate for the context. Since it could not be made, or even imagined by most people, it lacked value. A child's Lego model may be new, appropriate for her time and place, but it has relatively little value, except to the parents and child. Thus, creative ideas that have the three components—they are new, appropriate for their context, and valuable—seem to make sense in an organizational setting.

To distinguish between creativity and innovation, we might divide the definition's components. The first two components refer more to the creative steps of generating ideas that are novel and appropriate for the context; the third component focuses more on whether an idea is innovative, or whether it might become a marketable outcome with economic value.[6]

We used this definition with the organizations we studied in depth, and others we interviewed for broader perspectives. The definition made sense to them and helped us focus our discussions in several organizations.

As we mentioned in chapter 1, we talked to people in more than 50 organizations from different sectors, in different parts of the world. But to get a deeper sense of how creativity and innovation work, we carried out in-depth case studies on five of those organizations, speaking to more than 150 people over three years.[7] Those in-depth cases, from theatre and circus, to information delivery, software development, and sports, form the core of many of our observations in this book.

We spent months within each organization, reviewed initial findings with them, and then tracked them over time, meeting periodically with the leaders and other members within the organizations to get updates on their progress.

As far as we know, none has read Rosenzweig or Kennedy, but they understand intuitively the point that both make. The attitude we encountered was often one of never taking for granted that what works today will work tomorrow. Across all of the organizations we came to know well, the senior leaders consistently pushed an attitude of "how do we keep getting better" and "what would be the best way if we decide" rather than "we've found the one true way" or "I guess it's the best we can do."

DISCIPLINES AND "ACES": INTEGRATING THE PIECES

So what common features did the case organizations have?

We mentioned briefly in chapter 1 that six factors had surfaced across the organizations. In this chapter they are described as parts of our framework and discussed in relation to past research. We'll talk about each in more detail in separate chapters. The six factors form the framework we use throughout the book: a triangle of three "disciplines," a circle of three "aces."[8]

The framework, shown in Figure 2.1, has an inner triangle, with the three core disciplines that organizations need for building creativity and innovation. Its outer circle includes factors that can enhance, or inhibit, those creative disciplines. The three disciplines are stacked in the triangle, with the simplest,

Figure 2.1. The Three Disciplines and Three "Aces"

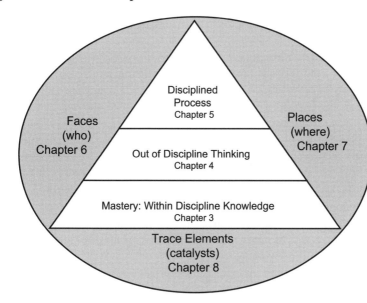

most common one at the bottom: within-discipline mastery or expertise. The next one, a step above, is out-of-discipline thinking, less common, more difficult to achieve, and yet critical for organizations seeking to remain creative. At the pinnacle of the triangle is a disciplined process, which refers to the stages, timing, and forms of collaboration that organizations use to enhance the opportunities for creativity and innovation.

The framework's circle includes three factors, or "aces," that underlie and enhance the disciplines' impact on success. The circle's three "aces" start with "faces" in an organization—the creative entrepreneurs, creative leaders, and creative team members who take ideas and turn them into reality. "Places" include the physical and organizational infrastructure that is reflected in offices, buildings, and location. Finally, "traces" include "trace elements" or catalysts of policies/practices, culture, and networks that spark and sustain creative and innovative endeavor.

In the rest of chapter 2, we briefly describe these components of the framework, review what we know from existing research about them, and what we're hoping to add to the knowledge base. This chapter gives a first link to past research, whereas references throughout the book add an additional layer of depth.

CREATIVITY AND INNOVATION: IDEAS WITH A "PAST"

Although we think of creativity and innovation as being around for ages, scholars began serious research on them only in the mid-twentieth century.[9] Some point to a seminal speech in 1950 by J. P. Guilford, President of the American Psychological Association, who called upon scholars to study more systematically and explicitly the elements that go into creative endeavor. And study they did, with a vengeance.[10]

Since 1950, much research has emphasized individual-focused creativity issues, such as motivation, creative problem solving and thinking, and the characteristics of creative persons.[11] Interest at levels beyond the individual has exploded in the last half century, and even more so in the last two decades, both in the academic world and the general press.[12] Harvard professor Teresa Amabile and her colleagues have explored creative activity within several companies and blasted many myths about creativity.[13] They have found, for instance, that creative people and groups are motivated less by tangible, financial rewards than by having a "worthy problem" to attack; that creativity is not limited to "certain people," but that anyone has the chance to be creative; that fear, competition, and time pressure can work against creative performance; and that creative people aren't dark and gloomy, but rather quite happy and enthusiastic about their work.

In addition, in the last decade, collaboration among scholars and practitioners across disciplines has gained ground. Interest in and understanding of the physiology of the brain and its connection to behavior and creativity has brought together people from psychology and biology to neuroscience and marketing to enhance what we know—and scrape away at what we do not know—about the brain's relationship to behavior, thinking, and creativity.[14] Finally, as we suggest in chapter 1, both creativity and innovation are receiving growing attention as critical resources and sources of competitive advantage for countries, communities, and organizations.[15]

3D CREATIVITY: DISCIPLINE, DISCIPLINE, DISCIPLINE

As we worked with organizations from different sectors and regions over the last few years, we found several characteristics that often built on past research. Our framework includes the three types of discipline that build on each other and form a basis for creativity and innovation in organizations. We'll talk about each and some of their research ancestry.

Discipline 1: Within-Discipline Mastery

For groups to be creative in finding or solving problems, they need members with expertise and knowledge about the problem. When the *Columbia* space shuttle failed, a presidential commission brought together experts with deep discipline knowledge, from a variety of fields. These experts, with knowledge ranging from aerospace to physics to law, gathered and analyzed data and reported on findings, which they presented to different audiences, from politicians to NASA officials to the general public.[16] Such within-discipline expertise is the basic building block that organizations seek when hiring and is the most common of the "disciplines" we found within the organizations we examined. Groups and organizations may hire, or develop, people with deep technical skill, yet our notion of "within-discipline" expertise takes the concept further.

Beyond the need for deep knowledge or "deep smarts" to understand and solve problems, within-discipline expertise offers other advantages. First, it generates informal internal competition among members who want to be (among) the best in their fields. Second, it provides a way to "speed up learning and working," in an innovative endeavor. Finally, it allows group members to move "beyond the fundamentals" to have the confidence, time, and energy to be creative.[17]

Being (with) the Best

People with strong within-discipline expertise are among the best, and they want to stay with the best. That, in turn, sparks internal competition. Following Boise State University's outstanding 2006–2007 football season, fans wondered who would replace the three-year starting quarterback, Jared Zabransky, who led the team to its historic win against Oklahoma. Just before the

2007 season began, senior Taylor Tharp got the nod. Even though he waited in the wings as backup for three years, the coaches made it clear that nothing was set in stone. They would watch other "competition" for the position—other quarterback hopefuls—and make no guarantees that Tharp would continue in first place. So if Tharp wanted to hold onto his post, he would have to get better, smarter, and more creative, as the season went forward. Many high performers exhibit this inner drive and competitive instinct, not seldom driven by insecurity, and often found in sports.[18]

Speeding Up Work

Within-discipline expertise provides the language, jargon, and cues for people within a field to streamline the work they do together. In some cases, speeding it up means more time to be creative. When a director says that an actor needs to "go into a character more deeply," the actor knows what to do. When a football coach talks of "the system" that his program uses, it means something quite specific to his coaches and players, and that could be very different from another program. When Wall Street's quantitative wizards talk about "tail risk," their conversation doesn't slow because they need to explain what it means.[19] In multidisciplinary environments this quick interaction is tempered by the friction of learning to interact, which, once developed, gives an added leverage. The mastery within a discipline, then, allows organizational members to use shortcuts to move tasks along faster.

Moving Beyond the Fundamentals

Last, within discipline also provides the chance to be creative, because the "fundamentals" are in place.

When it comes to teaching children how to drive in America, one parent seems to be the designated driver teacher. When Nancy's sons learned to drive, she taught them how to use standard transmission. One evening, she and her younger son started out at 5 P.M. for a high school graduation reception party. The house was two miles away, through neighborhoods and small inclines, normally a six-minute drive.

Forty-five minutes later, they arrived at the party.

The car stalled half a dozen times, rolled backward on two hills, and jerked its way through a few stop signs. Her son gripped the wheel and yelled at the clutch. Nancy looked out the side window to keep from laughing out loud.

Six years later, she and her son followed a jumpy Mercedes through downtown streets. The car had a huge "Student Driver" sign on its roof, and a bumper sticker on the back that said: "Stick shift. Please be patient."

"You just can't tell people how to drive a stick," her son said, "You have to concentrate so hard to learn it, to get the feel for it. But then, when you've got it, that's it. You don't really have to think about it."

Nancy's son captured one of the values of within-discipline expertise for creativity. Once the stick-shift mastery is there, drivers can "think about" ideas other than which gear to use, RPMs, and planning their drives to avoid hills and stoplights. A race car driver then pushes that basic mastery to the next level of understanding for how they can push the vehicle on all those dimensions as well as have a strategy for winning the race.

Driving is a simple example of the value of deep learning or expertise. But going beyond the fundamentals works for football players, actors, and engineers. A university football kick returner, now a professional football player, commented that within-discipline mastery is critical if players want any chance of future creative activity: "Very few players have really mastered the craft, in a sense. You can't have a young player, who really can't play his techniques that well, thinking about different creative techniques—he just hasn't reached that level yet." He also commented that mature players could be more efficient and effective in their actions. By understanding the fundamentals, they could find better ways to get the job done, using their "smarts" rather than simply brawn.

Learn the fundamentals, then be creative.

Discipline 2: Out-of-Discipline Thinking

When people talk of being creative, many Americans use the phrase "out-of-the-box thinking." For most, this means thinking in ways that are less traditional, not linear, or unexpected. Such thinking usually involves forming groups with members from diverse backgrounds and perspectives to tackle problems that might cross boundaries or disciplines. To do such nontraditional thinking often requires seeking or at least being receptive to ideas from outside one's normal area of expertise or discipline, and having the ability to exploit those ideas in a way that eventually leads to value.[20]

But out-of-discipline thinking, as we describe it, goes further than having group members with varying perspectives. We found that organizations pursuing innovative endeavors benefit from out-of-discipline thinking in at least three different ways depending on their approach. In addition, the ways those ideas and their users "find" each other ranges from being rather passive to quite proactive.

Types of Out-of-Discipline Thinking

In our case organizations and in the general press, at least three approaches to out-of-discipline thinking emerged in terms of how ideas come about: bridging ideas, blending ideas, and transferring ideas.

The inventor of the wildly successful Furby toys and the more recent "emotional" artificial life form Pleo, Caleb Chung, is a classic bridger. He has stepped across many disciplines over the years, and succeeded in several. He went from acting and doing mime as a younger person, to working in Mattel's R&D lab, to inventing in his own right, bridging art (design) and science (technology) almost seamlessly.

Some organizations find ways to blend ideas. Business schools in the United States have taken a beating in the last decade. Henry Mintzberg, a longtime critic of business academics and maverick thinker, argues that business school training is too narrow, quantitative, and irrelevant for problems facing future leaders.[21] Partly to combat student narrowness, some universities have created "D-schools," or design schools. Stanford University's Hasso Plattner Institute of Design, housed in a double-wide trailer, blends disciplines through courses by academics and industrial-design professionals, and mixes students from different disciplines to work on business problems. For Microsoft's Mozilla business development work, for example, a three-discipline student team—from business, product design, and computer science—worked together.

Finally, people and organizations may transfer ideas from one discipline to another. Dan Hawkins, former Boise State head football coach, considered ideas from math to use in preparing and calling plays. He looked to chaos theory to help mathematically assess the potential outcomes of particular plays, with certain players. He thought it might help coaches decide which plays to use against certain opponents' defensive plays or determine how many yards to anticipate against a particular opponent's particular personnel lineup.

How Ideas and Users "Find" Each Other

In addition to ways that disciplines come together, we found several ways that users and ideas "find" each other. Four approaches emerged: (1) taking what comes; (2) being a magnet; (3) casting a net; and (4) looking, with a purpose.

First, "taking what comes" refers to being open to ideas that may have value. A sports training coach mentioned that, in reading about how to manage money, he realized some attitudes could be valuable for young athletes, in terms of how to plan and carry out a goal. He used the ideas, which he was not looking for but was open to, as he helped athletes design their workouts.

Second, a person or group becomes a magnet when they are known as being open to new ideas. Several of the leaders in the organizations we looked at repeatedly asked, "how can we do things differently?" or "what's a different, more creative approach to solving this problem?" After a time, others in the organizations—as well as people outside—would approach the leaders and groups with ideas that might, or might not, have value. But because the "magnets" were willing to listen, they received more ideas.

Third, casting a net for ideas is a bit more proactive and involves being open, but with a broad, perhaps undefined, purpose. As groups sought to come up with new ideas, they might ask for input from a variety of people in or outside of the team. They had no expectations, but were open if something did emerge. They consciously kept the idea pool full.

Fourth, looking, with a purpose, occurs when groups have a problem to solve and seek ideas or solutions outside their normal disciplines. A software design team that goes through a series of increasingly focused user groups to solicit and then test ideas is looking for ideas to make the product easier to use. They are actively looking for ways to "grab the throats" of potential users and make them customers.

Discipline 3: A Disciplined Process

When we say that discipline and creativity go together, we often get the reaction: creativity is chaos, it's chance, it just happens. You can't have a process for it.

In fact, the opposite is found in organizations (and often people) that succeed in creativity and innovation.

Creative organizations we worked with have a *disciplined process* for creativity and innovation. For many people, structure, rather than being a constraint, can actually enhance creativity and freedom. Members of innovative organizations and groups don't "wait" for ideas to show up. They don't expect a so-called muse (that writers who don't write much talk about). And they don't think that "structure" stifles creativity. Instead, some of the best creative organizations structure whole or parts of the process of coming up with, experimenting with, and using ideas.

Key aspects of the creative process that have been written about and examined include: (1) stages or steps that individuals or groups go through to generate creative ideas and innovative outcomes; (2) how timing comes into play, in terms of where organizations put emphasis; (3) the types of ideas that emerge in the process; and (4) how collaboration works in creative organizations.

In Figure 2.1, a disciplined process sits at the top of the triangle, symbolizing that the other disciplines support it, that a disciplined process is often uncommon, and that it is the most difficult of the three types of discipline to achieve.[22] As the toughest discipline to achieve, and given its complexity and contextual nature, many of the organizational members we talked about spoke more in terms of "this is what we'd like to do or are aiming for." There is room for development.

Aside from being difficult to carry out, a disciplined process is also tough to capture—in discussion, observation, or on paper. The "stages" are wrinkled: they fold back on themselves and are iterative. The effort and person-hours spent on various stages may vary over time. What parts matter differ. Groups generate different types of ideas.[23] Finally, collaborative approaches differ within an organization and even across groups.

Stages and Timing

Scholars and practicing managers who write about the creative process often refer to a common set of stages, which initially were thought to be linear: preparation, incubation, illumination, and verification.[24] We know now that they are not linear, but often iterative, that creative groups and individuals may begin the stages at different points or return to them, and that those characteristics vary with the type of venture and the context at the time.

Research and practical results about time pressure or deadlines to encourage creative activity have been mixed. Some would argue that certain projects, such as the Manhattan Project or finding the cause of severe acute respiratory syndrome (SARS), happened more efficiently because of time pressure (to end a war, to end a health crisis).[25] But more recently, in business organizations at least, some scholars have found that time pressure may have an inverted U-type impact: Some urgency is useful but too much can overwhelm and backfire.

Yet we found that across different sectors, the basic model of stages still is useful for organizations and groups to explain their creative and innovative activities. We did find, though, that the timing of stages varied; there was a difference in the proportion of time (in person-hours) that organizations dedicate to early stages (generating ideas, initial experimenting) versus later stages (testing and preparing for launch).

Types of Ideas

German auto company BMW uses a very specific process for creativity and innovation.[26] One aspect of the process is filtering ideas, to weed weak from strong ones. The stronger ones move forward for more consideration, but the firm also stores the weaker ideas for possible future use. Key to the process was saving ideas, since some small ones could become more valuable later.

Likewise, we found that groups within our case organizations generated different types of and sizes of ideas. Organization members talked of the "big ideas," "tweaking ideas," and the "back burner" ideas. Each seemed important, came from different sources and was treated in different ways.

Members of one organization exhibited a multiwave approach. Employees describe a situation of high-volume, low-frequency waves (for big ideas) and low-volume high-frequency waves (lots of smaller ideas). In the organization, several people claimed that one or a few people generated big-wave ideas, while others were creative in continuous daily efforts and improvements than big shifts in products, services, or operations.

Collaboration

The notion of creative collaboration has often focused on the nature of the relationship among pairs or small groups of people—from casual to intense and long lasting. Longtime creativity scholar Vera John-Steiner talks of collaboration as being a type of continuum, starting with "distributed collaboration," where people interact casually and informally, exchanging ideas, these days through phone calls, e-mail, or MySpace pages.[27] Next, she sees complementary collaboration when people with different expertise work on a common problem. Third, John-Steiner claims that some collaboration replicates a "family" in nature, where people shift roles or trade skills over a long period and in complex endeavors, like building a bomb (the Manhattan Project) or creating a new business model (eBay or Google). Finally, she claims creative collaboration may also be integrated when a long-term partnership generates outcomes that become a legacy, such as Crick and Watson, Hewlett–Packard, or Clinton and Clinton.

We found, however, that collaboration also varies on other dimensions than length of time or depth of partnership. As we worked with our five case-study organizations, we uncovered at least four approaches, largely depending upon some external environmental factors, expectations regarding deadlines for developing an output, and perceptions about the roles of organization members. Some organizations may use different forms within different units or even in different situations. Thus, the patterns we found are generic, but at least give organizational members a starting point for understanding how they may be collaborating and whether it is an approach they wish to continue or change.

The four types of collaboration patterns that emerged were a star, pyramid, amoeba, and fireworks. Star collaboration, for instance, happens in organizations where ideas and decisions are more centralized; they flow through a core person or group before the organization moves forward with them in innovative work. Pyramid collaboration follows a mode where the uppermost organizational members do most of the creative and innovative work and decision making. A bit less centralized than the star form, it still assumes that creativity and innovation may not be evenly distributed throughout the organization. Amoeba collaboration pushes the expectation and activity of creativity and innovation throughout the organization and may change shape—in terms of who collaborates with whom—over time. Finally, a fireworks form of collaboration occurred where ideas sparked from different parts of the organization, and then groups, teams, or units worked on them and sparked more.

THE "ACES"

Figure 2.1 also includes a circle of three "aces," or factors that underlie and enhance (or inhibit) creativity and innovation. Our terms are *faces*, *places*, and *traces*. *Faces* refer to the creative agents within an organization who generate and carry out innovative ideas. *Places* refer to the physical and organizational infrastructures that affect how creative (or not) members of an organization will be. Finally, *traces*, as in trace elements, are the sometimes nearly invisible, "microscopic" yet critical catalysts in an organization that hold its creative spirit together and help it flourish.

Faces

At least three types of roles or faces are important within organizations seeking to be innovative: creative entrepreneurs, creative leaders, and creative team members.[28] These roles might shift across different people over time, but embody tasks that need to happen within creative organizations.

Creative Entrepreneurs

Some people have an unusual ability to be able to interpret and read the external environment as they identify opportunities that will help their organizations thrive. They tend to be good at "seeing": (1) seeing or making sense out of what others do not; (2) foreseeing or being able to anticipate opportunities before they are clear to others; and (3) reseeing, or finding old ideas that can be changed to become new creative ones. Often, creative entrepreneurs are real visionaries but are unable to sort ripe from less timely ideas or to turn a vision into action. Then, the fortunate organizations turn to creative leaders.

Creative Leaders

Where entrepreneurs see what is possible, leaders turn that into reality. Creative leaders have at least three key tasks.[29] They turn the entrepreneurial vision and ideas into something feasible, an output that others can see and find a role to participate in. Second, they form creative teams to carry out the vision and manage the diversity—whether "invisible or conscious" within a team. Third, they protect ideas and people when they are still in an early stage.

In the mid 1990s, when Digital Equipment and Compaq (DEC) merged, engineers in Galway, Ireland, feared they would lose their jobs and livelihood. Several engineers formed a group that ultimately ushered DEC into a completely new market area—supercomputers. A veteran from Digital's compiler unit and senior scientist from the UNIX group had the vision (creative entrepreneurs) to see that the firm had critical components throughout the company (e.g., the world's fastest chip, a motivated, yet undirected group of talent among the engineers at Galway) that could be marshaled to address a market need for supercomputers. Yet another person (creative leader) provided the strategic leadership for the creative group by helping it in its ability to integrate and build the supercomputer, interact with critical stakeholders and customers, and protect its work until it was steady enough to present to the rest of the organization.[30]

Creative Teams

In addition to entrepreneurs and leaders, innovative organizations need teams that will carry out the ideas. Such teams need members who are motivated, who have expertise or characteristics that support the project, and who are diverse.

Creative teams differ from some work teams in that their motivation may be contrary to what economists might predict. Some creative team members are motivated less by financial gain than by other factors. Typically, they are curious about and want to solve a problem, but not just "any" problem will do.[31] It needs to be "worthy"—of the group's time, effort, and mental and emotional investment. Groups that have achieved extraordinary and sometimes unrepeatable outcomes focus on such projects that mattered to them, and to some community beyond themselves. As group members, they see the value to a bigger world, such as Oppenheimer and his team at Los Alamos building the world's first atomic bomb, which at the time they saw as important for ending World War II faster, or NASA teams working to put a man on the moon and return him safely within less than a decade.

In addition, within the creative organizations we worked with, we also found that motivation came from a sense of "being on the fringe," being an unexpected player or contender within an industry or sector. Some researchers have talked of the underdog nature of entrepreneurs, but not often in terms of being creative.[32] Members of the studied organizations often mentioned that as a push to make them more innovative.

Third, expertise is critical among creative team members, without the team becoming susceptible to too much expertise. Such deep knowledge can sometimes dampen or thwart creativity because of (often unrealized) limits that expertise puts upon the team. Some call this a "curse of knowledge": when too much knowledge makes groups and individual perform worse.[33] Finally, the team mix and chemistry need to be right. For this to happen, many groups need to experience a classical group-formation process of becoming a team.[34]

Places

In our framework, the concept of places comprises both physical/spatial and social architectures. By spatial architecture, we mean the building, including its design or layout. By social architecture, we mean the ways that individuals and groups work together within the spaces. Several factors are important for organizations that seek to use place as a way to enhance creativity and innovation.

Very critical are the outcomes that place can offer to organizations. First, places become central meeting points and sparks for interaction and collaboration. They can also provide a place for competition among individual or group members, as well as among organizations. Second, places offer ways for organizations to express their cultures or identities. Plenty of recent discussion about organizations from Google to Cirque du Soleil suggest that place may attract top-notch talent, and firms should value that asset. In addition, sometimes spaces, especially ones that are temporary, can generate a mindset or an ability to deal with change. As theatre groups or sports teams change locations, people, or deliverables, such as plays, the members must be able to adjust rapidly and be comfortable with change. Last, we discuss how place can help be a backdrop to spawn experiences that may in turn enhance creativity and innovation in a community.

Traces

A final factor in our circle in Figure 2.1 that helps enhance creative and innovative endeavors is environment, broadly speaking, within and outside of an organization. We call these features traces, as in trace elements, to comprise three aspects: culture, policies, and networks or connections. Traces refer to trace elements, a concept in biology. Trace elements, such as boron, selenium, and iron, act as catalysts for chemical reactions for specific functions in the human body. The trace elements enhance proper growth, development, and physiology of an organism by sparking chemical reactions to happen more quickly and efficiently. Only tiny amounts are necessary—micro parts per million—but their impact is significant. Nearly invisible, they are crucial to generating positive reactions to hold together the successful functions of the human body.

Likewise, the equivalent of trace elements appear in creative organizations: they can be nearly invisible elements, yet essential, that act as catalysts and help creative and innovative activity function more quickly or efficiently within a unit. Similar to their role in a human body, they can spark reactions for optimal performance. Also, just as the human body uses different trace elements to generate different types of chemical reactions, we argue that different types of traces in organizations can support different sparks of creativity: specifically, we include trace elements of practice,[35] trace elements of culture,[36] and trace elements of connection, or networks.[37]

Trace Elements of Practice

Cirque du Soleil has made a worldwide reputation as an integrator of circus, theatre, and creative performances.[38] Part of its success rests on aggressive searching and recruiting of people who can offer acts that are unique or difficult to replicate. The creative choreographers and storytellers build upon those acts to generate performances that have captivated audiences for over twenty years.

The policies and practices of hiring people for organizations that expect creativity and innovation are critical. Often, they are the key tangible artifacts of an organization's push toward an innovative culture. They emerged in terms of being trace elements of finding people who fit the organization or team, trace elements of expectations placed upon members, and trace elements of reward for creative and innovative endeavors.

Trace Elements of Culture

Trace elements of culture cover several aspects, including not relying too much on a single or few idea sources and expanding the places and people from which ideas come, and finding ways to encourage the flow and surfacing of ideas. One surprise was that such cultures can exist in the most unexpected of organizations.

Early in our investigations, we sought out organizations that we did not expect to be leaders in creativity and innovation, just to see how they differed from the ones we were examining. One was Intermountain Gas Company, a mid-sized regional gas exploration and distribution firm in Idaho.

When Nancy sat down with the utility firm's top four executives, the room became tense. She looked them in the eye, swallowed, and said she was visiting because no one would expect creativity in such an unsexy commodity business, in an industry not known for being especially high tech, or exciting when it came to being creative. What did they think?

The room was silent. The executives raised their eyebrows. Bill Glynn, the CEO, sat back in his chair and folded his hands on his chest; the others looked at each other sideways. One leaned forward and said, "Let me. I'll start."

And they were off and running, for two hours. Example after example poured out of them of how they were finding new ideas and ways to solve problems.

One senior manager talked about how the firm needed a new computer information system. He investigated systems and found that other companies in their industry had spent over $20 million on the type of system his firm needed. He figured a way to do it for half that amount: "Then Bill [the CEO] told me I had half of what I asked for. And, you know what? We did it for even less than his budget. We just found ways to do it better and more efficiently."

The utility firm's top four managers talked about ways they had infused innovation throughout their business model and processes, their exploration methods in finding and accessing gas resources, and how they tried to solve all sorts of problems more efficiently. "We have to be creative to survive."

The managers then commented that they felt their firm was "on the edge" of creative industries, in several ways. Because of limited resources, they always needed to be looking for more efficient, effective ways to get things done. But also, being in a remote city, on the edge of what some might claim is the center of activity, they saw creativity as necessary to be noticed. And, being "on the edge," they felt being creative was in some ways easier.

"Look at Finland," one said. "Way out on the edge. Nothing but ice and smart people. We're also far away from everything. And perhaps, being far from the centers of what we think of as creative, we lack the 'clutter' of bigger cities—there is more peace, less noise, and more space." From their perspective, in smaller, remote cities, people feel they can have an impact if they are creative. So they are more likely to get involved. Interestingly, a world-renowned ballet company, the Trey McIntyre Project, recently moved from San Francisco to Boise, Idaho, in part because of Boise's "isolation," which presents fewer distractions from the ability to be creative.

The utility firm, unexpected as it was, exhibited trace elements in its culture. The expectation that "even" the financial and production people would come up with ideas was clearly implicit, and thus it surprised the managers when an outsider questioned whether theirs was a creative organization. Also, the culture sought to be porous and permeable, with ideas moving around easily—their comments about not having the clutter of big cities also reflected that people could operate without much distraction or obstacle.

Trace Elements of Connection

For years, senior management of a fast-growing high-tech firm spent hours outside the firm trying to read and anticipate changes that the company could take advantage of. The CEO met with customers; the head of strategy and marketing met often with potential and actual investors; the vice president of research and development mined conferences and contacts for insights into what directions technology might go. But finally, the three realized their efforts were never going to be effective. They were like a single straw in a milkshake, bringing in information and insights to the firm, but slowly and in a limited way. When they realized that the power of the firm lay in encouraging all levels to be information and insight gatherers and analyzers, the focus on creativity and innovation shifted to become the responsibility of all members of the organization. Simply by realizing that the firm's number of "touch points" with its fast-changing environment could expand as its employees used their networks boosted the firm's power. Members down the line became more involved in looking for ideas and solutions, rather than expecting or waiting for them to come from the top people, and they had pathways into groups that the senior managers did not.

THE CREATIVE ORGANIZATION'S DEVELOPMENT

During the time we worked with our core organizations, top leadership turned over almost completely in one (three out of twelve remained); a second was acquired by a much larger company; a third was working hard on a strategy for the next stage of development; and a fourth completed a strategic alliance that was in the planning stages when we began talking. All have tried endeavors that, for them and other organizations in their fields, are new and risky. To date, the organizations' results, in performance and creative endeavors, remain strong and look promising. Yet, given the warnings from Kennedy and Rosenzweig, we'll not make predictions about long-term innovative sustainability!

It has become increasingly clear that organizations such as these, in addition to being creative and innovative in their daily operations, face a challenge of transforming their organizations and how they apply the disciplines and "aces" to adapt to a changing context. With their own inner drive towards new ways of working and developing, they continuously put stress to their own creative architecture. And different parts of an organization can and should differ in their willingness to change over time.

One organization's manager put it this way:

> I think we [in management] are very susceptible to change. I am happy to take on a new role, or reconsider the strategy all the time, as we move along and develop. I think all of us in this room have had a number of roles, and we trust each other enough to shift positions as we see fit, and are comfortable in these changes. However, at one point we realized … not everyone likes or should have to face those changes, continuously. To be able to feel good about what you do, to experience progress and development, and to have the peace of mind to focus on your daily tasks—some things need to stay fixed. It is not unwillingness to change, but it needs to at least come in bursts, so that you know "now we change," and not continuously "are we changing or are we just considering changing?" That is something we work consciously with today.

A FRAMEWORK FOR CONTINUED READING

As you move along in the book, here are some of the key components and terms to keep in mind:

- *Creativity means finding an idea* that is new, appropriate for the context, and valuable—a successful idea.
- *Do you have the right "aces" up your sleeve?* If you think about it, creativity is related to knowledge and the situation in which it develops. By analyzing several companies and creative settings, we identified a framework for creativity composed of a triangle of three disciplines and a circle of three "aces."
- *The three disciplines* necessary to build and promote creativity and innovation are:

  1. *Within-discipline thinking*: Being with the best, speeding up work, moving beyond the fundamentals. First, learn the fundamentals, and then you can be creative.

2. *Out-of-discipline thinking*: Ideas often come from outside the field for which we have to solve problems and find new solutions.

3. *Disciplined process*: Structure enhances creativity and freedom by allowing repetition of things that work.

- *The three "aces"* that can enhance or inhibit creativity and innovation are:

  1. *Faces*: creative entrepreneurs, leaders, and teams.
  2. *Places*: physical infrastructure and location.
  3. *Traces*: culture, policies, and networks or connections.

- *Keep in mind: The creative organization is in constant flux*, and depends on this development to thrive and adapt. Nothing works indefinitely, and we have to figure out ways to best deal with conditions and continuously improve. What stage are you in and what should be the priorities at this stage?

NOTES

1. See Paul Kennedy. 1987. *The Rise and Fall of the Great Powers*. New York: Random House; Phil Rosenzweig. 2007. *The Halo Effect: And the Eight Other Business Delusions That Deceive Managers*. New York: Free Press: 154.

2. Several authors make the point that, repeatedly, companies find what works and stay with it too long, without recognizing changes in the environment. See, for example, three of the best-known works: Clayton M. Christensen. 1997. *The Innovator's Dilemma*. Boston: Harvard Business School Press; Clayton M. Christensen, Scott D. Anthony, and Erik A. Roth. 2004. *Seeing What's Next*. Boston: Harvard Business School Press; Peter M. Senge. 1994. *The Fifth Discipline*. New York: Doubleday.

3. Rosenzweig. 2007. *The Halo Effect*: 158.

4. Gary Hamel makes a strong argument for good management innovation practices to become part of regular, expected manager activities. This builds upon and is the toughest in the "innovation stack:" from operational, to product/service, to strategic, to management. See Gary Hamel. 2007. *The Future of Management*. Boston: Harvard Business School Press.

5. The three-part definition—novel idea, fits context, and has value—has been around for many years. Several scholars have used it repeatedly, most recently and perhaps most emphatically, Robert Sternberg, former Yale professor, now Dean of Arts and Sciences at Tufts University. For example, Robert J. Sternberg (Ed.). 1999. *Handbook of Creativity*. Cambridge, UK: Cambridge University Press; Others include Herbert Simon, "Understanding creativity and creative management," in Robert L. Kuhn (Ed.). 1988. *Handbook for Creative and Innovative Managers*. New York: McGraw-Hill Book Company: 11–24; Teresa M. Amabile. 1996. *Creativity in Context*. Boulder, CO: Westview.

6. Many researchers make such a distinction, essentially separating the production (creativity) from the adaptation and implementation (innovation) of ideas, products, or procedures that are novel and useful. See, for example, N. Madjar, G. R. Oldham, and

M. G. Pratt. 2002. "There's no place like home? The contributions of work and non-work creativity support to employees' creative performance," *Academy of Management Journal* 45 (4): 757–767; S. G. Scott and R. A. Bruce. 1994. "Determinants of innovative behavior: A path model of innovation in the workplace," *Academy of Management Journal* 37 (3): 580–607; C. E. Shalley and L. L. Gilson. 2004. "What leaders need to know: A review of social and contextual factors that can foster or hinder creativity," *Leadership Quarterly* 15:33–53. Finally, the father of "creative destruction," which argues that innovation comes from creative new ventures, Joseph Schumpeter. 1934. *The Theory of Economic Development.* Cambridge, MA: Harvard University Press.

7. For the five case studies—the Boise State football program, Cirkus Cirkör, Healthwise, the Idaho Shakespeare Festival, and ProClarity—we conducted semistructured interviews within each organization. We recorded and transcribed the interviews, which lasted from one to two hours; in some cases, we interviewed the same person (typically the top leader or leaders) more than once. We presented findings to each organization, have presented them to several professional organizations (both academic and professional) over the years, and have published several articles from the data to date.

8. Fifty years ago, psychologist George Miller wrote about being "persecuted" by the number seven: it's still with us—seven habits, seven digits in a phone number, seven deadly sins, seven wonders of the world. Humans have greater chances of remembering information that comes in chunks of seven, plus or minus two (between five and nine "chunks"), so that's one reason we have six factors! See George A. Miller. 1956. "The Magical Number Seven, Plus or Minus Two: Some Limits on Our Capacity for Processing Information," *Psychological Review* 63:81–97.

9. See, for example, Amabile. 1996. *Creativity in Context*; Teresa Amabile. 1999. "How to Kill Creativity," in Teresa Amabile, Peter Drucker, Suzy Wetlaufer, Dorothy Leonard, Jeffrey Rayport (Eds.). *Harvard Business Review on Breakthrough Thinking*: 1–59. Boston: Harvard Business School Publishing; Robert Drazin, Mary Ann Glynn, and Robert K. Kazanjian. 1999. "Multilevel Theorizing about Creativity in Organizations: A Sense Making Perspective," *Academy of Management Review* 24 (2): 286–307; Bernard A. Nijstad and Paul B. Paulus, "Group Creativity: Common Themes and Future Directions," in P. B. Paulus and B. A. Nijstad (Eds.). 2003. *Group Creativity: Innovation through Collaboration.* Oxford: Oxford University Press: 326–340; practitioner work, informed by research, includes examples such as Tony Davila, Marc J. Epstein, and Robert Shelton. 2006. *Making Innovation Work: How to Manage It, Measure It, and Profit from It.* Upper Saddle River, NJ: Wharton School Publishing; Jeff DeGraff and Katherine A. Lawrence. 2002. *Creativity and Work: Developing the Right Practices to Make Innovation Happen.* San Francisco: Jossey-Bass; Thomas L. Friedman. 2005. *The World Is Flat.* New York: Farrar, Straus and Giroux; Frans Johansson. 2004. *The Medici Effect.* Cambridge, MA: Harvard Business School Press.

10. Guilford's speech appeared in an academic journal: J. P. Guilford. 1950. "Creativity," *American Psychologist* 5:444–454.

11. Much groundbreaking research has come from psychologists, in particular, focusing on the individual level of analysis. Much of the early work on biological, cognitive, psychological, and information systems included attention to creativity, with an emphasis on children, students, and individuals in a work environment. See, for

example, Mark A. Runco. 2004. "Creativity," *Annual Review of Psychology* 55:657–68; Mark A. Runco (Ed.). 1997. *The Creative Research Handbook.* Cresskill, NJ: Hampton Press, Inc.; Robert J. Sternberg (Ed.). 1999. *Handbook of Creativity.* Cambridge: Cambridge University Press; Todd Lubart. 2000–2001. "Models of the Creative Process: Past, Present and Future," *Creativity Research Journal* 13 (3,4): 295–308.

12. See, for example, DeGraff and Lawrence. 2002. *Creativity and Work*; Paul B. Paulus and Bernard A. Nijstad (Eds.). 2003. *Group Creativity: Innovation through Collaboration.* Oxford: Oxford University Press; Kerrie Unsworth. 2001. "Unpacking Creativity," *Academy of Management Review* 26:297–298; Wendy M. Williams and Lana T. Yang. 1999. "Organisational Creativity," in Robert J. Sternberg (Ed.). *Handbook of Creativity.* Cambridge: Cambridge University Press: 373–391.

13. Teresa Amabile was one of the early scholars to focus on group level creativity and has consistently challenged assumptions about what encourages and discourages creativity. Most recently, she has studied "creativity in the wild," studying over 12,000 diary entries from employees over a seven-year period. See Beth Potier. 2005. "Longitudinal Study Explodes Myths about Motivating Creative Workers," *Harvard News Office,* February 10; and Bill Breen. 2004. "The 6 Myths of Creativity," *Fast Company* (December): 75.

14. Many articles in the popular press have come out in the last year, such as Jeffrey Kluger. 2007. "A New Map of the Brain," *Time,* January 18. http://www.time.com/time/magazine/article/0,9171,1580416,00.html; Kelly Greene. 2007. "Putting Brain Exercises to the Test," *Wall Street Journal,* February 3; "Blossoming Brains," *The Economist* (August 11, 2007): 71–72.

15. Examples of reports, books, and articles include the following: *The Global Competitiveness Report*, 2005-2006, www.palgrave.com/worldeconomicforum; Alan Cowell. 2004. "Nokia Falters, and the Finns Take Stock of Their Future," *New York Times,* September 4: B1, B3; Richard Florida. 2005. *The Flight of the Creative Class.* New York: HarperCollins; Richard Florida. 2002. *The Rise of the Creative Class.* New York: Basic Books; Richard Florida and Irene Tinagli. 2004. *Europe in the Creative Age.* London: Demos. Available at: http://www.creativeclass.org/acrobat/Europe_in_the_Creative_Age_2004.pdf; John Howkins. 2001. *The Creative Economy.* London: Penguin Books; Charles Landry. 2000. *The Creative City.* London: Earthscan.

16. Similar to many such groups, this one explicitly recruited a variety of discipline representatives, and sought to make the findings understandable to people outside the aerospace field. See the Rogers Commission to investigate the Columbia disaster—http://en.wikipedia.org/wiki/Rogers_Commission.

17. In any discipline, learning the basic concepts, techniques, and ways of approaching problems is crucial for going into more creative ground. Examples of inventors illustrate the importance of knowing the fundamentals before they "move beyond." Louis Pasteur (1822–1895), French chemist and bacteriologist, said in 1854 that "In the field of observation, chance favors the prepared mind." Depth of knowledge, preparation, and expertise that is solid and substantial, then, provides a foundation from which one can test ideas and develop new ones.

18. Marshall Goldsmith and Mark Reiter. 2007. *What Got You Here Won't Get You There: How Successful People Become Even More Successful.* New York: Hyperion.

19. According to Michael Lewis, tail risk is "whatever financial cataclysm is believed by markets to have a 1 percent chance or less of happening." It might be a

stock market fall of 30 percent or more, a collapse of the dollar, or a fast change in interest rates: whatever doesn't happen 99+ percent of the time. See Michael Lewis. 2007. "In Nature's Casino," *New York Times Magazine,* August 26.

20. See, for example, Glenn M. Parker. 2003. *Cross-Functional Teams: Working with Allies, Enemies, and Other Strangers.* San Francisco, CA: Jossey-Bass; Johansson. 2004. *The Medici Effect*; Tom Kelley. 2005. *The Ten Faces of Innovation.* New York: Doubleday Currency Books.

21. Many academics and business people have criticized business school "silo" discipline approaches. Mintzberg seeks to provide ideas for overcoming weaknesses in his book. See Henry Mintzberg. 2004. *Managers, Not MBAs: A Hard Look at the Soft Practice of Managing and Management Development.* San Francisco: Berret Koehler. Several business schools seek to overcome some of those weaknesses through partnerships with design schools. *BusinessWeek* profiled several. See Jessi Hempel and Aili McConnon. 2006. "The Talent Hunt," *BusinessWeek Online,* October 9. http://www.businessweek.com/magazine/content/06_41/b4004401.htm.

22. Several scholars and practitioners have talked of the iterative nature of the process. Peter Drucker, for instance, has long led management thinking and talked of a process for innovation. See Peter F. Drucker. 2002. "The Discipline of Innovation," *Harvard Business Review* 80 (8): 95–108. See also, J. Andrews. 1996. "Creative Ideas Take Time: Business Practices That Help Product Managers Cope with Time Pressure," *Journal of Product and Brand Management* 5 (1): 6–18; J. Richard Hackman, (Ed.). 1990. *Groups That Work (and Those That Don't).* San Francisco: Jossey-Bass; Mark D. Cannon and A. C. Edmondson. 2005. "Failing to Learn and Learning to Fail (Intelligently): How Great Organizations Put Failure to Work to Innovate and Improve," *Long Range Planning* 38:299–319.

23. Jeff Mauzy and Richard Harriman. 2003. *Creativity, Inc..* Boston, MA: Harvard Business School Press.

24. Wallas and Ghiselin posited the stages of creativity early in the last century, partly based upon their study of artists and scientists. This has become a fundamental view of creative stages and still holds some merit today. See Graham Wallas. 1926. *The Art of Thought.* London: Jonathan Cape; Bernard Ghiselin. 1952. *The Creative Process.* New York: Mentor Books.

25. For a different view on time pressure and deadlines: Warren G. Bennis and Patricia Ward Biederman. 1997. *Organizing Genius.* Reading, MA: Perseus Books; Amabile. 1999. "How to Kill Creativity."

26. See David Sutherland, Jochen Hartmann, and Markus Seidel. 2002. "From Roadmap to Roadway: Managing Innovation at BMW," in A. V. Vedpuriswar. 2002. *The Practice of Innovation.* Hyderabad, India: Icfai University Press.

27. John-Steiner has two landmark books about the creative process. One focuses on the individual, with emphasis on artists and scientists, and the other focuses on collaboration. Vera John-Steiner. 2000. *Creative Collaboration.* New York: Oxford University Press; and Vera John-Steiner. 1997. *Notebooks of the Mind: Explorations of Thinking.* New York: Oxford University Press (rev. ed.).

28. Research sometimes seems to lump creative entrepreneurs and leaders together. In *Organizing Genius,* for example, Bennis and Biederman offer both examples of people who have a vision and lead it to fruition, and examples of people

who tend to be more leaders than entrepreneurs. We sought to separate the three roles—entrepreneur, leader, and team member—to call attention to the critical positions and roles that each plays.

29. Bennis and Biederman call a group leader of a "great group" a "guider," someone to set tone, keep the group on track, understand how to get the most from positive friction, while giving members the autonomy to solve a problem. Others refer to a "creative agent," or someone who acts as a buffer for a creative group—between the group and its environment, which may be within an organization or outside of an organization. This boundary spanner encourages interaction and experimentation, and in a sense, acts as an entrepreneur for the group, finding opportunities, taking risk, exploiting resources to achieve the goals to taking advantage of the opportunity. See Nancy K. Napier and Mikael Nilsson. 2006. "The Development of Creative Capabilities In and Out of Creative Organizations: Three Case Studies," in *Creativity and Innovation Management* 15 (3, September): 268–278; Scott Shane. 2003. *A General Theory of Entrepreneurship: The Individual-Opportunity Nexus.* Cheltenham: Edward Elgar.

30. The story is available in a teaching case study. See Nicholas Athanassiou, Edward F. McDonough, Francis Spital, and David T. A. Wesley. 2003. *Compaq High Performance Computer (A).* London, Ontario, Canada: Ivey Publishing.

31. Amabile. 1999. "How to Kill Creativity"; Bennis and Biederman. 1997. *Organizing Genius.*

32. Practitioner Web sites and books, as well as some research, suggests that stories of the "underdog" winning against a big competitor in business, sports, or politics are mythic, especially in a country like the United States. Such underdog stories also are emerging abroad, for example in transition economies and among Irish entrepreneurs. See, for example, E. G. de Pillis. 1998. "What's Achievement Got to Do with It? The Role of National Culture in the Relationship between Entrepreneurship and Achievement Motivation," in P. D. Reynolds (Ed.). *Frontiers of Entrepreneurship Research.* Boston: Babson University; Jill H. Kasen. 1980. "Whither the Self-Made Man? Comic Culture and the Crisis of Legitimation in the United States," *Social Problems* 28 (2): 131–148; Justin Tan. 1996. "Regulatory Environment and Strategic Orientation in a Transitional Economy: A Study of Chinese Private Enterprise," *Entrepreneurship: Theory and Practice* 21:31–44; http://www.zeldawisdom.com/dearzelda/dearzelda_070314.shtml "being the underdog helps because no one sees you coming" http://soupornuts.wordpress.com/2007/06/19/great-heart-the-quality-that-distinguishes-underdogs-and-entrepreneurs/.

33. The curse of knowledge is a prominent concept in Dan and Chip Heath's book, *Made to Stick.* See Chip and Dan Heath. 2007. *Made to Stick.* New York: Random House.

34. Bruce W. Tuckman. 1965. "Developmental Sequence in Small Groups," *Psychological Bulletin* 63:384–399.

35. See, for example, M. D. Mumford. 2000. "Managing Creative People and Tactics for Innovation," *Human Resource Management Review* 10 (3): 313–352; C. E. Shalley and L. L. Gilson. 2004. "What Leaders Need to Know: A Review of Social and Contextual Factors That Can Foster or Hinder Creativity," *Leadership Quarterly* 15:33–53.

36. J. M. George and J. Zhou. 2002. "Understanding When Bad Moods Foster Creativity and Good Ones Don't: The Role of Context and Clarity of Feelings," *Journal of Applied Psychology* 86:513–524; J. Zhou and C. E. Schalley. 2003. "Research

on Employee Creativity: A Critical Review and Directions for Future Research," in J. J. Martocchio and G. R. Ferris (Eds.). *Research in Personnel and Human Resources Management* 22:265–217. Amsterdam: Elsevier; A. R. Jassawalla and H. C. Sashittal. 2002. "Cultures That Support Product-innovation Processes," *Academy of Management Executive* 16 (3): 42–54; P. Jeffcutt. 2000. "Management and the Creative Industries," *Studies in Cultures, Organizations and Societies* 6:123–127; Amabile. 1999. "How to Kill Creativity"; K. Kamoche, M. P. Cunha, and J. V. Cunha. 2003. "Towards a Theory of Organizational Improvisation: Looking Beyond the Jazz Metaphor," *Journal of Management Studies* 40 (8): 2023–2051.

37. See Johansson. 2004. *The Medici Effect*; Janet Bickel. 2007. "The Role of Professional Societies in Career Development in Academic Medicine," *Acad Psychiatry* 31:91–94.

38. Douglas Belkin. 2007. "Talent Scouts for Cirque du Soleil Walk a Tightrope," *Wall Street Journal*, September 8.

Part II

THE THREE DISCIPLINES

Part II, chapters 3–5, forms the core of 3D creativity and innovation, outlining the meaning of discipline in creative organizations. Each chapter discusses a creative discipline important for innovative and creative activities.

Chapter 3 considers within-discipline thinking—mastery of a field or area of expertise—and its benefits and implications. Chapter 4 focuses on out-of-discipline thinking, or finding ideas that are outside a core field. It covers why such thinking is important, how individuals and organizations approach out-of-discipline thinking, and how ideas and their users "find" each other. Finally, chapter 5 examines the notion of a disciplined process—how organizations generate and test out ideas before launching them, why some may put more emphasis on some stages of the process than others, what types of ideas emerge, and different types of collaboration.

Together these three disciplines form a platform for creative action within an organization.

Chapter 3

WITHIN-DISCIPLINE THINKING: MASTERY FOR CREATIVITY

Richard Klautsch puts in his time lifting weights, practicing drills, and refining his moves. He runs on the treadmill, watches videos of previous plays and works hard to be part of a successful team. Over the years, he's tried different positions, reads the field well, and others trust his judgment. Sounds like any university football or basketball player, right? Not quite. Richard Klautsch is a Shakespearean actor.

Like any athlete, Klautsch knows that being at the top of his field means devotion to his discipline. So, he stays in shape, trains his voice and movements to convey a character's lines, and watches films and plays to learn from others, to see what he has done well—and not so well—so that he'll stay as sharp as he can be.

WHAT YOU SEE AND WHAT YOU DON'T

Any organization needs members who are good at what they do, who have the expertise and knowledge that set them apart in their fields, and are the best people they can afford. A university looks for a teacher who's had several teaching awards; a software firm looks for a marketing director who's worked in other information technology firms; a theatre director seeks out a set designer she knows from previous experience to be one of the best in the industry.

Think about your resume. The largest section is "experience," what you've done and achieved in your career. Or, remember the last job application you filled out, or asked a potential new hire to complete: lots of questions and lines to fill on what jobs and experience came before the present one. Experience, expertise, and mastery within one's discipline are desirable—typically, the more, the better. We are talking about mastery that comes from deliberate and devoted practice over a long period—expertise as reflected in consistent, measurable, superior performance resulting in an output of concrete results.[1]

But expertise can also include less tangible, tacit knowledge about issues gained in the experience of many years of work. Brain research on judgment reports that deep expertise develops often over years of experience, where a person sees and solves similar problems.[2] Contrast a newly minted financial analyst and an experienced banker: each receives an inch-thick pile of financial information on a firm. The less-experienced analyst may need hours to review the data to find specific information that raises questions about a firm's performance. An experienced banker, who has seen many such reports and has field experience with a variety of companies, may review the extensive information and identify, within minutes, some of the possible problems in a firm's situation. As one banker with deep within-discipline knowledge says, "I've seen this sort of situation before and I can 'feel' where the trouble is." This combination of tangible knowledge and skills in financial ratios and analysis, plus less-tangible judgment gained from experience, forms the basis for deep within-discipline knowledge. It is in this combination of having run through a number of these situations, reflecting on what you learned, analyzing the situations, and practicing the moves, that you develop expertise.[3]

Organizations expect to hire people with deep technical skill, knowledge, or expertise. Some organizations, such as Google, have made it a key requisite to the company's development to attract smart people.[4] But the notion of within-discipline knowledge pushes further. As our framework, Figure 2.1, shows, within-discipline knowledge rests at the base of the discipline triangle, as the most common and fundamental of the 3Ds of creativity, and has at least three components, which we will discuss in this chapter. First, people with deep within-discipline knowledge often become among the best in their fields and typically are relentless learners. They also understand and seek to reap the benefits of being "with the best," as part of an extraordinary team or group. There is a strong connection between the individual and the organizational mastery. Next, within-discipline knowledge speeds up critical activities that support group creative efforts, by helping group members act, learn, and adjust faster. Third, as individuals and groups learn and excel in the basics of their discipline, they often feel freer to try new ideas and take risks. In other words, with less focus on the specifics of a discipline, people may move beyond the fundamentals to become more creative.

As we discuss the importance of mastery, it is important to consider the difference between deep and diverse expertise. For an organization, it is often crucial to have a broad skill set to apply in a certain situation as it develops over time, which some of our examples show. That requires skilled individuals who are able to work with and combine their own deep skill set with that of others—individuals with the ability to know what they know and what they do not know, and confident enough to allow others with the expertise to do the work they cannot.

To measure expertise is not easy, as these are often complex competencies. However, giving recognition to people who make extraordinary contributions drives performance. A recent article reviewed the ten people with the most patents in the United States. These ten people were unknown to the wider general public, but they attested that their organizations had put a premium on acquiring patents and subsequently rewarded them for their work.[5]

WITHIN DISCIPLINE: BEING (WITH) THE BEST

Best in show. Olympic champion. Oscar Award winner. Many people want to be the best in their fields—and that extends to working in organizations. Being part of an organization that people know and think highly of, like Google, Nokia, or Wipro, can give one a springier step, a sense of pride and loyalty. And to be in a top organization implies that the people within it are among the best in the field. So both being the best and being with others who are the best pushes organization members. First, they need to prove to themselves and others that they deserve to be among the best; next, to stay on top means they are constantly learning; and finally, they never want to drag others down (or be pulled down) by not keeping up with the best.

Prove It

In high-performing, highly creative organizations, key participants—whether software engineers, football players, or managers vying for promotions—need prove themselves by "selling" their abilities and expertise. Achieving a within-discipline skill or mastery is especially common and critical when people vie for similar positions. The result is ongoing internal competition. It happens every spring, for example, when football teams look for new starting players for the next season.

In January 2007, Boise State University completed its best season ever with an unexpected defeat over a hugely favored University of Oklahoma. The Boise State team then lost eleven key players, including the longtime starting quarterback, who moved on. The team was in the spot all university sports teams face at the end of one season and before the next. How to build another successful team?

In spring training 2007, Boise State coaches evaluated four potential quarterback starting candidates. How would the coaches choose? The process, of course, is a long one, where coaches and trainers observe players in many settings—in the weight room, in player-run passing drills, and in the film room—to see who will be the next quarterback. An undercurrent of competition pushes young men to be the best. In a sense, they were auditioning for a job.

Like quarterbacks, actors audition. But unlike quarterbacks, they do it continuously, often nationally, and sometimes internationally. To be tops in their fields, like Richard Klautsch, actors realize they also need to be in peak condition. The best continually push to expand their range of abilities and hone their skills as professionals. Also, because the competition is so fierce among many fine actors, some develop other characteristics that support being one of the best in the field even though those characteristics may have little to do with within-discipline or expertise as we commonly think of it.[6] Some argue that being "easy to work with" can be a competitive advantage. In the words of one actor we interviewed: "Everyone wants to work with people who are open to new ideas and who perform with integrity—and [who] are pleasant to be around. That's a good calling card to getting more work."

In its work, Cirkus Cirkör has learned that bringing in performers from around the world who are very skilled at what they do means that they sometimes need to put up with quirky behavior. The organization has learned to adapt to the best in the field—rather than expect them to adapt to the organization. The circus leaders have had to learn how to work with each individual based upon his or her needs. If you expect people to be the best you also need to give them the recognition they deserve.

Relentless Learning

In addition to encouraging people to prove themselves as being among the best, within-discipline knowledge and expertise encourages people to want to remain with the best. This often means constant and relentless learning. In the software industry, R&D members work in a field of ever-present change and competition with other firms. Their within-discipline knowledge is soon obsolete without vigilant and continuous learning. For employees in firms that value creativity and top-level performance, being the best demands commitment and an unspoken internal willingness to remain in top form. That attitude and expectation permeates all levels.

But what happens if within-discipline expertise is unavailable or uneven within a group working on a particular project?

One firm's product-development team solves the challenge of unavailable within-discipline expertise by trading knowledge. The team typically oversees three tasks: product design/development, quality assurance, and user experience. A team sometimes lacks extensive expertise in all three areas, requiring members to trade skills and expertise across teams. For this to work, of course, members must trust that colleagues working within the firm are up-to-date in their within-discipline knowledge and thus are among the best in the industry.

Such constant learning and constant improvement often entails learning from others on the team and going beyond the sources of information and knowledge that are most accessible to seeking other avenues. One football player talked of looking for ways to learn beyond what the coaches taught: "You can draw from players who are really good but do different stuff—I mean, you're kind of stealing stuff from people.... I watch NFL corner[back]s play and pick up stuff ... just by watching people that are better than you. And creativity can happen that way."

Cirkör consciously schedules experts and circus students to practice together during certain hours. In this way the students can learn from those who are more experienced, but they also see that they can acquire the skills to one day become a star. For the experienced, it is a constant reminder that if they do not keep up the hard work, many are there to take their place.

In addition, team members learn to trust that they've each pushed themselves further. An actor described feeling like he was making himself vulnerable to another actor in a scene. To do so required great trust—in the other actor, in the output of their joint work, and in the overall confidence of the director overseeing their work. So each person continually improves to be one of the best and to work with the best.

When Things Go Wrong: Missing or Messing with Expertise

When strong group members have deep expertise, they expect it from others. So when members lack such knowledge, an imbalance occurs within the group, which can cause a type of jerkiness during the creative process. Conversation and idea flow may slow, stop altogether, or go in directions that sideline an original discussion. Bob Keiser, a software engineer who frequently seeks input from his colleagues, found that when others who are "interested" show up at the meeting, the results can be frustrating: "We need people who are extremely knowledgeable about the subject, at least at some level. They don't necessarily have to know the details, but they have to … understand enough to communicate. [If they don't,] the next thing you know, they're asking questions, which is good, but it kind of ends up distracting the process."

In contrast to people who lack within-discipline knowledge but want to learn, others may have the knowledge but be unwilling or unable to move beyond it. Rather than asking questions to learn beyond a narrow discipline, they stay within a discipline silo. One manager hired an employee who, he claimed, shouldn't have been talking to customers because she didn't fully understand the product or the technology. As a result, in her interactions with customers, she ended up providing what he called a "silo" of information, or parts of what the customers needed to know, not an integrated body that covered both product and technology knowledge.

If the within-discipline knowledge imbalance is too great, distrust and sometimes outright indifference may emerge. High-performing groups show patterns of deeply skilled individuals that are put together to work as a team. Groups with low expertise but ability to work as a team do not perform as well. However, to put skilled individuals together generates friction and more work, initially, to build trust, develop work routines, and so on. That means adequate time is required to get things started.[7]

An example of an imbalance happened in a regional professional theatre in New England that hired a stage manager and assistant manager with little within-discipline expertise to oversee a production of twenty actors, many quite experienced. The cast and the managers clashed, as it became clear the managers were in over their heads. Some cast members tried to help the stage manager, who resisted, feeling he was being overruled (likely true). Eventually, as one actor described the situation, the result was disappointing for all: "[What I learned is] if everyone does their jobs, and cares about the production, there's no problem. The result [here] was that many [actors and support] people who worked on that show will never work for that theatre again."

Finally, in some situations, different people bring different types of within-discipline expertise to a project, but the success of the project depends upon one group or person being able to convey that expertise to others, who have to work with it or implement it. Sometimes the originator of an idea is negligent in providing enough guidance on how to carry out the project. The expert simply could believe that her job is complete once the idea has been formed. In each case, the expert gives the impression of expecting the implementers to be able to "read her mind," likely an improbable wish for most of us. Ideas require some sense of familiarity, a notion of how and where they could fit within the overall structure of the host organization, for others to take them on.[8]

During preparation for a theatre production, the painter and builders worked with a set designer who was knowledgeable about his field, but unorganized and unclear about what he expected from the technicians. For them, his designs were sketchy and vague, forcing them to wonder what he wanted. Further, because he was often unavailable when technicians had questions, their work slowed. The painter didn't know whether the paint should have a "heavy" or "light" feel on the set, which was important because the difference would affect overall tone of the set and color intensity. Even worse, the set design plans were so unclear in one area that technicians couldn't tell whether to build a tree, a cart, or a building.

Thus, having within-discipline knowledge is great, but when people work together, the ability to convey that knowledge to others can make all the difference.

WITHIN-DISCIPLINE KNOWLEDGE: SPEEDING UP ACTIVITIES

Unless you're in software, theatre, football, or geophysics, you're likely to be unfamiliar with terms like *agile development, tech week, the O-line,* or *void spaces.*[9] Yet, experts in any field use jargon and within-discipline lingo almost without realizing its power.

While it baffles people from outside a field, within-discipline language has important purposes. First, jargon allows faster communication among members in the group that understand it. Biologists, physical therapists, or financial analysts can talk in their disciplinary shorthand to each other and know precisely what they mean. When they talk to people outside their fields, of course, experts adjust their language to a lower common denominator way of speaking—using language that lay persons understand, but which may lack the precision or richness of the jargon. So within-discipline knowledge and expertise offers users an advantage of speed—in acting, learning, and adjusting.

Fast to Act

Within-discipline language allows participants to become a team, understand the tasks at hand, and move faster in pursuing them. This has several payoffs. First, it can help organization members answer the question of "what do we do now?" Next, within-discipline knowledge allows an expert or group to create some output quickly; in cases where time is a competitive advantage, the ability to act quickly helps a team or organization succeed. Finally, in some settings, jargon may even become a form of code for members.

Where Do We Go Now?

When outsiders first hear actors talking about "going deeper into a character" or "building the concept," they often think, "What a pretentious profession!" Yet, such abstract phrases (to a nonactor) have meaning on many levels that help guide subsequent decisions of actors or directors. For director Risa Brainin, "building the concept" refers to deciding a key question: "Why this play, for this setting and this audience, at this time?" Once a director answers those questions, she has a "concept" for the play—the time period, the tone, whether it will be more traditional and stylized or more informal and natural. In the business equivalent, it clarifies the mission—what the organization will do, why, and for what customers. From that concept flow decisions that are tangible and understandable to anyone involved, such as the type of stage design (modern London, ancient Greece, or Middle Ages), costumes to match, sound/music, and whether the actors will be formal or more informal in their presentation of lines.

Likewise, in the football world, "building the system," is similar. It means creating an internal culture and set of processes for training, practicing, and more, that shape the future direction of a program. For players and coaches, "the system" has meaning; for outsiders, it sounds like an abstract phrase. Thus, within-discipline language and concepts can clarify goals and subsequent tasks that organization members will pursue.

Now We Know What to Do, Let's Do It

Second, within-discipline knowledge can speed activity, especially under deadlines. A medical information company frequently holds planning sessions and typically has 80 percent of the same people from session to session. An advantage, of course, is that the group knows core products, their history, and can quickly build toward the next steps because of some of that historical knowledge. As one manager put it, "[Participants] know what the campaigns are and what information we are looking for or we are trying to get out of that day."

Watching two acrobats rehearsing for a coming performance is interesting, but hard to decipher for an outsider. As the director gives them ideas of what she wants them to do, they work together to create an act. Not much is said, but there's a stream of small movements with the arms, placing each other in different positions, pulling the rope to the side and then winding it up in a spiral, small nods, "Yeses," "If you can ...," "Hmmm," "Let's try ...". These coded signals give enough information to try the act again in a new way. There is a common language that, as you work together over time, you know how to interpret.

In theatre, where budgets are slim, speed is critical in building sets, creating costumes, and rehearsing actors. This requires the art of "enough" discipline. In contrast to the designer whose drawings are vague and require that the technicians go back for clarification, or worse, make decisions that might go against what a designer wants and risk having to redo them later, some designers are so explicit that technicians can build sets faster and more accurately. With accurate drawings, the time needed to build sets drops, allowing time for the designer to get input from the builders. An admiring technician described his dream designer: "He sat down at the drawing table and drew it all out—to the nuts and bolts, literally. [You'd need] a magnifying glass it to see it.... At times he needed to see [the part we built] and changed a few things but it was always for the better. And he asked for our opinions ... got input from us and respected our opinions."

Codes and Signals

Finally, while some within-discipline jargon is common across professions, in some types of organizations it may vary. For example, in college football, many ideas and plays are common, but each program develops its own language or code for plays, drills, or patterns. When coaches or players move from one team to another, they learn that a play called "Wild Bill Two" in one program may be "Slight Swing 55" on another team. Such variation happens in part because teams play in front of their competitors. To foil the opponent, coaches and players refer to plays using their own codes and signals. For example, to convey a play to a quarterback, two players send hand signals from the sideline. One is the real play, the other is fake. So even if opposing coaches and players were able to decode the hand signals, they still wouldn't know which signal conveys the upcoming play.

Another example of the importance of codes or values comes from Health-wise, a nonprofit health information deliverer; the "Healthwise Way" is a form of code for helping employees make decisions about their actions. The company uses "teamwork, doing the right thing, and respect for others" as fundamental values for the way people work and act. The details of those concepts are conveyed through orientation meetings with new employees, cited frequently in meetings, and posted around the headquarters building.

Cirkör acknowledges that all organizations have their own codes and language that govern their actions. However, when people join from other organizations, they adopt the approach of being "humbly ignorant." They say, "We understand you have all this language, but if we may be *humbly ignorant* we do not understand that code nor will we adopt it to work together. Instead we want to create our own logic and ways of working in this collaborative venture." This approach allows them to break people and organizations free from ingrained perceptions of how things "should be" to work, and to start ventures fresh.

Fast to Learn

Sometimes, creative work and fast learning occur together. Many of us have people we tap to help us think through tough decisions or knotty problems. Even, or maybe especially, members of creative groups and organizations realize that they can't figure out problems alone very often. Software manager Bob Keiser saw it as critical to bring in other people as he sorted through a problem. But also, since the two he most often "drug in" were relatively new to the firm, he was using his brainstorming, problem-solving sessions almost as training for them: "There were two main guys that I would drag in a lot [to help me figure out problems.] It was very important that they start learning the whys and the backgrounds of all this. Plus, I can't figure it out on my own. I don't know what the heck the stupid product is supposed to be, right? So you need more than one mind to evolve this thing and pull it off." Implicit in his comment was the idea that smart, creative people can learn fast. He wanted input for solving his problem and he wanted to illuminate for others the organization's challenges so they could learn to learn quickly. This was especially important in an organization where employees tend to remain for many years. In this firm, once engineers joined the firm, few left—not so for a university sports team.

A university football program typically has four years or, at most, five, with a given player. Coaches frequently talk about the challenge of bringing new players "into the system" and helping the players "get it" as soon as possible. So bringing the players in as freshmen and convincing them of the importance of spending time to learn their discipline is crucial. One player talked about how he reached a point where he had the within-discipline knowledge that helped him move to another level in his work: "From experience, watching film and trying to get better … one day it just clicks. You just go out there on the field and it seems a lot easier—you're not trying as hard and not thinking as hard." Likewise, speedy learning works well when an organization has prepared members to shift roles or positions. The Boise State football team, similar to the New England Patriots, has a philosophy of developing players to step into several positions. Thus, their within-discipline language (and training) has allowed them to learn new positions quickly. While most teams may have one or two players for a position, this one typically develops up to four or five as backups.

The team's multiposition tactic offers two benefits—when injuries occur, alternative players are ready to step in and are up to speed. In addition, players with that wider expertise may have more chance to play, again because they are ready. Rather than relying on the same ten to twelve players as first string, this team has several who could play. When injuries occur, coaches become more creative in how to staff the personnel on the field. It also allows for more flexibility. One coach explained: "A lot of teams will have ten players that are going to play ball.... For us, [in one game,] the free safety got hurt ... but I don't think anybody batted an eye. We said, we'll just take another guy and throw him in there." Having more players as backups increases the depth and range of abilities, makes players more flexible physically and mentally, and widens the options open to coaches.

Finally, depth of player skill and ability—in other words, extensive within-discipline expertise across several people—has another advantage. Because so many players could step into different positions, the opposing team is likely to be more confused, because the "personnel" (players who come onto the field for a given play) are less predictable and thus harder to prepare for and respond to.

Fast to Adapt

Finally, within-discipline knowledge and expertise can allow members of a team to adjust behavior and actions quickly. The Boise State football coaches "overprepare" players—they practice and drill in the techniques and knowledge of the game to the point where players are so comfortable with the knowledge, they can adjust more quickly and are unfazed when changes emerge.

The ability to adapt to new situations and team members is also a key point in selling oneself, especially in the arts world. A musical designer with years of experience in London has watched modern dance troupes from Europe to Asia. He finds Helene Peterson, cofounder of the Drop Dance group, one of the best choreographers he has seen worldwide. Even though she is an accomplished dancer herself, she excels at choreographing routines for actors and nonprofessional dancers.

Peterson is inventive in the dance steps, but perhaps more importantly, she reads the actors and dancers, matches steps to their abilities, confidence, and personalities. In a sense, she adapts her within-discipline knowledge to understand and translate what she knows for the users of that knowledge. She knows how to design dance steps and movement, depending on the actors, no matter who they are. She is able to draw upon deep expertise, yet is extraordinary at adjusting her approach—and the choreography—for actors who are not dancers. As a result, she is in high demand for choreographing dances and plays.

A circus group that was on tour a few years ago was asked one afternoon while at an event if they could do an impromptu show, because there was a gap in the schedule. Within an hour the circus group had created a perform-ance that allowed them to dazzle the audience. One of the members expressed it in this way: "Because we had the building blocks and the skill set of the group, we could quickly put something together. Since we had rehearsed together prior to going on tour, we knew each other well, we all had parts of an act, and could quickly and almost without words communicate what had to be done to put together a performance."

MOVING BEYOND THE FUNDAMENTALS

We spent hours talking to actors, directors, and designers. They are tall and short, old and young, balding and full-haired, male and female, Asian American and from Delaware, gay and straight, and introverts (surprisingly) and extroverts (not surprising, but apparently not typical). None were overweight.

Then Nancy talked to football players.

"Good height, good weight, good legs." That's the best compliment a coach will give a player. But that abstract phrase meant little until the inter-views began. Football players are BIG—more than twice the size of some of the actors, maybe three times their size. Even their chairs are large: the confer-ence room where the program holds meetings for the full team has stadium chairs at least six inches wider than the norm.

One college football player, now a professional football player for an NFL (National Football League) team, was an offensive lineman, or, as he would say, "on the O-line." Articulate, comfortable with media interviews, he had a turn of phrase for much of what we talked about. And one phrase he used related to the value of his knowledge to help speed learning and to "go beyond the fundamentals." By this, he meant that he had put in the time and work to know how to block, tackle, shift position, read the players in front of him, and know where to be to protect the quarterback, all the basics of his position. As he reached the point where his within-discipline knowledge became part of him, he could free his mind to "go beyond the fundamentals," and be more creative or improvise in how he does his offensive line job.

Moving beyond the fundamentals in their disciplines allows people to do two things. First, it allows them to move outside of their expected perform-ance limits. Second, it allows them the chance to add depth, sometimes unseen or unexpected, to their outputs or performances.

Stretching Performance Limits

Within-discipline expertise seems to liberate individuals and groups to move outside of what they might normally expect they could or should do. In a way, they exceed performance boundaries to develop new approaches that fit their situations or personalities. In the football team, for example, coaches insist that players have basic skills and plays committed to physical and mental memory before they may play multiple positions. The coaches then overdrill or overprepare players (in the good sense).

According to football coaches, such overpreparation allows players to move to more creative plays, because they know and are relaxed about the fundamental ones. One defensive player commented that he had played for almost a year and a half before feeling comfortable enough that he didn't "have to think so much about what was going on." In his mind, he had reached a point where he knew what was expected of the defensive group and then he could start improvising and trying a few new things.

Actors also talk about learning more than they need to, which in turn improves and deepens a performance. In theatre, the audience sees only what appears on the stage. What makes a performance stronger, though, is the attitude of directors and actors toward preparation and pushing beyond the fundamentals.

In a particular play, two or more actors may work on the backstory in a scene to decide what it means for their characters, especially as they interact. For instance, *King Lear* revolves around the relationship of a father (Lear) and three daughters. At no point does the play itself mention the three daughters' mother. Yet, for one production, the director asked the three actors playing the daughters to discuss, and agree on, what had happened to "Mrs. Lear." Since each daughter likely had a different relationship with her mother, that could have influenced the individual relationships with their father, as well as their relationships as sisters. For this play, the actors agreed that the mother had died in childbirth when the third daughter (Cordelia) was born, many years after the first two daughters. This agreement helped clarify the bitterness in Shakespeare's language that comes out among the daughters and between the daughters and their father. While none of this appears in the play itself, the three actors felt it added to the depth of knowledge of the play and, according to one of them, allowed her to be more creative in how she played the character.

Other actors talk of going deeper into a performance by making the work nearly invisible, or "erasing the track." One actor talks about the challenge and importance of making the lines her own: "I don't think people understand how creative theatre work is. Most think the hard part is learning the lines. But it's really 'making those lines human'—sounding like they're your lines. Because when we do it well, it's invisible. Our job is to erase the track."

Seeing the Big Picture

A second aspect of moving beyond the fundamentals, once deep knowledge is second nature, is that creative group members can begin to see beyond their own jobs, to see what they call a "bigger picture." A software manager pushes engineers to reach for and see the larger product and output they are working on. In his view, the more of the problem engineers know about and see, the more innovative they can be. As he says, with small parts or pieces of a problem, their creativity is "going to be strained by what they're working with. Then, their world is small, right? And so, it's all about broadening it." Compare this to the Toyota approach, where creativity and innovative approaches within one area can come to have large effects on the overall performance of a process.

Football players talk of learning more about the bigger picture as they learn more about their own jobs. A former university player who became a professional football player commented on the importance of a quarterback learning broader vision: "Occasionally, a quarterback is so experienced that he'll see [several receivers] on the field. But a young quarterback has tunnel vision ... and will have a quick release so that he can get rid of the ball. But ... for a more experienced quarterback ... his vision becomes greater."

John Naisbitt, well-known futurist, has recently tried to understand what it is he does that makes him good at describing developments with an impact on society. He has identified his mindset as the key thing that allows him to describe and analyze the world around him. So, for him, mastery is seeing the big picture.[10]

Opening Up to Creativity

Offensive linemen, play directors, circus actors, and engineers—their common thread has been to learn the fundamentals and then creativity will come. One football player's comment applies to them all. We close with a comment from Chris Carr, a former Boise State receiver who now plays professionally for the Oakland Raiders. For him, within-discipline expertise leads naturally to moving beyond the fundamentals, team creativity, and performance. As he says, "To be successful, it is drilling and repetition—staying within the framework of your scheme. But [sometimes] there's 'exception to the rule'—sometimes you have to improvise. [And] it makes a great team great. You have to have good skilled players who can go outside the scheme and do things that no one person can do."

WITHIN-DISCIPLINE MASTERY

The core idea in this chapter is that any organization aspiring to be creative should, as one part, focus on developing within-discipline mastery. Individuals within the organization need to continuously build their skill sets to be the best they can. The organization needs to ensure that these individuals are pushed, coached, praised, and tested to try new things and work together to develop innovative and creative ideas, products or performances. As a manager and member of an organization you can take different steps to develop this discipline. How do you address the issues raised in this chapter?

- *How can you master your field?* The more you are experienced and knowledgeable in one field, the better. What is the field you should master? How do you keep track of your performance? Who can be your coach and who is the star you should learn from and aspire to be?
- *What does it take to be with the best and be the best?* Competition among peers and restless learning prompt excellence, creativity, and innovation. The ability to clearly communicate knowledge is almost as crucial as the mastery of knowledge itself. Deep within-discipline expertise and good communication boost the creative process. What would be your training regimen to be better at it? How do you boost internal competition, yet keep people to play nice and work productively together?
- *Do you have the codes and language that give you speed?* Fast communication and trust is possible through the use and development of a common and discipline-specific jargon. That prompts fast action, learning, and adaptation to the environment, all elements that are part of staying or becoming cutting edge. Are you all on the same page? Can you identify common ways of expressing things that would enable quicker communication as well as communicate a shared purpose and belonging?
- *How do you push the boundaries to extend the reach and range of the expertise in the organization and its members?* With mastery of the field, individuals and groups can focus less on the discipline itself and move beyond the fundamentals. This "liberation" enables them to see the big picture and be more creative.

As a football player said, "to be successful, it is drilling and repetition. But (sometimes) you have to improvise."

NOTES

1. K. Anders Ericsson, Michael J. Prietula, and Edward T. Cokley. 2007. "The Making of an Expert," *Harvard Business Review* (July–August): 114–121.

2. In recent years, researchers in neuroscience, management, and medicine have begun to understand more about the brain and creativity, and some have raised questions about how expertise may work against a broader way of thinking. See, for

example, Nancy C. Andreasen. 2005. *The Creating Brain: The Neuroscience of Genius.* New York: Dana Press; Jerome Groopman. 2007. *How Doctors Think.* New York: Houghton Mifflin; Dorothy Leonard and Walter Swap. 2005. *Deep Smarts: How to Cultivate and Transfer Enduring Business Wisdom.* Boston: Harvard Business School Press.

3. Ericsson, Prietula, and Cokley. 2007. "The Making of an Expert."

4. Gary Hamel. 2007. *The Future of Management.* Boston: Harvard Business School Press.

5. Kevin Maney. 2007. "Masters of Invention," *Portfolio* November: 37–38.

6. Increasingly, organizations and researchers emphasize the importance of social skills and tempering negative displays of competitive behaviors. This can be seen in some of the ideas from works such as Daniel Goleman. 1995. *Emotional Intelligence: Why It Can Matter More Than IQ.* New York: Bantam Books; Robert I. Sutton. 2007. *No Asshole: Building a Civilized Workplace and Surviving One That Isn't.* New York: Warner Business Books; and Marshall Goldsmith and Mark Reiter. 2007. *What Got You Here Won't Get You There: How Successful People Become Even More Successful.* New York: Hyperion.

7. Taylor and Greve found that deeply skilled teams in the cartoon industry produced the best results. They also found that these teams showed high levels of friction and required enough time to work together prior to performing. The teams that performed worst were those with new people without a deep expertise that could still work well as a team. A. Taylor and H. R. Greve. 2006. "Superman or the Fantastic Four? Knowledge Combination and Experience in Innovative Teams," *Academy of Management Journal* 49 (4): 723–740. Presentation by the authors at the Academy of Management, Philadelphia, August 2007.

8. Davenport, Prusak, and Wilson found in their research that certain individuals in an organization are crucial to the finding and adoption of new ideas that develop organizational performance, such as Six Sigma and Knowledge Management. One of the key steps these individuals undertook to give the ideas traction was to shape them in the language of and in line with key objectives of the host organization. They called this "Packaging." See Thomas H. Davenport, Laurence Prusak, and H. James Wilson. 2003. "Who Is Bringing You Hot Ideas (and How Are You Responding)?" *Harvard Business Review* (February): 58–65.

9. Briefly defined, the terms are as follows. *Agile development* is a Microsoft-created process that allows developers to create "features" or almost discreet parts to a program, in smaller chunks, with regular testing and review; one goal is to decrease final time for beta-testing and increase creative time. *Tech week* is the final testing, fixing period (can be a week or more) right before opening night in theatre when the play is fully integrated, including all actors, staging, music, lighting, and props. The *O-line* is the nickname for the offensive line of football players who stand on the line of scrimmage and whose job it is to protect the quarterback. Finally, *void spaces* are the pockets in geologic matter (subsurface of the earth) where material such as water or oil or granite exist.

10. John Naisbitt. 2006. *Mind Set! Reset Your Thinking and See the Future.* New York: HarperCollins.

Chapter 4

OUT-OF-DISCIPLINE THINKING

I roamed the countryside searching for answers to things I did not understand. Why shells existed on the tops of mountains. How the various circles of water form around the spot which has been struck by a stone, and why a bird sustains itself in the air. These questions and other strange phenomena engaged my thought throughout my life.

Leonardo da Vinci

Following his long career in the film industry, a retired Hollywood producer bought a farm in Iowa. One day, after swatting at flies and having no luck hitting them, he began thinking about, and then reading about, fly eyes. He learned that flies' compound eyes can sense rapid motion and also have a wide range. He used that information to create a wearable camera, shaped somewhat like the goggles in the movie *Matrix*. He shopped the idea around, figuring that sports, especially football, might be a possible market. He claimed that a football quarterback wearing the "fly eye" goggle "camera," which is more a sort of projector, could "practice" a full game, including snapping and throwing. But most important, as the camera "showed" plays in the game, the quarterback could learn how to read the field and position of other players—by himself, alone, in a room.

The producer, an expert in the field of film and cameras, took knowledge from entomology, a discipline he knew little about but could see value in for his field, to create an unusual wearable, self-contained projector that could have use in a third field, sports. Like Leonardo da Vinci, curiosity engaged his thought.

The story illustrates the complex and challenging process of coming up with an idea in one field, transferring it to another, and transforming it into value for the experts in a new area. Along the way, new knowledge and expertise needs to enter into the process, often through collaboration, to develop the idea further and build capabilities. This is something few organizations manage well. And it is hard to make it a success.

In this chapter we will describe approaches for employing out-of-discipline processes, the value of doing so, and the tough work and choices involved.

In most professions, we are trained to find an area of expertise and then build credibility, knowledge, and skill within it. It makes sense, given the explosion of knowledge within all fields, our access to information, and the need for specialists who can understand the intricacies of a given field. Medical patients quickly move from the general internist to specialists; business managers seek consultants in lean production or mergers and acquisitions; dancers specialize in ballet or modern dance in a given period of their careers.

Yet, the dangers of being bombarded with so much knowledge in a given field, coupled with the complexity of the world's environment, demand broader thinking. Some organizations and professions are beginning to acknowledge the need for wider perspectives. Executive MBA programs are focused on helping functional managers become general managers, developing their understanding across disciplines. The medical profession is increasingly acknowledging that by following a single thread in diagnosis, from a specialist's area, doctors may miss the bigger picture, which could provide more accurate diagnoses.[1]

Out-of-discipline thinking challenges and also complements the dominance of expertise and within-discipline knowledge. The retired film producer epitomizes the ability to go beyond a field to generate new ideas—whether as a way to solve a problem, create a new product or service, or simply to pursue another career. Yet many examples, from both the past and today, illustrate the public skepticism that comes when scientists, artists, business people, and others reach outside of a discipline or, worse, when they question or undermine the foundations of the accepted view of a discipline. Those bringing new ideas or methods are often laughed at, reviled, or condemned in one way or another.

The literature is also filled with examples of the difficulty organizations face as they aim to transform themselves. Past evolutionary progress makes them blind to new venues of development and unable to absorb new knowledge and practices. Yet the ability to think outside of a discipline will become increasingly fundamental to an organization's ability to adjust and adapt.

In this chapter, we talk about out-of-discipline thinking and the ability to draw upon fields outside one's primary area of expertise to find and create useful ideas. A step higher on the discipline triangle, it is more challenging to do and somewhat less common in organizations. First, we'll talk about why we need out-of-discipline thinking in organizations seeking to enhance their creativity and innovation. Next, we'll discuss three types of commonly used out-of-discipline thinking processes. Finally, we'll talk about how ideas and users can find each other, and the discipline required to do so.

OUT-OF-DISCIPLINE THINKING: CHALLENGING THE STATUS QUO

Louis Pasteur's theory of germs is ridiculous fiction.

           Pierre Pachet, French physiology professor, 1872

Out-of-discipline thinking has a rocky history. More often than not, outliers of science, art, and even organizational studies have been viewed skeptically, often with derision, rather than welcomed quickly or at all. Lucas Turin's theory of smell, based upon molecular vibration, directly challenges and raises the hackles of scientists who hold the reigning view: that we sense different smells because molecules have different shapes.[2] Picasso's striking shift from realism to cubism and beyond was difficult to comprehend for many artists and consumers used to impressionism and the "pretty paintings" of the late 1800s and early 1900s. Mary Parker Follett (1868–1933), long-neglected organizational consultant and scholar, posed ideas that drew from political science, social work, public administration, and business to suggest new approaches to management that are only now gaining attention and recognition.[3]

Lonely are those in science, art, and organizational management who hold views that integrate ideas from different disciplines, or who stretch beyond the prevailing assumptions. Systems for measuring career development and organizational success are focused on maintaining the current system, and often fail to capture and reward the ability to transgress borders. Yet, when such people or ideas fall between the cracks, because of the difficulty of fitting a person or group or idea into an existing category, it means a diminished capacity to capture and develop such critical ideas.

One example of the importance of capturing off-the-wall ideas is found in the work of two medical researchers from Perth, Australia. In the early 1980s, they suggested that bacteria cause ulcers, and that antibiotics could help cure them.[4] The scientific world yawned. The idea came from two medical scientists, one who was not yet an M.D., and was dismissed as implausible; it made little sense to other scientists, since it came from outsiders unknown to the general research community. These two scientists were based in Perth, a city on the edge of the known scientific, and geographic, world. Like Turin and his unusual theory of scent, Barry Marshall and Robin Warren tried repeatedly to publish their findings, with little success.

Then they became desperate.

Eventually, Marshall decided to experiment on himself, and drank a glass of the bacteria he believed to be the culprit of ulcers. Most likely to his colleagues' horror—but to his own delight—he immediately showed early stage ulcer symptoms. He then began a regimen of antibiotics and bismuth and eventually recovered. He showed that bacteria could cause ulcers and antibiotics could help cure them.

Even though world scientists remained skeptical, Marshall's self-experimentation and results were dramatic enough to compel others to reexamine the idea. By 1994, the National Institutes of Health in the United States endorsed their claims and, in 2005, the two formerly unknown, noncredible scientists received the Nobel Prize in medicine.

As Mark Twain has said, "A person with a new idea is a crank until the idea succeeds."

Who Needs Out-of-Discipline Thinking?

In the "flat" or "spiky" world of twenty-first century organizations, thinking beyond borders—geographic and disciplinary—is increasingly important for survival, let alone sustainability. The ability to identify and grasp ideas that depart from a discipline's traditional modes of operating, thinking, and framing problems, as well as the ability to prioritize ideas, should be fundamental and expected, rather than a characteristic we consider unusual. Different groups, whether organizations, scientists, entrepreneurs, or groups within organizations, may find out-of-discipline thinking to be a skill useful for achieving their goals. But each may be driven toward it, or use it, to meet different types of needs.

The cases that make up the core of this book are all smaller organizations, and several are headed by the people that have taken them to a top position. Driven by their need to develop and grow, it would seem natural that they start looking outside for new ideas and input. Yet, small organizations are often limited by their lack of resources and the necessity to attend to daily operations. But these organizations have stayed open to new ideas.

The inclination of large organizations to grow stale makes their outside focus even stronger, for several reasons. First, changing environments create conditions in which historically successful approaches may no longer work. Organizations, particularly mature and larger ones, need to look to new approaches and strategies to survive, let alone thrive. Second, experts in some fields, from science and cognitive areas to entrepreneurial startups, increasingly acknowledge that major advances will come from finding the problems—and solutions—that fall on the intersections among and between fields, not within single fields alone. Finally, we know that creativity in groups happens more effectively when group members are diverse, or come from different backgrounds. The diversity may lie in physical, tangible differences, such as ethnic, age or gender makeup, or disciplinary backgrounds. We'll examine how different groups need and use out-of-discipline thinking.

Mature firms can be vulnerable when they use historically successful approaches.[5] This happens if they become insensitive to environmental changes, which may occur for a variety of reasons. One of the biggest vulnerabilities is believing past successes will carry them forward. But many are adapting and getting better at timing appropriate responses.

Microsoft and IBM are classic examples of mature firms that have moved beyond their successful disciplinary history to exploit changes and find new directions. In the early 1990s, Microsoft and IBM, leaders in proprietary software, began to realize the industry itself was changing. The founders of the idea of open source software, including MIT's Richard Stallman, were turning up the heat. Stallman's "GNU manifesto" envisioned software that was developed, revised, and used for free by many, rather than held closely by a few powerful firms. It was, of course, the basis of what we now call open-source software.[6] As IBM's researchers realized they couldn't fight the changes coming from open sourcing, they looked for ways to eventually complement it—by developing advanced software "on top of" the open source code.

The reliance on, and difficulty to break free from, the past is also a reason why many entrepreneurial ventures spring out of established firms. Some firms, like Baxter, become known as generators of entrepreneurs and new ventures.[7] Ideas spring out of needs or opportunities identified by some in these large organizations. To allow them to develop, they are taken outside the structure of the firm. The knowledge, gained while in the larger firm, gives the entrepreneur deep knowledge about the industry, access to capital, relationships, and knowledge. These factors provide better conditions for growth.

Growing competition forced managers at Netflix, the DVD movie provider, to think differently. As Blockbuster, long dominating the U.S. retail store movie rental market, seriously challenged Netflix's leading position in the DVD mailing service market, Netflix had to adjust the way it interacted with customers. It took an approach that a decade ago would have been expected; in these days of outsourcing to low country bidders, it seems like heresy.

Netflix had traditionally used only e-mail to interact with customers. Yet as Blockbuster moved in, Netflix found a new way to interact. In 2006, Netflix dropped its e-mail customer service altogether and started a call center, with a difference.[8] Rather than outsource the call center to India, Netflix set up shop in Portland, Oregon. A call center, rather than e-mail service, keeps the firm closer to customers. It provides a "human voice" and thus perhaps a greater chance of retaining customers. The firm located the call center in Portland because its managers found people there to be "unfailingly" polite. Taking an old idea, one that had nearly left the discipline of customer service, Netflix brought it back to life.

Finally, market survival—or domination—faces many firms today. Richard D'Aveni, strategy expert and Dartmouth Tuck School professor, argues that firms will need to pursue several tactics to secure a stronghold in their markets.[9] One is "shape shifting," or finding new ways to change the borders and nature of the competitive landscape. Sometimes, it requires that a firm learn about a new field or discipline. Apple, for instance, redrew the boundaries of industries, as it moved from the iPod to the iPhone. Rather than remain solely in the music delivery industry, Apple crossed the border into the mobile-device market, combining what it had done well for years with a new field that allowed it to expand its existing markets and take customers away from another industry's existing market.

In 1959, Oxford don C. P. Snow published *Two Cultures and the Scientific Revolution*.[10] In it, he argued that scholars from the natural sciences and from the humanities inhabited two different intellectual cultures that did not interact or communicate with one another. Furthermore and more startling for the scientists, Snow claimed that from the 1930s on, the literary and humanities scholars designated themselves as "the intellectuals," essentially excluding scientists and their contributions from the intellectual landscape. Think of it. Virginia Woolf is an intellectual, but Albert Einstein is not. By this, Snow meant that the humanities scholars found ways to write for and interact with the public more readily than did scientists, who rarely reached out beyond their scientific colleagues. In an updated version a few years later, Snow was a bit more optimistic. In *The Two Cultures: A Second Look*, Snow suggested that a third culture would emerge, in which the scientists and the humanities scholars would in fact communicate with one another.

Some people think Snow still has it wrong.

John Brockman, founder of Edge.org's Third Culture Web site, says Snow's dream of a "third culture" in which literary and scientific intellectuals would exchange ideas failed.[11] Instead, Brockman claims scientists never did start talking to the humanities scholars (perhaps they were peeved at being ignored), but rather began speaking directly to the public, building understanding and appreciation for the wonders and joys of science. Think of Carl Sagan, Stephen Jay Gould, and Richard Feynman.[12] Partly because of these men and others with a willingness to reach out, Brockman claims a different type of "third culture" has now emerged.

Brockman's "Third Culture" includes thinkers—mostly scientists but also artists, philosophers, and even some brave humanists—who address big societal and scientific questions that can "redefine who we are." They do it by reaching outside of their disciplines.

Indeed, in Brockman's world, discipline boundaries may become moot.[13] Brockman's 2003 edited book, *The Next Fifty Years*, and his more recent *What Is Your Dangerous Idea?* bring home the point. In *The Next Fifty Years*, twenty-five scientists, ranging from cosmologists to mathematicians to biologists to psychologists, offer predictions of what the main problems and developments will be in their fields and beyond. Many suggest that major advances within fields, such as biology or physics or psychology, will give way to advances that combine knowledge and insights across several fields to solve problems that are very much in the world, rather than strictly in theory. Bioengineering will help quarterbacks throw footballs more effectively. Neuropsychology could help counselors develop more successful methods to work with autistic children. Already, mathematician Ian Stewart says changes in computers, bioinformatics, and financial engineering will blur pure and applied math. Because problems will not stay within a traditional narrowly defined discipline, solutions need to be developed the same way—to the increasing interaction or even clash of disciplines confronting each other.

Likewise, in *What Is Your Dangerous Idea?* 108 contributors from neuroscience to physics, art to philosophy, posit ideas that "are defended with evidence ... by serious scientists and thinkers ... but that challenge the collective decency of an age" (xvii). As in Brockman's earlier book, the weaving of ideas across disciplines is promiscuous—and imperative—for creativity and innovation.

Out-of-discipline thinking also matters in entrepreneurial ventures, where clashing ideas and interactions may lead to new business ideas and problem solutions.[14] When he was at Stanford, Professor Martin Ruef found that the most creative entrepreneurs tend to interact more with people they do not know well, often people from different walks of life, backgrounds or fields, than with close colleagues or business associates. The best of them sought out distant colleagues and strangers and built what are called "weak ties."[15] Ruef and others have found that these weak ties offer more breadth of information—from other fields and disciplines. Creative entrepreneurs hear and learn from people or sources in fields other than their own, and are able to connect them. Ruef claims the weak ties allow entrepreneurs to experiment more easily because they are less constrained by expectations within their own circles or disciplines. The information from various sources, then, is input for creative entrepreneurs to generate innovation, if the entrepreneur has an ability to integrate those disparate bits of information.

At the same time, the "out there" idea is more likely to be considered if the person proposing it is in a central position, one where he or she can gain attention or set the agenda. The more central you are, the more likely your information is taken into consideration. However, and here's a catch, as you get more central, that is, advance in your organization based on great new ideas, you are less subjected to new information that you found earlier because you were on the fringes. Thus, balancing the influx of new ideas with the ideas already there, and balancing a central existence with life on the fringes, become critical.[16]

Broader ideas come also when organizational members go outside to cocreate with another organization. In addition, the process of working with an outsider group sometimes offers a way to gain new perspective. In a sense, an outside group may help "reflect" the organization's strengths and how best to build its strategic capabilities. Cirkus Cirkör has through numerous cocreation processes gained clarity about what their core interests are and how to better structure them for mutual benefit and growth. To develop your organization through interaction with other organizations, whether municipalities, businesses, or other artistic organizations, requires this clarity to build for the long term.

Finally, out-of-discipline thinking has happened for years in creative groups. Research on group creativity reminds us that diversity of group members' thinking is critical for generating ideas and perspectives that can lead to breakthrough improvement.[17] The assumption, of course, is that diversity in tangible characteristics such as age or gender will generate diversity in thinking. Diversity can refer to having a mix of ethnic, cultural or gender backgrounds, of various disciplinary fields, or of age and experience.

While this makes common sense, some organizational groups—such as software programmers and engineers (who often are similar in age, race, gender, and experience)—do not have obvious wide-ranging diversity. In such a situation, organizational leaders need ways to encourage diverse thinking to overcome such limits. American insurance firm United Heritage is steeped in business within its domestic market. Nevertheless, its CEO, Dennis Johnson, insists on sending its senior managers on three-week-long "sabbaticals" outside of North America. The managers must visit a place that would allow them to develop their professional expertise, such as an investment manager going to London, but otherwise the options are wide open. Thus far, the firm has sent half a dozen of its managers (some of whom had never been outside of the United States) to different places and is beginning to see payoffs of broader perspectives and new ways of approaching problems.

Other firms, like Hewlett-Packard, which have long transferred employees abroad, have noted the impact of such exposure on creativity. One manager commented that living abroad helps people "be more creative as they expand their environmental understanding ... as [they] learn and experience more, [they] simply come up with new ideas, challenge assumptions, and see more opportunities." Such experience is critical for any group seeking to enhance creativity.

So how do organizations, groups, and people reach out of disciplines?

Types of Out-of-Discipline Thinking

In late 2006, the *New York Times* reported three seemingly unrelated stories.

December 17, 2006: Noah Charney, doctoral student at Cambridge University in England, has invented a new field of work. By combining knowledge in art history, criminology, psychology, and logic, he helps police track stolen art—and thwart potential thieves, who plague the $6 billion international market of stolen masterpieces.

November 1, 2006: Mr. V. Mortensen, Director of the Center for Multireligious Studies at Aarhus University in Denmark and owner of Perceval Press, published an anthology called *Theology and the Religions: A Dialogue.* He also writes and publishes art books that combine some of his photography, poetry, and essays about war and music. Mr. Mortensen, whose first name is Viggo, has also acted in a film or two, including one called *The Lord of the Rings.*

October 22, 2006: Pastor Randy Frazee of Willow Creek Community Church, in Barrington, Illinois, near Chicago, offers twelve neighbors an evening of barbeque, conversation, and community. Complementing the church's regular Sunday morning services, the more intimate meetings in neighborhoods demonstrate a new marketing strategy that includes messages sent via text on mobile phones, blogs, and podcasts.

These ostensibly disparate cases are examples of people and groups that actively seek to use or develop ideas from multiple disciplines. Each story illustrates out-of-discipline thinking, where individuals or groups move beyond their field of primary expertise and knowledge to tap into ones further afield—as vocations or to bolster their activities.[18]

But they also illustrate three types of out-of-discipline thinking: bridging disciplines, blending disciplines, and transferring and absorbing knowledge from one field into another. Individuals whom we have called, in the past, "Renaissance men," move across disciplines and succeed at each. They bridge or step from one field to reach other ones—like Mortensen the actor, Mortensen the writer, and Mortensen the businessman/publisher—and succeed in each. Next, some individuals and groups have the ability to blend disciplines, integrating knowledge from more than one discipline, which sometimes creates a new discipline in itself. Charney's interest in art history and criminology, as well as statistics and psychology, were not enough for him. He also had the ability to see how to blend the fields to address a vexing problem, and in the process created what some believe is a new discipline. Finally, some groups and individuals reach outside their own fields and industries for ideas, analogies, or methods that they then transfer and apply within their own organizations. The Willow Creek pastor drew ideas from outside of religious institutions and created a business model in a setting not normally considered a "business."

For an organization to do this strategically requires a broad mindset and a disciplined process, to ensure the balance of deep knowledge and that the opportunities and obstacles involved are managed. Across the sectors we have studied, certain individuals recurred as "outside lookers." While this was a strategy early on, increasingly they now work on the premise that such tasks need to be distributed more widely.

We'll review the types and their potential in the next section of the chapter.

Bridging Disciplines to Identify New Opportunities

Viggo Mortensen, actor, author, and publisher, is a modern example of a discipline bridger: He is able to jump from one to another discipline and be successful in several. The bridging of disciplines can range from art to science to the ability to succeed in different economic, political, or organizational contexts. Examples of individuals that have done this can be found across many sectors and countries. First are the original so-called Renaissance men, especially Leonardo da Vinci, master at physiology, engineering, drawing, and sculpting, and later, Thomas Jefferson, who was an architect, author, statesman, and gentleman farmer. Recent historical examples include Winston Churchill, failed (then successful) politician, military man, writer of history, and painter. Dwight Eisenhower was a World War II general, university president, and U.S. president. In the entertainment world, even Clint Eastwood is a bridger, stepping into roles as an actor and director, and also as a politician, as mayor of Carmel, California, for several years.

Current-day equivalents face more daunting levels of knowledge to master, yet they seem to exist in some shape. Diane Ackerman is a long-time poet who writes about science and makes it sound like poetry.[19] In her review of the book *Contemporary Poetry and Contemporary Science,* she sees experts from science and the humanities meeting more in the realm of daily questions and applied problems, than in theory. Questions dealing with such exotic subjects as neuroethics, the senses of animals, and stem cell research demand people who can use their brains as strong mental bridges.

Another example of how bridging disciplines has opened up a new opportunity for an individual is provided by Charlie Fee, a producing artistic director of a regional theatre, who stands with feet in both the artistic and business camps. He has an acting and directing background, but he grew up with a father who was a finance professor. His ability to combine artistic and business skills is rare in the theatre world. When one theatre conducted a nationwide search for a new artistic director, it learned that, out of more than sixty applicants, Fee far surpassed other candidates because of his ability to bridge two major disciplines and generate ideas that are unique in the industry.

Cirkus Cirkör provides an example of how this happens for organizations. Long a respected circus company, Cirkör early on realized that the disciplines in a circus performance and the process of learning them and interacting through them was a great opportunity to broaden their agenda and develop people, organizations, and innovations. Today, Cirkör is engaged in several educational programs, works with disabled youths, runs kick-off and off-site events for companies, and has found that circus is a great vehicle for engaging young people with difficulties adapting to traditional schooling.

Thus, bridging disciplines not only opens new opportunities for the organization or individual, it also provides innovative learning experiences for those on the receiving end.

Blending Disciplines to Transform a Field

Blending disciplines involves using knowledge from two or more dissimilar areas to create a new perspective. Sometimes, a new field or discipline may emerge; other times, the blending may help solve problems that each discipline examined separately and unsuccessfully. In either case, it is the process of blending or meshing the fields that generates a new outcome.

Art Thieves, Beware

Cambridge doctoral student Noah Charney has blended multiple disciplines to create a new one altogether, one he hopes will be recognized as its own scholarly discipline. His interest and abilities in several fields range from art history to criminology, psychology to criminal profiling. He approaches the problem of stolen art with statistically based data analysis, assessing information about stolen art from earlier centuries to see how historical thefts might provide insight into modern-day heists. Most intriguingly, he also pays attention to the motivations of art criminals, an aspect he claims police have neglected.

In June 2006, Charney organized a public conference to offer some of his research results. It drew from a range of groups, each holding different perspectives about art thievery. The attendees included FBI and Scotland Yard art theft agents, Italian police, and academics. Police helped the academics understand who real art thieves are, often dealers in the drug and terrorist worlds. Academics helped police and art agents understand the value of data analysis and art history to understand where an art piece was in its historical and cultural context. Such knowledge helps piece together past thefts, and perhaps, predict which types of artwork may be future victims. As the *New York Times* reported, the benefits of Charney's blending of knowledge from many disciplines as a form of "interdisciplinary bridge-building became apparent."[20]

Men, Brains, and Cars

Why do men nearly drool when they talk about sports cars—the speed, the handling, the look? In 2002, Daimler-Chrysler sponsored a study to find out. The research, which blended disciplines of marketing and neurobiology, examined how men's brains acted when shown photos of sports cars versus limousines and small cars. The result: men's brains are simply encoded or wired to think of sports cars as sexy status symbols.[21]

A subsequent study expanded the idea to examine how people react to well-known versus less well-known brands of cars and insurance. Researchers at the Ludwig-Maximilian University examined twenty men and women using a technology called functional magnetic resonance imaging (fMRI) to learn how their brains reacted to various brands. The researchers found that strong brands generated different reactions than weak brands; more importantly, they discovered that the brain took less effort to recognize well-known brands.[22]

Neuromarketing was bound to happen. As researchers learn more about the connections between brain physiology, cognitive activity, and behavior, astute business people can readily see marketing applications. The blending of disciplines, creating a new one of neuromarketing, opens doors for research and opportunities in both disciplines, but of course raises ethical and related questions that we've not faced before.[23]

Sun-Powered E-Mail

A final example of blending disciplines links a high-tech firm in Boston with villages in the jungles of Cambodia. In 2004, First Mile Solutions LLC, a Boston-based startup firm, introduced Internet access to the rural jungles of Cambodia by linking Linux computer and solar energy power technologies.[24] The Internet Village Motoman project, funded in part by the World Bank, American Assistance for Cambodia, and Japan Relief for Cambodia, is a form of "pony express" in Cambodia, where less than 1 percent of the population has Internet access. The project's "e-mail men" drive routes throughout rural Ratanakiri Province, bringing their solar-powered computers to various access points. They then gather and deliver e-mails to villagers. The so-called DakNet, from the Hindi word for *postal*, has allowed villagers to contact the government about problems and search for jobs. It has even allowed villagers to exchange medical diagnostic information with Massachusetts General Hospital and the Harvard Medical School in Boston. Again, having the vision to combine computer technology, solar-powered technology to run the mobile device that stores e-mail messages, and understanding the geographic constraints, entrepreneurs have created an innovative way to provide communication and access to information to villagers in rural parts of this developing economy.

Blending disciplines creates new opportunities and pushes the boundaries in established fields or industries. Finding customers or people in your organization ready to adopt what is emerging comes next.

Transfer across Disciplines or Fields to Push Boundaries

A third way to use out-of-discipline thinking is to take ideas from one discipline and apply them in another. Examples range from jails to information "shopping" to theatres.

Inmates and Car Production

Toyota Motor Corporation is famous for its lean production system. Companies from all over the world learn from it and try to adopt all or parts of the process in their own firms. But what happens when a jail manager takes a look at lean production?

When Patrick Findley took over management of the Los Angeles Police Department's jail system in 2005, the jails had a serious bottleneck problem. Processing new prisoners into jails, especially in the evening, took hours. Officers had paperwork to complete and each prisoner was entitled to dinner. For years, inmates received heated frozen dinners, which took much time to prepare. What Findley saw, beyond cranky prisoners, frustrated police officers, and long wait times, was a production processing problem. So, after a course about Toyota's system, he applied some of the car company's production system ideas to the challenge of processing inmates. One solution: reduce the time delay and resulting bottleneck by serving ready-made sandwiches instead of cooking frozen dinners.[25]

Shopping for Medical Information

Healthwise, an online health information provider, wants its Web sites to be as easy as possible for people to use. But people use Web sites at different times for different reasons. Sometimes, they zero in, when they have a specific question or problem they want to research. They need the answers quickly and want to spend their time efficiently. Other times, users browse, to see "what's there," similar to a shopper in a grocery store. Not a traditional discipline, shopping expertise and approaches have become fodder for anthropologists and marketers to understand more about how people navigate and experience shopping.[26] So as the health-information Web site creation team sought ways to understand how to design the site to meet both browser and zero-in shoppers, they sought insights from the company receptionist—known for her shopping expertise: "We invited our receptionist ... to contribute to this process [of Web site design] because of how she shops.... We really explored how she shops—how a store is organized, what catches her attention when she walks into a store. Is she looking up? Or sideways? What words [and displays] get her attention?" In learning how a good shopper reacts in a store, the team began to consider how to design a site, in terms of words, layout, and design. Customers who seek specific information fast can follow straightforward steps to reach an answer; others who want to browse can follow links that broaden or narrow their looking—similar to shopping.

Julius Caesar and Nike?

A marketing director for a theatre spent several years working in a sports program within a university. On joining the theatre, she brought ideas from sports marketing, which a senior manager thought might have promise. Sponsorships, for instance, are common within the artistic community, but typically for specific plays or events, rather than for individual artists.

Many sports firms sponsor athletes—from tennis star Serena Williams to soccer star David Beckham. So, what if companies sponsored individual actors? The image of Julius Caesar with a Nike swoosh on his costume might make audiences swoon, and, of course, the director is not advocating that. But he wondered whether some ideas from marketing of sports might work in theatre? For example, firms could sponsor individual actors, giving the actor a supplement to what is typically relatively low pay. This could make working in the theatre more attractive to the most talented actors. The sponsoring organization, in turn, would have the chance to meet with the actor individually or perhaps include him in a company event.

The theatre has not yet implemented the idea. Nevertheless, the director's knack for looking beyond his discipline for ideas that might transfer to the theatre illustrate his openness.

Looking beyond the boundaries of established practices can open up opportunities that greatly benefit your organization. When you do find an opportunity, start thinking how best to introduce it to ensure acceptance. Additionally, as the implementation of Toyota's philosophy and other organizational practices has shown, it is one thing to see what is to be done, but it can prove a great deal tougher to get it all to work. Elements of tacit knowledge and organizational culture can have a strong influence on your ability to transfer an idea, knowledge, or practice from another field.

How Ideas and Users Find Each Other

As in the piling up of hypothetical alternatives, creative accidents follow the law of probabilities—the more we fish, the more likely we are to get a strike.

Alex Osborn, father of the concept of brainstorming

Out-of-discipline thinking starts with a basic premise: that groups and individuals are open and receptive to the notion of finding ideas, especially ones from outside their disciplines. Without being willing to consider new ideas, out-of-discipline thinking is of little value. So how do people within organizations find ideas, especially these eccentric out-of-discipline ideas that may find shape later?

We have found five ways in which ideas and idea users connect, reflected in the following quotes, from a theatre director, a coach, a health information manager, and a senior R&D manager:

1. *Take what comes:* "[O]pen yourselves up to anything by not closing out anything.... Being able to listen to thoughts that anybody has."
2. *Be a magnet:* "We got hooked up with this idea when [a colleague in another organization] said they should run it by me. He said I'd 'be all over this.' A lot of people are not receptive to some of this stuff but I'm sort of into that."
3. *Cast a net:* "So we have a good team that feels ... safe about giving out any ideas. And we invite other people ... who may not have anything to do with this project to give us their ideas."
4. *Go look:* "He reads a lot about the military because there's a lot about analogies there ... about fast response [that could apply in our industry]."
5. *Coproduction:* "Working with the municipality over the next year, we will be using different parts of what we do in certain parts of the community, and that will give them new input and ways of working, and us a process for development and learning ... we could then use this process elsewhere."

These quotes show a range of openness to ideas, from passive willingness, to active searching for ideas, to collaborative engagement in the development of ideas. The different approaches complement each other and can together provide a balanced inflow of ideas over time. Next, we'll talk more about each approach.

Take What Comes

Painter Philip Guston is typical of consistently creative people: they do the work even when they feel uninspired. Guston goes to his studio even when he doesn't want to, in hopes that the "angel" of inspiration will come any way. Sometimes the angel does not come, but sometimes she does. But as he says, "what if I hadn't gone to my studio that day, and the angel *had* come [and I wasn't there to meet her]?"[27]

Sports coaches can be like Guston and take what comes, when they are not looking for it, and turn it into something useful for players. Football's "special teams" coaches and players are, as many coaches will say, an unusual breed. They can be offensive or defensive units and appear only intermittently during a game. The players' jobs revolve around kicking and running: they do kick-offs, kick returns, punts, punt blocking and returning, and field goals and blocks. Because of those tasks, they sit "between" offensive and defensive positions, and must understand both.

They differ in other ways as well. Special teams coaches rarely become head coaches. Their players often have not played the sport long since they often move into the sport after playing soccer. As a result, while other coaches, players, and fans typically understand the goals and activities of other position groups, like defense and offense, many may not fully understand, or fully respect, the role of the special teams.

Yet, good special teams coaches and their players can make or break crucial points in a game. Thus, coaches are often on the lookout for ways to improve and make the special teams a competitive advantage for a team. But sometimes ideas come unexpectedly, even when coaches don't go looking. One special teams coach found an idea when he heard golf and tennis coaches discussing how to improve their players' rhythm on strokes and swings. He realized some of those ideas could help kickers build rhythm into their "swings."

Likewise, football conditioning trainers may not be in the spotlight compared to offensive coordinators, but their work at preparing and training players can build endurance and mental strength. One such trainer believed he was open to ideas, but learned that his assumption about which ideas would help were backward.

Although his main background and experience was in football, the trainer worked with athletes in several sports, including women's volleyball and tennis, and men's wrestling. He anticipated that he would be able to use his deep knowledge from training football players to help other athletes improve. He found, to his surprise, that he learned more from the other sports that was useful for football. For example, although many football positions require steady forward force, some need more bursts of energy (certain receivers, for example). So, he learned from volleyball players, who consistently need frequent energy bursts, and transferred knowledge to help football players generate the "bursts" they needed. Because each coach—special teams and training—was receptive and able to notice ideas, he was able to take what came by and adapt it for football.

A high-tech organization in one field happened onto a technique that its new employees brought with them from another firm. It hired software developers who had learned *agile development* during their tenure at a former employer. Agile development focuses on developers' monthly efforts on writing and testing chunks of product features, rather than working on an entire product, and doing all the testing at the end. The concept of smaller, self-contained features (which might be used in a given product or a later one), and constant testing with broader user groups, was an unanticipated bonus for the firm that had hired the software developers.

Managers certainly saw value in the technique in software development. But they realized it might also be a useful conceptual process elsewhere in the organization. This was another case of "take what comes." The developers essentially "walked in the door" with the agile development process expertise and the firm could build on it elsewhere. The organization managers had not actively sought the new idea, but took what came and turned it into an advantage.

Some of the traits we have found in organizations that are good at this are: confidence in new ideas and abilities both as an organization and as people in the organization to not fall into Not-Invented-Here behaviors; agility to pick up and transform what you do and how you do it; slack; and a great process for identifying what is useful. Seeing results from practicing and testing this approach makes it grow on you.

Be a Magnet

Some people and organizations just seem to draw ideas to themselves, without much effort. Such magnets build a reputation for being willing to listen to ideas, no matter how strange or unlikely.

Former Boise State head football coach Dan Hawkins, now at the University of Colorado, is one of these magnets. His regular question to players, coaches, and anyone who observes the team is, "How can we improve?" Some players admitted they were at first reluctant to offer suggestions, not knowing if the coach was serious, but his openness to anything, strange or not, has now become legend. He presses other coaches for ideas, asks questions they might not, and has gained a reputation as someone open to hearing any kind of "wacky" idea.

So when he heard about a young Ph.D. student who was looking to apply chaos theory to sports, the coach was ready to listen. The doctoral student claimed the theory could help project outcomes of plays using probabilities based on data over time. During one summer, the coach and the chaos theorist tried to figure out how to apply the idea to upcoming games. Although the technique ultimately failed to be one Hawkins could use, he was willing to spend time exploring with the student about how it might work.

The great advantage for the coach is his attitude as a magnet, and the likelihood that other more useable ideas have and will likely come his way.

Planting new questions and ideas among people he meets allows Hawkins to get the ideas, nurture them until they fit into his work, and then harvest them. Naturally, as you get all these great ideas you need to sift through them and pick the ones you want. A sense of timing gets you a long way, as you identify the opportunity and get it in the open window.

Don't forget to repay the debt. Getting great ideas is good, but creative leaders give back. Acknowledging great ideas and their creators, and giving resources and feedback, allow ideas to grow. And such leaders will remain idea magnets.

Cast a Net

Casting a net typically starts with being open to and then seeking new ideas, albeit casually. Two common ways this happens include allowing time for something to come up, and seeding the pot through outside influences.

Sometimes, we search for ideas without a specific problem to solve, but more to see what might be interesting. Some organizations and individuals build "dabble time" into their work days and weeks. Google and 3M are famous for urging employees to spend time musing on new product ideas. A high-tech R&D manager uses a "5 percent rule": he allocates about 5 percent of his time to "just look" for ideas, on the Internet and in books, and by talking with others in and out of his field. If he finds something new, he investigates it. If it sounds like one worth integrating into his group's tasks, then he goes after training to see if it makes sense for the organization.

Clay Young, a senior vice president for ProClarity (now part of Microsoft), deals with financial analysts and stakeholders. He seeds the idea mill for himself and others with books of all types, but especially history. Fascinated by history in high school and as an honors student in college, he brought his interest into his marketing career. He views reading and learning from history as mental exercise, but also sees parallels for modern-day business. He finds that history, in particular, forces one to question the assumptive models in any decision-making process: "[History helps you] learn about the assumptive models … in people's heads that are the root of decision making. If you can think about the assumptive models and then [can] step back and [ask,] 'Yeah, but is that right? Are those assumptions correct?' So that's one thing that we constantly have to do [in our industry]."

Some organizations are a bit more formal, explicitly using books for new ideas. One firm assigns top managers a recent business book before the annual retreat. An insurance company, for instance, assigned Bill Gates's *Business @ the Speed of Thought* to encourage all of its senior managers to consider how the digital economy affects their units—whether from the perspective of human resources, marketing, or operations.[28]

Another manager has created a book club within his firm. It offers him and his team a way to look for ideas and to encourage openness to ideas, regardless of whether they will work or not. Anyone on the team who wants to participate reads the chosen book and then discusses it at a monthly meeting. If the group finds an interesting idea within a book, typically a small unit will experiment and try it out for six weeks. If the idea has merit, then the new approach may spread to other parts of the organization; if not, the group drops it and moves on. The range of books has been wide over the years, including, for example, *Blue Ocean Strategy*, *The Cluetrain Manifesto*, *The World Is Flat*, and *The Future of Work*.[29]

Go Look, with a Purpose

Some ideas and users find each other when users seek out information from other disciplines for a particular purpose. Often the idea seeker wants to solve a problem, learn new skills, or better understand some stakeholder group. At least two types of "looking with a purpose" appear common: (1) looking for ways to better understand customers, and (2) finding ways to improve processes.

Understanding Customers: Electronics and Fashion?

Royal Philips Electronics, the Dutch giant in technology, approached British fashion designer Sara Berman in 2004. She assumed that the firm wanted her to build technology into clothes, to develop some new form of wearable technology. Rather, the electronics firm invited Berman to join its "Simplicity Advisory Board." The board included experts in many different fields, from health care to architecture, industrial design to fashion. Each had only a little knowledge about the technology or products that Philips produced, but each had considerable expertise in design and concern for simplicity.

Philips sought to make a major shift in its approach to brands. It wanted to move from being a high-volume electronics giant to being a design-led firm, with a focus on health, lifestyle, and technology. According to chief marketing officer Andrea Ragnetti, the firm wanted to embed "simplicity into the company's DNA, [and] needed an element of vision."[30] As Philips seeks to create products that are intuitive, easy to use, and able to meet specific needs, it drew from design experts who knew little about technology but lots about simplicity and how that could be built into products. Also, it needed more understanding of what consumers want and how they will use products, all of which specialists from fields like fashion and design, far outside of technology, knew how to assess.

When Philips sought to introduce higher-quality image medical equipment, it turned to a board member, radiologist Peggy J. Fritzsche. She agreed that the medical equipment's image quality could be better and more detailed, but noted that the tradeoff would be more complex equipment. Her concern was that as radiologists needed more time and effort to learn the new technology, they would spend less time on diagnoses. So Fritzsche suggested that Philips make medical imaging equipment more intuitive. This would reduce the time doctors spend on the technology and increase the time they could spend with patients.

Although the firm's initial intent was to simplify just its products, the notions of simplicity are beginning to move through the organization. Managers and employees alike have begun to ask how processes, organization structure, and interactions can be made simpler and more effective. Yet, as fashion designer Berman says, simplicity can be deceptive. We think it is easy to achieve and yet it is actually quite complex, especially when it moves beyond the realm of product design. So for Philips to simplify organizational processes and make long-lasting change could well be tougher than simplifying products.

Understanding Customers: Wal-Mart and God?

Religion has become big business, including challenges of building and retaining market share. Baylor University, in conjunction with The Gallup Organization, reported results of a survey that surprised few church leaders: people eighteen to thirty years old today have weaker religious affiliations than those over sixty-five.[31] Church leaders who want to build market share are seeking to bring in younger unaffiliated people. Just like many industries, some churches have begun to use hard-core business strategies. Some have studied firms like Wal-Mart and consumer products companies to learn how to reach current and potential members.

Willow Creek Community Church exemplifies how several churches in the United States enhance their recruitment, retention, and management of their flocks. From its 155-acre campus, Willow Creek's senior pastor, Bill Hybels, has long used branding and word-of-mouth marketing strategies to build his flock into the 6,000-plus member mega-church it is today. Over the years, Hybels and other pastors in the church have explicitly learned about business from some of their church members.

The church's recent marketing approach, for example, has focused on building closer spiritual connections with members, quite a shift from approaches that churches used when they tried to attract the then twenty to thirty-year-old baby boomers. In the 1960s and 1970s, churches wanted potential members to see religion as fun and inviting. Rock bands, coffee bars, and self-help workshops were the norm as methods to attract young people.

Today, however, church leaders see a different mood among young people who want more serious spirituality and more closeness with other church members. Willow Creek's neighborhood pastors and leaders organize community dinners of up to twenty people who meet for spiritual discussion during the week. The smaller, more intimate settings create a sense of community, and the church leaders hope that this will attract younger and other nontraditional audiences.

Finally, some churches aggressively use techniques from successful consumer product firms. For example, in 2008, the United Methodist Church begins a new print and cable TV ad campaign: "Open hearts. Open minds. Open doors." While the campaign content is interesting, the message delivery will distinguish it from others: It will reach potential and actual members through mobile phones, the Internet, and live events. Thus, religion and its form are shaped by business as the disciplines come together.

Understanding Customers: Advertising without Borders

When Sony Corporation looked for an advertising agency with energy and new ideas, it hired an Amsterdam-based firm called 180.[32] Why did Sony, based in Japan, go halfway around the world to a firm called 180? Partly because of location: 180 is in Amsterdam, a city that exudes diversity and creativity. The Netherlands generally has long excelled in reaching out to other countries for trade. Its small domestic market forces business firms and others to seek opportunities beyond its border, one reason its citizens learn so many other languages.

Also, as a magnet for other cultures, especially people who emigrated from former colonies like Indonesia, Amsterdam and other Dutch cities are increasingly known for their culturally diverse population that brings different viewpoints into the country. The founder of the Dutch marketing firm StrawberryFrog says, "Amsterdam allows us to be in touch with the world without being swallowed up by any particular culture." That's why the firm calls itself "Your friendly global neighborhood advertising agency." Partly because of that global yet local attitude, many ad agencies in Amsterdam create wordless ads, understandable by people from different cultures and languages.

Sony has recognized the value of understanding other cultures as it designs and markets products, and what better way to tap into that than by using an ad firm that draws on such ideas, right from its front doorstep.

Improving Processes: Airline Pilots and Operating Room Teams

What do airline crashes have to do with saving patients? Some hospital administrators and doctors think quite a bit.

The similarities between emergency medicine and flying airplanes are more than may appear at first glance. Both include highly trained Type A professionals, who sometimes make life-and-death decisions, use sophisticated technology to do their jobs, and face periods of boredom punctuated by moments of panic. And, over the years, they have made large mistakes costing many lives.

A 1999 study by the Institute of Medicine, a branch of the U.S. National Academies, reported that up to 98,000 patients die every year from preventable human errors—not deaths from disease or heart attack or cancer, but *preventable* human error. Further, recent publicity about amputations of the wrong limbs and teams who leave medical equipment inside of patients after surgery has not helped the industry's reputation for safety.[33]

Likewise, in recent decades, the airline industry has faced its share of reputation damage, from major crashes to drunken pilots. Many of the crashes happened because of human error. As a result, the airline industry focused increased attention on safety measures and how to improve safety records, and many of its safety problems have declined in recent years.

Given the similarity of situations, hospital managers are looking beyond the medical field to airlines for insights into how to enhance safety measures. Some compare the hospital operating room to earlier airplane hierarchy: surgeons are the captains; attending physicians and nurses are the copilots and attendants. Given this structure, communication patterns and orders in operating rooms have tended to follow those strict hierarchical lines. In contrast, the strict hierarchy culture in airplanes has changed. As airlines have been more diligent about understanding the effects of fatigue and how to manage during crisis, pilots, copilots and attendants have improved their collaboration and found new ways to communicate more effectively.

Some health-care administrators are using such lessons from airlines. Hospitals want to understand more, for instance, about the impact of fatigue in an operating room, and how a medical team can communicate better, especially during emergencies. Just as airlines have checklists to help before takeoff, so too are hospitals looking at what sorts of guidelines and routines may be useful. Following crashes, airlines and federal agencies systematically assess what happened and why; hospitals, in turn, are seeking to anticipate what could go wrong and understand what does, starting with more thorough and comprehensive briefings of participants.

Some of those out-of-discipline ideas seem to be working. Several medical journals in the United States and Britain report that hospitals using airline approaches have fewer malpractice suits, faster patient recovery times, and fewer infections after surgeries.

Improving Processes: Scrunching Steps

Sometimes, necessity or difficulty leads to breakthroughs. When Shawn, a program manager whose world consists of writing program proposals and solving problems on a computer, found himself unable to type, what could he do? Shawn has a chronic muscular disease that has made it progressively more difficult to type or be seated for prolonged periods. When he realized his disease's implications, he began to seek ways around his problem and, in the process, learned to "scrunch steps." He has developed remarkable new skills. Perhaps his experience could lead to new product and process ideas of value to others. It certainly is a good example of creativity in action.

> At one point I had to stop typing for several months and ... I finally decided I had to find a way to cope with this. I found voice software. And trained myself to use it. Now I can dictate much faster than I could type. And not only that, I have trained myself how to program so that I can actually manipulate code in the computer. I can do things with a voice command that other people can't with a keyboard and mouse, [unless they take] several steps. So I have actually "scrunched steps" necessary to accomplish certain procedures. At first, it was a real drain on my productivity, but after I took some time out to come up with some innovative new ways to accomplish things, I was a lot more productive than I ever would have been than if I had just continued down that same path.

Improving Processes: Changing Time Mindset

Two final examples focus on how people from different disciplines can help change mindsets about time. In one case, an organization faced an increasingly fast changing, volatile industry. A senior manager felt that some of the organization members had not fully realized the shift in time speed within the industry. As the organization was looking for a new hire, one promising candidate, and eventually the one who joined, came from another industry that has a much different mindset about competition and urgency. As a result, she brought a different mindset about pace of work and productivity. By coming from a different and very fast-paced industry, where she was used to quicker turnarounds and multiple deadlines, she helped to instill a somewhat different "time mindset" and additional urgency among her team members.

Finally, an actor/director found his theatre expertise useful to project management in another industry—university administration—and helped shift mindsets about deadlines. When he worked as an assistant to a vice chancellor of a major university's medical center, the theatre director was in charge of event planning and organizing several large meetings. Whenever he learned about a project and its date, he thought "opening night." He planned for it as he would for a theatre production. He worked from the due date (opening night) backward, to set tasks and deadlines. Unfortunately, the medical center staff did not always think as theatre colleagues might. The director was shocked the first time the medical center administrators said, "Oh, don't worry about that event. We're going to move that deadline back a bit."

In theatre, of course, it's not possible to "move opening night back a bit." As the director says, the theatre world produces "absolute 100 percent on-time delivery." So his theatre world discipline—in terms of meeting deadlines, planning, solving problems before opening night—became an advantage in the world of medical administration, as administrators chose to use it!

Coproduction

When different groups or organizations work together on something, based on each organization's knowledge and competence, they use out-of-discipline thinking and often create something new and quite unexpected. Sometimes the coproducers are already close partners. Sometimes they barely know each other. Coproduction processes rely on mutual interaction and a trial-and-error process, where each participant adopts and adapts his or her knowledge, ways of working, and perceptions of how things can and should work to form a new, coproduced outcome.

Such coproduction happens frequently in such venues as the Edinburgh Fringe Festival. Festival organizers invite actors and other artists to work together, under "rules" that change year to year, to generate a new performance.[34] Another, more common example of coproduction is open-source development of software. In this case, individuals or groups that may not know one another, be in the same location, or do any work together beyond a particular project, collaborate to produce and test new software. Initially coproduction mostly focused on the development process, such as new products or software. But in industries such as services, creative industries, and increasingly for highly customized products, cocreation and coproduction may include the customer or user. Prahalad and Ramaswamy describe several interesting ways in which companies interact across the value chain to become consumer-centric.[35] Some of these ideas build on an information infrastructure that allows the customer access to information, choices, and prices at multiple stages. The customer can combine and assemble the products, services, and experiences at a point of their choice—out of a selection of connected suppliers. The systems are designed for this adaptation and customer cocreation of deliverables. They argue also that the intersection between the locus of knowledge and of innovation is important to understand in order to identify what types of solutions emerge, including when knowledge and competence is distributed widely.

Coproduction as a venue for creativity and innovation allows new opportunities to be brought in and developed. Simultaneously, you need to manage cocreation and coproduction processes for different reasons. One, they can be very time and resource consuming depending on the compatibility of the organizations involved. Second, as new ideas and development paths evolve, you can easily stray from your own path, and this needs to be managed to ensure you keep track of your strategy and vision. Finally, ownership of outcomes can be a sticky issue unless you have a good agreed upon process for resolving them.

DISCIPLINE TO MANAGE THE OUT-OF-DISCIPLINE PROCESS

The out-of-discipline process that brings ideas, knowledge, and new practices into an organization is not simple. Rather, we have found that there are profound challenges and obstacles involved if you are to transform this process into opportunities for your organization. In this section we will touch upon some of these challenges.

Timing and Sequencing Is Important

With the strength of existing structures and our tendency to celebrate and focus on the things that have been successful, there is a strong tendency to listen to people in central roles and to centralize "ideas" management. To be able to maintain an open mind requires both processes and roles that help us stay focused on its importance. Do you already have or have you considered implementing: specific structures and processes to bring in new ideas, as well as look outside for opportunities to apply your knowledge; places or meetings where such ideas are aired and developed through open dialogue; the culture and the roles where such initiatives are celebrated?

Networks have proven important to belong to and know. We will discuss this further, but it is fair to say that this is one critical way of ensuring exposure to new things. This led one of the organizations we studied to change its original centralized approach. Instead, now they work to get all members of the organization involved in looking for new ideas.

As these processes start to work and bring in new ideas, you need to manage the timing and sequencing of how they are brought into the organization. In some cases, new ideas are allowed to develop continuously, and when the time is right they can be put into play. Other approaches include using markets for ideas, or pilots for launch, or customer-adaptable features that allow you to gauge interest in a certain idea. One of the case companies is considering opening its development lab up to potential customers for early feedback.

Today, a lot of development is done through projects. As a vehicle to be creative and innovative, their limitations in resources and time are useful. Yet, to form a comprehensive strategy based on projects can also be a challenge. In some cases the projects are financed by outside parties, and the challenge is to create a lasting effect in terms of structures, strategic impact, and knowledge that remain yours after the project is finished.

Matching opportunity with readiness requires agility and an artful sense of timing. Making many opportunities and projects into a whole requires you to consider interaction between them over time and the sequence in which you should do things.

All In a Baby-Step at a Time

Creative and innovative processes are social processes. Through trial and error, you start a journey without quite knowing where it will end. Think about text messaging. It was a tool for business people. Who would have considered that these snippets of text would become a major social interaction tool for young people globally?

To start this journey, it often helps to see a live example, a prototype, or hear someone talk about how they have worked the process. One example is TeknIQ, a program aimed at raising competence levels in small and medium-sized enterprises about opportunities with intelligent products and embedded systems. Salespeople who want to get companies to participate in the program use a prototype from another participating organization in the program. As Sven-Arne Paulsson, the program's director, says, "You can talk all you want, but putting a real example on the table at the start gets the discussion going in the right direction." Everyone recognizes that the road to get to the prototype is long, but by seeing it, you get more comfortable taking in ideas from the outside to develop your organization. It is a question of credibility.

As things start to develop, the creative process relies on opposition, too—you need to keep communicating, and you need to allow for open debate, to get new things out in the air, or to give the room to grow to a point where they are ready to start.

Out-of-discipline thinking is risky. As you take the steps of discovery, make sure you monitor rewards and ownership. Ensure the people and organizations you work with are rewarded and paid well for what they bring.

Key individuals play a number of roles across the creative process, from bringing new ideas, stewarding them into the organization, transforming them into useful ideas, to implementing them. As in all new ventures, the number of failures will be large. Subsequently, you need to be aware of risks and roles different members play. Then set up systems so key individuals are protected from damage and the risks and rewards are in line.

Creative Takeaways

Let us review some of the concepts in this chapter:

- *Look at the world through fly eyes.* Think about it: flies have an extremely wide range of vision. The complexity of the world today demands broader thinking, wider perspectives, and understanding across disciplines. Creativity could be limited by the blinders of a single discipline; going beyond that discipline and having a wider vision helps the creative process.

- *Look at the intersections.* We need out-of-discipline thinking to achieve our goals and stay cutting edge, since solutions and opportunities are sometimes found at the intersection among or between fields of expertise. Master your discipline, but also try to look for new opportunities by looking at reality from a different perspective.
- *Develop "weak ties"* to connect with people coming from a different field of expertise and benefit from the mutual exchange of ideas. Being less constrained by your discipline's borders, you'll start experimenting. Diversity of experiences, views, and expertise in a team is beneficial to the creative process.

Out-of-discipline thinking can take the form of:

- *Blending disciplines*, eventually creating a new one.
- *Bridging disciplines*, excelling in different areas (Renaissance man)
- *Transferring and absorbing ideas* and concepts from different disciplines.
- *Be receptive!* To let ideas find us and for us to find them, being open-minded is key. You can either take what comes, be a magnet for ideas and creative people, cast a net to find ideas, go looking around with the purpose of finding something inspirational, or coproduce the new.

NOTES

1. Jerome Groopman. 2007. *How Doctors Think.* New York: Houghton Mifflin. Groopman offers a compelling view of how doctors can reach conclusions too quickly, in part because they narrow down and focus on one or a few options, rather than think more broadly.

2. Turin's theory of smell goes directly against the mainstream, long-held theory. As a result, many in the scientific world consider him a renegade and dismiss his attempts to publish the theory in scientific journals. He's made a name for himself, rather, in trade press books. He published a widely popular guide to perfumes, in French, which brought him to the attention of the secretive high-end perfume firms; it is due out in English in April 2008: Lucas Turin and Tania Sanchez. *Perfumes: The Guide.* New York: Viking Adult. Turin became known to the general public from two previous books: Chandler Burr. 2004. *The Emperor of Scent.* London: Arrow Books; and Lucas Turin. 2006. *The Secret of Scent: Adventures in Perfume and the Science of Smell.* New York: HarperCollins.

3. Mary Parker Follett was an early management and organizational scholar who suffered the plague of not "fitting" into a discipline. Her contributions included the importance of the group within organizations, arguing for the importance of conflict

and diversity in organizations, the role of authority in organizations, and participatory decision making. A review of citations about her work shows that scholars in more than half a dozen fields have used her ideas, including those in business, psychology, sociology, political science, public administration, and interdisciplinary studies. See Brain R. Fry and Lotte L. Thomas. 1996. "Mary Parker Follett: Assessing the Contribution and Impact of Her Writings," *Journal of Management History* 2 (2): 11–19.

4. The story of Barry Marshall and Robin Warren's unpredictable, yet persistent, journey to Nobel fame focuses on their willingness to look outside the normal approaches in medical research, and also to their being outsiders, on the fringes of their field (also geographically). The account of their work appears in many sources. See, for example, Barry Marshall (Ed.), 2002. *Heliobacter Pioneers.* Carlton South, Victoria: Blackwell Science Asia; Gary Hamel. 2007. *The Future of Management.* Boston: Harvard Business School Press; and, C. Heath and D. Heath. 2007. *Made to Stick.* New York: Random House.

5. Many scholars and business writers have talked about the dangers of not recognizing and adapting to environmental changes. One of the most often quoted is Harvard professor Clayton Christensen, whose book discusses the danger of firms continuing with approaches that worked in the past, and listening to major customers' requests for improvements, which can leave firms vulnerable to newcomers that fill in market gaps that mature successful firms neglect. See Clayton Christensen. 1997. *The Innovator's Dilemma.* Boston: Harvard Business School Press.

6. Yoram Wind, Colin Crook, and Robert Gunther provide an overview of the open-sourcing threat in their book: 2006. *The Power of Impossible Thinking.* Philadelphia: Wharton School Publishing.

7. Monica C. Higgins. 2005. *Career Imprints: Creating Leaders across an Industry.* San Francisco: Jossey-Bass.

8. Katie Hafner. 2007. "Humans Regain Jobs from Mice," *New York Times,* August 16: C1, C11.

9. Richard A. D'Aveni. 2007. "Leaders of the Pack," *Wall Street Journal,* March 3–4: R9.

10. C. P. Snow. 1959. *Two Cultures and the Scientific Revolution.* Cambridge: Cambridge University Press; C. P. Snow. 1965. *The Two Cultures: A Second Look.* Cambridge: Cambridge University Press.

11. Brockman has been relentless in pushing the idea of reaching for big ideas, bringing together smart people from many different disciplines, and pushing the boundaries of what is possible. His initial ideas for the third culture started with "The Reality Club," a group of top thinkers who asked hard questions of themselves and society at large. His book on the third culture is a good starting point for interested readers. See John Brockman. 1995. *Third Culture: Beyond the Scientific Revolution.* New York: Simon & Schuster.

12. Sagan (1934–1996) was a Cornell University astronomer and astrobiologist; Gould (1941–2002) was a paleontologist, evolutionary biologist at Harvard; Feynman (1918–1988) was a nuclear physicist and 1965 Nobel Prize winner. All three were prolific writers of scholarly and popular science books, opening up worlds of astronomy, evolution, and physics to the public.

13. Brockman pushes the idea that thinkers in all fields need to consider what they can learn from others. A recent edited book, *What Is Your Dangerous Idea?*, nudges this

thought even further. Both of the following books are worth reading: John Brockman (Ed.). 2003. *The Next Fifty Years.* London: Phoenix; and Richard Dawkins, John Brockman, and Steven Pinker (Eds.). 2007. *What Is Your Dangerous Idea? Today's Leading Thinkers on the Unthinkable.* New York: HarperPerennial.

14. In research on Stanford alumni who were entrepreneurs, Martin Ruef found that the most creative entrepreneurs tended to interact with a more diverse group of people—not colleagues that they worked with or knew well. Rather, the entrepreneurs sought out and interacted more with acquaintances and strangers. Mary Petrusewicz. 2004. "Note to Entrepreneurs: Meet New People," *Stanford Report*, January 21.

15. The idea of "weak ties" is usually attributed to Mark Granovetter, who described the idea in a seminal article: Mark Granovetter. 1973. "The Strength of Weak Ties," *American Journal of Sociology* 78 (6, May): 1360–1380. One recent author claims that the Renaissance's success was in large part due to interactions of disciplines and cultures—when people in science and art and commerce were able to intermingle, unusual and big ideas emerged. See Frans Johansson. 2004. *The Medici Effect.* Boston: Harvard Business School Press.

16. Jill E. Perry-Smith and Christina E. Shalley. 2003. "The Social Side of Creativity: A Static and Dynamic Social Network Perspective," *Academy of Management Review* 28 (1): 89–106.

17. Creativity and diversity has a long history in the research world. Because generating ideas requires groups to diverge—brainstorm and consider many alternative perspectives—researchers have argued that diversity in group members is critical. The diversity in members—whether ethnic, gender, age, educational, or disciplinary background—presumably brings in perspectives that may offer fresher ways of approaching and solving problems.

18. Each story illustrates people and groups with skills beyond a single field—sometimes far from their original one. Mortensen's budding publishing house as a business venture, Charney's blend of art with science applied to detective work, and Willow Creek's adaptation of business marketing techniques are examples of what is fast becoming necessary, if not common, in many settings. See J. Maslin. 2006. "A Star's Unusual Role: Indie Publishing Mogul," *New York Times*, November 1: B1: 8; Tom Mueller. 2006. "To Sketch a Thief," *New York Times Magazine*, December 17: 54–57; Fara Warner. 2006. "Prepare Thee for Some Serious Marketing," *New York Times*, October 22: B1: 4.

19. Diane Ackerman, poet, naturalist, and essayist, commented in a recent book review about poets and scientists that the chasm between the fields seems overwhelming only to the outsider, the person who has not sought to make connections. As a young scholar studying neurobiology, with a bent toward poetry, she found a soul mate and thesis supervisor in Carl Sagan, the noted Cornell astronomer who sought to bring his knowledge to lay people—creating bridges for broader understanding.

20. See the complete article: Mueller. 2006. "To Sketch a Thief."

21. A. Richard. 2006. "What's the Ultimate? Scan a Male Brain," *New York Times*, October 25: E10.

22. The study, presented at the November 28, 2006 meeting of the Radiological Society of North America (RSNA), caused a flurry of articles and media attention. According to the senior researcher, Christine Born, M.D., radiologist at University

Hospital, Ludwig-Maximilian University in Munich, Germany, it is the "first functional magnetic resonance imaging (fMRI) test examining the power of brands and found that strong brands activate certain areas of the brain independent of product categories." See http://www.rsna.org/rsna/media/pr2006-2/name_brands-2.cfm.

23. Cognitive neuroscientist Michael Gazzaniga, who is also a member of the U.S. President's Council on Bioethics, worries about the implications that may arise as the ability of scientists to understand and potentially influence brain and behavior increases. In particular, he wonders how to handle questions relating to brain enhancement, influencing decisions (e.g., buying decisions), and personal responsibility (e.g., "my brain made me do it"). See Michael S. Gazzaniga. 2005. *The Ethical Brain*. Washington, DC: Dana Press.

24. See a case study write-up about First Mile Solution's programs in rural areas such as Cambodia and India: http://www.firstmilesolutions.com/documents/FMS_Case_Study.pdf.

25. For more detailed discussion of Findley's application of Toyota's principles to jail inmate processing, see Mike Spector and Gina Chon. 2007. "Toyota University Opens Admissions to Outsiders," *Wall Street Journal*, March 5: B1: 4.

26. Consultant and "retail anthropologist" Paco Underhill has made a near science out of watching and understanding how and why people shop. His ideas are laid out in two books: Paco Underhill. 2000. *Why We Buy: The Science of Shopping*. London: Texere Publishing; and Paco Underhill. 2004. *Call of the Mall: The Geography of Shopping*. New York: Simon & Schuster.

27. Gail Godwin. 1995. "Rituals and Readiness," in *The Writing Life: National Book Award Winners*. New York: Random House: 10. Godwin is not alone in talking about the discipline of just showing up at the desk, at work, at the easel, in the lab. By putting in the hours, readiness may lead to creativity and inspiration. But without that regular "putting in the time," it will never come.

28. Bill Gates and Collins Hemingway. 2000. *Business @ the Speed of Thought: Succeeding in the Digital Economy*. New York: Warner Books.

29. See W. Chan Kim and Renee Mauborgne. 2005. *Blue Ocean Strategy*. Boston: Harvard Business School Press; Rick Levine, Christopher Locke, Doc Searls, and David Weinberger. 2000. *The Cluetrain Manifesto*. Cambridge, MA: Perseus Books; Thomas L. Friedman. 2005. *The World Is Flat*. New York: Farrar, Straus and Giroux; Thomas W. Malone. 2004. *The Future of Work: How the New Order of Business Will Shape Your Organization, Your Management Style, and Your Life*. Boston: Harvard Business School Press.

30. Kerry Capell. 2006. "Thinking Simple at Philips," *BusinessWeek*, December 11: 50.

31. Warner. 2006. "Prepare Thee for Some Serious Marketing."

32. 180 is one of several advertising and other consumer product marketing firms based in Amsterdam, in part because of this city's diversity. Jack Ewing. 2006. "Amsterdam's Red-Hot Ad Shops," *BusinessWeek*, December 18: 52.

33. Kate Murphy. 2006. "What Pilots Can Teach Hospitals about Patient Safety," *New York Times*, October 31: D6.

34. Bill Taylor. 2007. "Finding Innovation at the Fringe," *Harvard Business Online*, August 28.

35. One article, of several, where these ideas are discussed is: C. K. Prahalad and Venkatram Ramaswamy. 2003. "The New Frontier of Experience Innovation," *MIT Sloan Management Review* (Summer): 12–18.

Chapter 5

DISCIPLINED PROCESS

Exhilaration is that feeling you get just after a great idea hits you and just before you realize what's wrong with it.

Anonymous

J ust imagine: "creativity in a can." Open, add water. Cook a bit and simmer. Taste it and add some spices. Stir and simmer. Ask someone else to taste, and you've got a finished product. For nearly a century, this process is what many scholars have assumed individuals follow as they pursue creativity.

In the early part of the last century, educational psychologist Graham Wallas laid out four stages of the creative process: preparation, incubation, illumination, and verification.[1] In preparation, an individual becomes well-versed in an area of expertise, similar to mastery or within-discipline knowledge. In other words, open the can and add water. Incubation is a phase when individuals think about or stew, often unconsciously, rather than directly fret about a problem. Archimedes' "aha moment" in a bath came after he had mulled, or let incubate, the question of measuring volume. In other words, cook a bit and simmer. Third is illumination, or the moment when a person recognizes possible solutions to a problem. In some cases, the person may draw upon ideas from outside his discipline, as Archimedes did when he connected his problem with sitting in a bath. In other words, taste and add some spices. Finally, verification happens when individuals test ideas to see if they stand up to use and scrutiny. In other words, stir and simmer and have another person taste.

Wallas's step-by-step, linear approach has held sway for years. Others change the titles of the steps, but most follow a similar pattern of finding or receiving a problem, mulling it over, coming up with and testing possible solutions, and verifying or using them.[2] But we now know that the process is not absolute or linear, and that it may work somewhat differently in groups than with individuals.[3] Many people describe it as iterative, having almost what could be "wrinkles"—where stages and steps fold back onto each other. Sometimes, groups retrace, reframe, and rethink a problem, rather than move forward. In addition, while earlier the main notion was that creativity happens only in early stages, we now understand that creativity and innovation appear all along the development process.

A manager at Healthwise described the process of creating content and the process of delivery for a new product. Using Wallas's stages, we note (in italics) what seems to be happening:

> We do an all-day planning session with somebody from the outside and other teams from inside just to learn about that health issue from the perspective of someone who deals with it [*preparation*]. And over the next couple weeks we meet 4–5 times for an hour to an hour and a half going back through those [points] and better finalizing what to do [*incubation*]. At that point, the writers start coming up with plans as to how they [will write up content for each of the points] [*illumination ... but not quite*].
>
> But we got through a lot of the process and still hadn't figured out how to deliver on all of that type of information. We don't know the order or how to do it from the beginning [*return to incubation*].
>
> And so, we went away [again] and started thinking about the kind of information that would be provided and let people think about it in the back of their heads for a while [*incubation, round 2*].
>
> A lot of it we couldn't force. We couldn't come up with the solutions when we tried to at the beginning. [We had to accept that] it was really OK to think through this. And then ... finally it just jelled [*illumination again, and later, verification*].

In this case, the process generally followed a pattern of "good wrinkles" or steps that "folded back upon" themselves. Group members repeated some steps and returned to see what would work, and what areas they had missed.

Given the manager's description, the process appeared rather chaotic and unsystematic. But we've titled this chapter, "Disciplined Process" because managers and members of successful creative endeavors frequently comment that there is indeed a pattern or discipline to their process, sometimes recognizing it only after they sit back and examine what they have done. Across the organizations we have examined, patterns of activities and stages do occur, routines are followed, and there are structures to that process that the people in the organizations have created over time. We place the process at the top of the triangle (see Figure 2.1) to show its importance, as well as its relative rarity compared to some of the other disciplines. A potential reason for its rarity is the integral role the "aces," in chapters 6–8, play in a disciplined process, but more on that later.

To identify the process and routines for the future, a starting point can be to go through the process, after the fact, to find the routines, disciplines, and structures already there. Here's what the same Healthwise manager learned going through the process that she now applies to subsequent creative efforts. Italics illustrate what we inferred from her comments:

> We learned that we needed to do that all-day planning and then give dedicated time over the next two weeks to solidify that and [then the rest works out more easily] [*planning and finding ideas*]. They spent a lot of time on the first one; I think there were eight of them redoing the design. Now we have a much better idea of how ... to work. Going forward ... will be much more straight forward. So this is part of the definition process [*learning and evaluating*].
>
> We are getting better at specifying the timeframes ... and shrinking time ... by using guidelines and better definitions of what each document does and what it doesn't do.
>
> There's a much clearer idea up front of what things should be so we don't have a bunch of rework [*routines and processes*].
>
> The other thing we learned was that ... there are parts of our work that it [makes sense to] have a big group do it and there are parts that it is better to say, "OK, little group, go and work on this and bring it back to the big group. It is almost like you have too many ideas or too much input, which is really good to get people to buy in, but sometimes it's distracting [*many ideas—what types to use when?*].
>
> So another lesson is to know when we want everyone's creative ideas and bring lots of different perspectives and [when to do] work in smaller groups [*collaboration in different creative stages and for different purposes*].

In the rest of the chapter, we examine four issues that the manager raised when she reflected on what she had learned about putting discipline into the creative process. First, we'll talk about the patterns we found in different organizations relating to stages in the process as they generate ideas, experiment, test, and use them.

Next, we'll talk about the timing in terms of the amount of effort that groups put into various stages and reasons for the differences across types of organizations. In particular, we'll look at situations where some organizations put in differing amounts of "person-hours" during the creativity and innovation process. Some focus on the initial, front-end stages that encourage idea generation and experimentation, whereas others seem to focus more on later back-end activities of testing, doing trials, or practicing with the ideas.

Third, we'll discuss the nature of good ideas. Some people, when they think of creative and innovative endeavors, point to the most glamorous or celebrated creative results outputs—like the iPod, the pyramids, and the airplane. But do novel ideas that fit the context, and have value, always have to generate something big?

Not at all.

From our observations and those of others, members of organizations appear to generate different types of innovative outcomes.[4] Some are quite new, others are tweaks or improvements on existing outputs, and still others may be back-burner ideas. We'll offer examples of where some of the different types of ideas come from in our cases.

Finally, we'll talk about collaboration in creative and innovative endeavors. While organizations may be similar in the stages they go through while developing an idea, they seem to vary on their approaches to collaboration, ranging from being driven from a central core to more "amoeba"-type arrangements.

THE PROCESS THAT MAKES NO SENSE

After describing her approach to creativity, the Healthwise manager said, "So, I don't know if that makes sense. But that was the process." She's not alone in wondering how to "make sense" of the creative process. Some of that frustration comes from the difficulty of describing a process that is not always step by step. By viewing the creative process as "only" a linear sequence of steps, we may miss key points. We focus on each organization as a whole, pointing to key elements as we go along.

We write in linear form, so we'll start with a linear-stage model, building on Wallas's and others', but add aspects that come through across five sectors: theatre, American football, software, health information delivery, and contemporary circus.[5] The organizations' creative processes have roughly similar stages of identifying or finding ideas, testing and experimenting with ideas, and beta-testing or final reviewing, before implementing them.[6]

Theatre: Creating a World

Regional professional theatres in the United States have one main creative output: stage plays. Most struggle to maintain economic viability. Unlike in much of Europe, where public funding supports many ensemble and regional theatres, tight budgets in the United States force theatres to mount plays with limited numbers of actors, curtail rehearsal times, and ask local patrons to provide housing during the run of a play.

Often, theatres follow rigorous timelines, typically six to eight months for the full process, from the decision to mount a specific play to opening night. Usually a theatre's artistic director, with input from a board of directors, chooses a slate of plays for a season. The artistic director typically directs at least one play, selects and hires directors for the others, and may also choose some of the designers (for the set, costumes, music, lighting). Alternatively, the director for a given play chooses designers.

For a specific play, the director and designers become an initial core creative team. Once this team is in place, the creative process begins in earnest. In a sense, the director becomes the creative entrepreneur—setting the overall vision for the play—and the designers are creative leaders, forming groups that will help to implement the vision.

Opening night in the theatre world is sacred. Its deadline is unchangeable and affects the thinking and behavior of everyone involved in the production. As we mentioned in chapter 3, the opening night regimen creates a strong work ethic among top theatre artists and technical members. Theatre, as most performance arts, does not have the same opportunity to prototype. They need to perform from day one.

The director and designers start with an overarching concept for the play (see Figure 5.1). Typically, the director thinks about (incubates) and generates the main concept for the play, after receiving the offer to direct the play. Risa Brainin, theatre professor at the University of California–Santa Barbara, shapes her vision by thinking through a key group of questions: "Why this play, at this time, for this audience?" From that, the core team can structure what some call the play's "world." The world comprises the time period for the play, which in turns drives decisions about the costumes, set, music and sound, lighting, and style of delivery, whether formal or naturalistic. One director's vision or "world" of King Lear might be set in ancient Greece, with actors in togas, twittering birds in the background, moon lighting, and formal presentation. Clearly, it is quite different from another director's vision of King Lear in modern-day Chicago, with actors in suits, carrying cell phones, and rushing across city streets with taxi horns in the background. Because each conveys a different world, the related creative decisions vary.

Directors differ in the amount of control and guidance they offer during this part of the creative process. Some steer concept development, but ask for input from designers. Others make major decisions on their own, before

Figure 5.1. Play Production

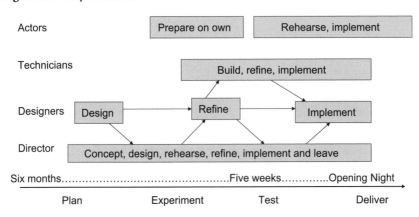

meeting with designers, and then ask designers to develop their portions, using the concept. In the end, though, directors put their imprint onto the concept and are ultimately responsible for the production's outcome, both artistically and technically.

Generally, individual designers work independently and in parallel, but not full time, during the next several months. The director acts as the central point for exchanging and approving final ideas from designers. If the budget allows, a director may hold face-to-face meetings with some or all of the designers, which allows designers more opportunity to integrate their segments. Once the director agrees to the design elements, technicians begin to construct the physical world: the set, props, and costumes. The sound, music, and lighting usually come later during the process.

About six weeks before opening night, the actors arrive. By then, most of the designers' creative and planning work has finished. The actors, through rehearsals, begin their phase of experimenting and testing out to see what works for the play. Although it seems that actors join the creative process late in the overall time scheme, in fact they know several months before they arrive for rehearsal which parts they will play. The best ones show a strong within-discipline expertise right from the start, as they have been at work long before they show up. As one veteran puts it: "What [directors] don't always know is that we've been working as well.... I am usually off book [know my lines], I've looked at other productions, read reviews, actors' biographies, and know all about the role."

Rehearsals begin five to six weeks before opening night. Some directors start rehearsals by trying to build camaraderie and rapport with and among the actors, who are another creative team. One director uses short exercises to build a cohesive team. People outside the theatre world may view actors as extremely confident since they are so capable of speaking on stage before hundreds of people with little apparent fear. In fact, many actors talk about how exposed they feel when they rehearse and when they act. Thus, building a team of actors willing to be open to one another becomes a critical part of the creative process.

On a King Lear production, for instance, the director and many actors did not know one another, so the director used several short exercises to help actors become comfortable with her and with one another. Some of the actors felt the exercises used valuable time on something not directly related to the play. The director recognized the time pressure, but felt that taking time initially to build a team would save time later during rehearsal. Later, the actors admitted that the team-building process had helped.

Once rehearsals begin, the number of people involved increases noticeably. From a team of a director and perhaps four to six designers, the creative team expands to more than sixty people, including technicians, stage, music, other support staff, and actors. The director and actors work together, typically six days a week, on specific scenes, on choreography, and on voice and accents. Rehearsals are the time to experiment. Actors test out how to say lines, move on stage, and show emotions. Directors may vary in the latitude they give actors, preferring not to "tell" an actor how to deliver a line. As one director says, "If I tell him, then it is my line, not his. I want him to own it, to be the character." This director offers more emotional suggestions, such as asking an actor to "make someone uncomfortable," which demands the actor put herself more into the decision. Other directors offer more specific suggestions on what movements to make or how to say a line.

In addition to more people being involved, the number of interactions explodes. Individual actors working together and groups of actors working together, for example, means more complex interactions. Actors need to understand their own roles but also those of others in their scenes. Likewise, designers and technicians associated with them—from set builders to costumers to musicians—integrate their parts with the actors' movements and speech. So, the creative process increases in complexity: more people, more interactions, and opening night pressure, with no revision. All the elements must work in harmony for the play to succeed.

The creative process shifts to a final phase before "launch." During tech week, all members of the play's production—the director, designers, technicians, and actors—integrate the entire play. The integration happens at the theatre site, in this case outdoors. Actors wear costumes, the lighting and sound/music enters, and actors perform on the set with props. During tech week, the artists and technicians work an average of six hours per night. The actors and director work through each scene of the play, sometimes doing the same scene several times in an evening. Some directors focus on insuring that the technical aspects work, like how to move a prop or piece of scenery, how to secure a microphone on an actor's costume, or how to deal with lighting changes, especially in an outdoor theatre. Other directors focus more on the actors' delivery and depth of emotion. At this stage in the creative process, some new ideas may emerge, such as the need for a different way to use a prop or editing of lines. Generally, however, these ideas are more tweaking than significant changes.

Finally, the play previews before a live audience for one or two nights (or more, if on Broadway!) before it opens officially. In the theatre world, this is a form of beta-testing. The director watches the audience for its reaction to decide whether to make any changes. If the audience doesn't laugh as expected, or if the laughter takes longer than anticipated, the director may change the timing. If the audience seems bored—people shift in their seats, yawn, or worse, fall sleep—the director may change the pacing.

When we first talked to directors, we asked about whether they read critics' reviews and make changes in the play after opening night. Not possible, said the directors. Once the play opens, nothing changes. As one director says, "we have delivered the play, in the best way we see fit." In fact, the day after opening night, the director and designers typically leave town. The actors and stage manager are responsible for keeping the play as it is, intact.

Even though play timing, use of sets or props, and entrances or exits do not change, creativity still continues. Some actors say that by having the structure "set," they feel they can move to greater levels of creativity and emotion in their roles. In chapter 3, on within-discipline mastery, we discussed moving beyond the fundamentals, and that is just what actors say happens. So, actors who have mastered their discipline reach a point where they no longer think so much about lines or movement, but rather focus on making a character more emotionally connected to the audience and the play itself. One actor describes it this way: "Some people may say creativity starts to end ... once the performance begins.... But I think it continues.... As an actor ... you achieve your greatest amount of freedom after you've agreed on a set way that something is to go."

Also, even though a play stays "the same" night after night, the audience does not. Several actors find that, especially in an outdoor theatre, the sky is light enough at the play's start that they can see the audience's faces. While disconcerting at first, some actors find that the audience interaction with the actors and the play can strengthen (or dampen) the emotional power of the play. As one actor said, "Every night you have an unmarshalled variable in the audience ... sometimes attentive and sometimes not.... You have to pull them in, play to them more, be aware of their listening. That's a creative element every night." But theatre is not the only empty black box space. In Boise, Idaho, it happens as well in the open, on a blue field.

Football: Flawless Execution

Most fans think of football as a series of weekly exciting (they hope) games during a four-month-long season. But four months of weekly preparation and practice is, of course, misleading. Coaches start preparing for a season months ahead, even before recruiting, but certainly during spring practice. Following a season's close, coaches review what worked and what did not. During the spring, they prepare and plan to play against future opponents. Yet a specific game plan, as well as experimenting and practicing for a particular opponent and game, occur mostly during the week immediately preceding the game. As a season progresses, coaches gain more recent and relevant information about upcoming challengers, from videotapes of opponents' games and insights from other teams that have played the team. So, general planning and preparation happens over the winter and during spring and summer training, but the bulk of preparation, planning, and practice for specific games (the initial stage of the creative process) happens within a short, typically seven-day timeframe.

For football, the creative output is a well-thought out game plan that is executed in a way that leads to victory. That means offensive, defensive, and special teams groups must know their parts, interact with other participants, and be able to handle unexpected opportunities (or threats) in split-second time.

American college football teams usually play games on Saturdays, which gives a team six days to prepare for the next game. Boise State University's preparation and planning process is very structured. In fact, one coach commented that clear structure enhances creativity: "I know the structure and I know the parameters. Then [we don't have to] think about that part.... We used to ... sit down on a Sunday and come up with our practice plans for the week. Now, we set timing and general practice plans before the season begins. We will monkey with them a little bit but they're pretty much cast in stone. You don't have to waste a bunch of brain time thinking about what we are going to practice."

Coaches follow a predictable schedule during the week to prepare a game plan (see Figure 5.2). On Sunday and early Monday morning, the head coach, position coaches from offense, defense, and special teams, and the quarterbacks review videotaped segments. They evaluate and look for what worked and what did not. During Monday afternoon and Tuesday before practice, position coaches identify possible play options for the upcoming game. The defensive and offensive groups work independently, with little integration, since their players are not on the field at the same time. In contrast, the special teams players are active during both defensive and offensive parts of the game, in kicking or returning the ball. As a result, the special teams coaches and players need to understand and interact with both offensive and defensive groups. The head coach checks in with all groups, offering input in the area where he has expertise, such as the offensive line, without telling coaches what the final plan should be.

Football's equivalent of rehearsal is practice, which begins on Tuesday afternoon. By Tuesday afternoon's practice at 2 P.M., coaches have decided on most of the upcoming game plan. For the game plan, each position coach identifies four to six options for each play. For example, when a team is at a second

Figure 5.2. Game Plan Preparation

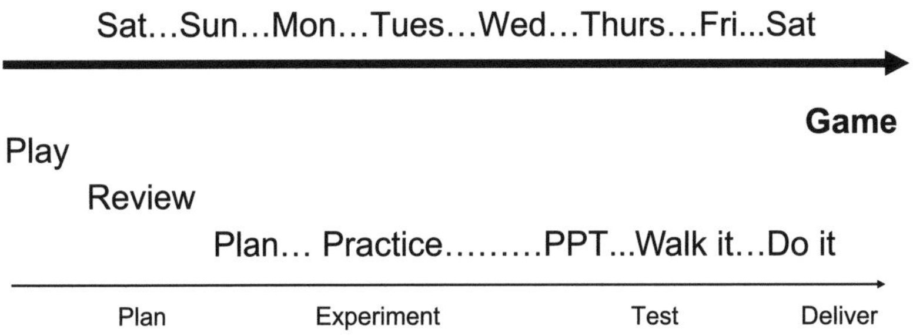

down, with eight yards to go for a first down, the offensive coaches could well have four different play options.

When weekly practice begins, coaches estimate that they have developed 70 to 80 percent of the upcoming game plan. Most planning has been done, because, like in theatre, the players as a group need as much practice or drilling—or rehearsal—time as possible. Players must memorize moves, test out execution of plays, and find flaws and correct them.

Practices on Tuesday and Wednesday focus on experimenting, testing, and seeing how well players can complete plays. By the end of Wednesday's practice, coaches say their game plan is 95 percent complete. During those two days of practice, coaches may remove plays that are too hard for the players to implement, or tweak others to achieve what coaches hoped for.

While coaches typically add no new plays to a game plan after Wednesday evening, they sometimes do. Boise State coaches say that they are able to add plays or bring in plays from earlier in the season for a particular new game plan, because they overprepare players. They reason that if players learn and practice many plays, they will be less rattled should the coaches include a new one during the week—or even during a game. Also, having more play options available may give the team an edge over opponents. Finally, coaches mix up the practices, as a way to build player flexibility and ability to deal with change.

During practice on Thursday, the team uses a form of beta-testing, like theatre's tech week. This team calls it "Practice Perfect Thursday." The players go through the game plan, play by play. They must complete each play in a specific order without making any mistakes. If they do so, the group moves to the next play. For example, if there are six plays in a given option, the players may complete the first play perfectly, then move to the next and complete it flawlessly. If a single player bungles the third play, the entire group has to start again from the first play, and repeat the drill until each in the set of six is faultless. No player wants to cause a mistake, and so peer pressure is high. This reinforces one of the elements of within-discipline mastery—working hard to be among the best. Football players have their equivalent of a preview evening on Friday, with a walk-through of the game plan and a written test on plays. Saturday is game day.

The football crew has grown very adept at using within-discipline mastery and a disciplined process to stretch their performance and surprise their opponents through new plays and combinations.

Software: Scrum, Anyone?

A global business intelligence software firm's creative output is a constant stream of programs or solutions for users, who may be customers, programmers, or partners. In the firm that we studied, the creative process takes about six months. Like theatre and football, the general creative process for software includes planning and preparation, as well as practice, or, in this case, testing. The creating stage includes developing an overall vision or concept for a product and forming a list of product features. The testing or practice stage comprises testing those features with both internal and external users before integrating them into a final product for testing and release. Once a product is ready for release, it moves from the product architect and product development team to the technical product manager, who works with customers and users after release (see Figure 5.3).

In contrast to football and theatre, where coaches and directors may speed up the creative idea generation stage to allow more time for rehearsal or practice, software firms seek the opposite. In the past, software firms typically needed about 30 percent of total development time for integration of product features and beta-testing at the end of the creative process. But, in development, the less time a firm needs for testing, the more time it can have for the creative aspects, and, as one manager says, "That's where our value comes."

On one of Nancy's early visits to the case firm, the vice president of R&D glanced at his watch and said, "Want to go scrum?"

What sort of invitation might that be, at 10 A.M.?

Scrum comes from rugby and is a way of "restarting" the game, when players cluster together. In agile development, scrum refers to a regular meeting of the developers and managers working on particular features of a piece of software. The manager in this firm led the way to five developers standing around a cubicle. The scrum meeting lasted about eight minutes, and focused on what each member had done in the previous twenty-four hours, would do in the upcoming twenty-four hours, and what obstacles she or he had encountered trying to get the work done.

Then, the group dissolved for another day.

Figure 5.3. Software Development

IDEAS, TURNING INTO PRODUCT FEATURES.............MOVING TO MARKET

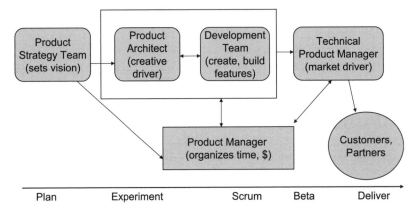

This firm, like others, has found a way to increase time available for creativity and incorporate the process of eliminating obstacles to getting work done and building testing into the development, using an approach called agile software development with scrum.[7] The process allows designers to choose and work on a limited number of product features, usually two to four per month. They experiment and test, identify and remove obstacles throughout the development process, rather than waiting until the product is fully designed. This reduces time spent on integration and beta testing products.

One concern for this software firm was how to encourage creativity and innovation at all levels and remove obstacles that might inhibit it. In its early years, the firm depended upon its upper-most managers to develop the new ideas for products. Once they realized that the approach failed to tap the creative power throughout the firm, they restructured to find ways to reduce obstacles to creativity at all levels within the firm.

Also, the firm has reorganized to encourage creative endeavors to be somewhat more unfettered. To remove obstacles from the creative process, the firm separates logistics and project management from the creative product development part of the process. A product manager sets and monitors the schedule and budgets for a particular product. A product architect is the creative driver, translating and implementing the broad vision for a product from the top manager team to the product development team. The team then comes up with the features and solutions for the new product.

Separating project management from product development allows creativity within product development to be relatively unrestrained. By not focusing on money and deadlines, the product development team feels better able to take risks and try ideas it might otherwise drop because of scheduling or budget concerns. The vice president of research also says that the separation infuses into the process what he calls "acceptable tension." If, for example, the product development team has an idea that will enrich a product feature, but it needs more time than allocated to develop the idea, a conflict emerges. The team can either finish on time or add a new creative piece. The resolution of such a conflict, then, goes up the organization to the senior vice president. He can decide whether to "finish now" or "slip the deadline." This way, the creative team is not hindered by concern with deadlines at the outset.

Organizational structures to maintain and manage the "creative tension," and refocusing development teams on ideas and solutions rather than schedules and budgets, are some of the components that make the software company's process creative, yet disciplined.

Health Information Delivery: Understanding Your Process

A fourth example of how the creative process works in stages comes from health-information delivery. Key players include all levels of the organization involved in various activities. Often the initial abstract idea comes from the senior manager and CEO, who has long held the untitled position as key innovator.

Interestingly, while theatre and football do not necessarily designate a "R&D group," each of our organizations had an implicit R&D function, typically in the creative entrepreneur's head.

The health-information organization chose to designate and recognize explicitly the need for finding and experimenting with new product or service ideas. As it realized ideas were emerging and no clear unit had responsibility for following them, management decided to restructure into two major segments. One large group focused on its existing core product and service areas, with writers, programmers, medical experts, and others continuing to update and refine existing knowledge bases. A second group formed to consider new product and service areas, as a separate "research and development" area, to investigate more ideas that might (or might not) result in useable products for customers. Creative and innovative endeavors operated within each group, as well as across organizational levels.

An example of the process for forming ideas, experimenting with them, and launching them involves a new product—the interactive coach (see Figure 5.4). Instead of patients seeking information from the Internet or print-based media, the interactive coach allows them to "speak" online with a "coach"— video of an information provider—at times that work for the patient. The process, underway, has involved people from multiple disciplines and skills (e.g., artists, producers, information technology experts, medical specialists) as

Figure 5.4. The Development of Interactive Conversations— How Processes Evolve over Time

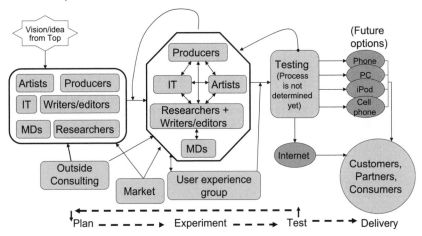

they brainstorm what type of information is important for patients, in what form, and at what time. The discussion starts with brainstorming within a multidisciplinary group, before the members separate to carry out their portions, testing them along the way and then meeting again as a larger group to identify and solve problems, find new approaches, and test among some user groups. The groups expand and contract, depending upon the task at hand, the needed skills, and the need to revisit certain decisions. The notion of large-small-large groups, as well as more focused disciplinary efforts balanced with groups of people from several different backgrounds, is part of the challenge for the leadership team to manage.

Circus: Beyond the Product or Performance

Rather than describe one more process in which the immediate outcome is what we have come to expect these organizations to deliver, whether software, theatre performances or football games, let us use the circus case to describe that "other type" of creativity and innovation these organizations are so good at.[8] What other type? Creativity and innovation that results in business models that for Cirkus Cirkör give the financial stability and opportunities to develop both the organization, create competitors as well as competent people to evolve the art form, and engage in regional development not because it is "good," but because it develops the organization. The capability to create new ways of operating relies on the artful management of specific routines, which we will describe. All our cases rely on this ability, expressed in different ways.

When we met people throughout Cirkör's organization, we asked them: "So, what is so creative about you [the circus]?" Most of them gave variations of the same answer: "Well, hmmm, it's what I do, but it is also what all others are doing. It is all creative!" And herein lies a part of the puzzle. The first time Mikael met Tilde Björfors, artistic director and founder, and Kajsa Lind, senior vice president R&D, they gave a ten-minute speech about Cirkör and what they do. They noted a number of things: putting on performances, training next-generation circus artists, running summer and winter camps for young and disabled people, setting up regional collaboration programs, delivering events to others, and so on. And then they said:

> In everything we do we work with the artistic process. We have guiding words that direct how we work and what we do. Cirkus Cirkör's guiding words are collective individualism, quality madness, and cheeky commitment. But we are comfortable in the process, we have done it many times, and as the going gets rough or people feel lost and confused, we can stand strong and say, "It is always like that in this stage, it will pass and then it will be good." That gives a very good basis to collaborate with others.

So let us turn to some of the recurring routines that create discipline in this process. One recurring routine manages the financial or business conditions surrounding a venture. In general, a performance is financed through several sources of funding. Planned around a performance are often smaller performances or opportunities for the audience to test and experience doing circus tricks and to interact with the artists. The multiple stakeholders surrounding the performances and its activities often have different motives and objectives for their participation and (financial) support. A key discipline thus focuses on balancing these stakes to ensure delight among financiers, the audience, and family and friends that participate in all these activities.

Closely linked to this routine is that of assigning and grooming people for different roles. This is a balancing act between the individual's interest, current priorities, and his skill set. Here is where the within-discipline mastery meets the disciplined process. The "who" meets "how" and "what." Adding to this puzzle is the character of circus life—international, traveling, and filled with people inspired by adventure and an inquisitive mind. This is a constant balance since the inflow and outflow of people is continuous, and the contracts are generally short.

Roles and relationships make up the third routine. Within Cirkör they have grown into a few different approaches that make them flexible. One, they have chosen to split executive management from the creative entrepreneur, that is, they have different persons in those roles. This combines the opportunity to think strategically and develop Cirkör broadly, with a focus on delivering and developing the operative organization. Two, within a fairly stable management group they shift positions rather freely, as they are comfortable with and trust each other, but need different organizational roles for different stages. Third, there is a certain clarity and openness on some of the competencies and who holds them in the management team. This allows them to have a constructive discussion on who should engage in different processes. It also helps them discuss why their understanding and approach differs in the processes in which Cirkör is engaged.

These are examples of routines involved in a disciplined process at Cirkör. While the cases have different approaches, together these routines make up a disciplined process for delivering innovative organizational and management solutions—solutions that allow them to grow on the fringes.

Think about your process for creativity. What does it look like? Reflect back on how you have worked recently. Do you see similarities with what we have described here? Differences? Based on this, how would you design your process to move a new venture forward? What steps, what routines become fundamental to fuel and manage the process, and where is time best spent? The last part of that question is next.

For the process of delivering outcomes (products, services, performances), even with the variations in amount of iterative action, "wrinkles," the

Figure 5.5. Stages of Creative Processes

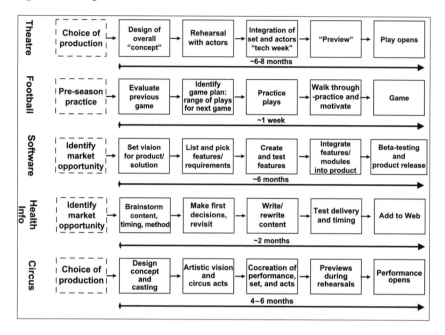

organizations follow somewhat similar stages—generating ideas and planning, experimenting, testing/practicing, and launching or delivery (see Figure 5.5). Despite the general similarities, though, some aspects do differ, including the way the groups allocate time on various tasks or stages of the process.

TIMING, WITHIN STAGES

"How do those coaches get ready for a new game, in a week?"

A software manager who is a big football fan wondered how coaches could come up with new ideas and prepare for a game in only a week, when it takes his firm about six months to create and test a new product.

As we suggested, using agile development, the software firm could increase the time available for creating a highly competitive product and decrease the time spent testing it to be sure it works. But still, the manager wondered how football coaches create a game plan and test it out to see if it works, in just a week?

Part of the answer is having routines, such as creating the practice schedule in the spring, rather than at the beginning of each week's practice during the football season. But in addition, the football team knew how much effort it needed to put into different stages of the innovative process.

Front-End or Back-End Focus

We did a simple analysis of the proportion of time that the five case organizations spend on front-end or back-end creative process activities. For our rough analysis, we defined front-end activities as the steps of creating ideas, planning, and picking possible solutions. In Graham Wallas's terms, this would include preparation, incubation, and illumination periods.

For our analysis, back-end activities include verification, the process of trying out, testing or practicing possible solutions to see which might work best for launch. We talked to people in our case organizations about what happens, when, with whom, and how much time—in person-hours, days, or weeks—they spent on front- and back-end activities.

The R&D manager's question turned out to be a good one. Organizations do indeed differ in how they allocate time and effort during the creative process. Theatre, the circus, and football organizations spend less time on the front-end and much more on the back-end activities. They spend no more than 25 percent of the process time on front-end activities and 75 percent or more of their process time is spent on back-end activities, testing, and practicing.

The reverse is true for software and health-information delivery. In the software and health-information-delivery organizations, the figures were almost opposite from the others: about 85–90 percent on front-end activities, and 10–15 percent on back-end activities (see Figure 5.6).

Why might the person hours for the organizations' activities be so different?

Several explanations come to mind. First, (most) theatre and football efforts do not demand completely new creative outputs. Both start from a base of

Figure 5.6. Amount of Time Dedicated to Planning and Creating versus Testing

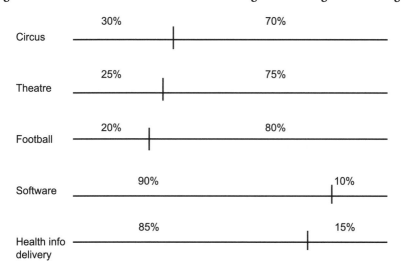

historically performed activities, a play script or rules for a game. Unless directors and actors develop and write a completely new play, which occurs only rarely, most artists (directors, designers, actors) in theatre interpret an existing work.

Likewise, in sports, coaches draw upon the history of previous games, their own and others. They also (re)use existing plays, or tweak them to become somewhat different. In some sense, the sports team may similarly "interpret" an existing play, in this case specific actions that the offensive or defensive teams would pursue.

Second, both theatre and football are forms of public performance. The members execute or implement the ideas and actions in front of an audience. Any given performance happens just once, in front of just that audience, and cannot be revised or repeated in the same manner, once completed. As unpleasant as a product recall in software development might be, it is "possible." It isn't possible to recall a play or football game, once delivered.

The notion of a one-off performance is a critical component of the process. This means that, in each case, the artists in a play or the players on a team have one try to make the production or game perfect. Even though a play occurs for several nights, it occurs only once in front of any given audience. The same is true for a football experience—once in front of a given set of fans. Thus, they have one time chances to create and deliver a product. A key element of success, then, is execution or delivery, which comes from much time devoted to rehearsal or practice.

Finally, in each case, unlike the other organizations we looked at in depth, both theatre and football have large numbers of people involved in back-end activities: during the practice/rehearsal stages and the final production or output. The production of a moderately sized play may ultimately draw upon one hundred or more people—from the actors (who the audience thinks of first) to the designers, and music and lighting technicians, to the costume and prop and set builders, to the ticket and administrative support people. "Many people" means lots of coordination. Likewise, in a modestly sized football program, well over one hundred people are ultimately involved in mounting a game: one hundred players, nearly twenty coaches, athletic trainers, security, medical and administrative support people—all play specific roles to create and execute a good performance.

Thus, the number of people involved and the number and complexity of interactions among people during the back-end testing and execution of a game or play rises dramatically once the front-end activities end. The back-end activities present very different and new types of challenges: to ensure that each person accomplishes his or her role in concert with others. This human interaction brings with it different levels of ability, knowledge, or expertise. In each case, while technology may play some role (e.g., in sound, lighting, or music; in transferring information from coaches to quarterback), the primary component of achieving the creative output is based upon human performance.

In contrast, software or health-information-delivery organizations may create new content or delivery options each time they work on a creative outcome. As one manager said, they need time, effort and mental power devoted to generating ideas for the design of content and delivery of products. Because some testing is built into and occurs during the front-end activities, the final testing or back-end work is shorter. Further, in health-information delivery and software development, even though many people may be involved at different stages, ultimately the process includes relatively fewer people (not 50–100!), working independently or, periodically, in conjunction with each other.

In sum, the different focus—front end versus back end—depends partly upon the degree of novelty and type of creative outcome, partly upon testability of the outcome, and partly upon the complexity of human interaction. Choosing the approach relies on understanding what you are developing, how you develop it, and degree of novelty, and then adapting your organization and process to best support this development.

IDEAS: SHAPES AND SIZES

Creative ideas come in many shapes and sizes. Some observers have described the types of creativity in terms of the process and "size" of the idea. DeGraff and Lawrence, for example, describe four different profiles of creativity exhibited by individuals, groups, and organizations, and which fit the desired type of creative outcome.[9] The four profiles are Imagine, Invest, Improve, and Incubate. The Imagine profile focuses on radical new ideas, yielding the big breakthroughs, such as what the Walt Disney Company did with cartoons from the 1940s on. The Invest profile organization selects and pursues specific initiatives and devotes many resources to a particular idea for development, such as IBM and mainframe computers in the 1950s and 1960s. The Improve profile makes small adjustments to an existing model or idea and generates major payoffs from it, such as McDonald's improvement in systems, standards, and structures. Finally, the Incubate profile focuses on long-term development, particularly in building a community of people, such as Alcoholics Anonymous. The four I's are helpful, and we found evidence of at least three in our case studies—Imagine, Invest, and Improve.

But when we asked our case organization members what types of ideas they generated and what the sources were, they frequently talked in simpler terms. They tended to speak of "big ideas," "tweaking ideas," and "hmmmmm" or "back-burner ideas." We'll describe each in the following section.

Big Ideas

Big ideas can move an organization forward in a dramatic way. Truly novel and radical for the organization, they may sometimes matter beyond the organization. For example, thirty years ago, Healthwise's CEO built his nonprofit organization by providing information that would "help people make better health decisions." That mission has driven the organization's pursuit of ideas ever since. It has also helped reframe the way the health-care delivery looks at patients and their role in staying healthy and fighting illness and injury.

Another "big" idea example comes from theatre. Charlie Fee, the producing artistic director of the Idaho Shakespeare Festival (in Boise, Idaho), also leads the Great Lakes Shakespeare Festival (in Cleveland, Ohio), more than 2,000 miles away. He developed a business model other theatre groups are watching. By mounting two plays in each theatre (two in Idaho, two in Ohio), and then remounting them at the other site, he has developed an approach that saves money, employs the same artists for longer periods (allowing each theatre to increase the caliber of people it can attract), and leverages some support functions. He watched mergers and alliances within business—and a few in the arts world—and developed this one, which has received much attention and interest.

Tweaking Ideas

Some people we talked with also mentioned smaller ideas that were more tweaking of existing or older ideas. Chris Petersen, Boise State's current head football coach, commented that he has "no new ideas," he just reuses old plays that he gets from watching tapes and then tweaks them a bit: "We may see somebody else doing it, or we may see something on tape, and we say, Well, what if we did this and this?"

Then again, Petersen admits he doesn't want to be predictable; he wants to "look different from game to game to game." That means, if the team has success with a play, he won't use it again the following week (or sometimes for many weeks) because he knows the opposing team will be working on a defense to thwart the "new" play. So even though a play may be a "tweak," it can become fresh enough to foil an opponent.

Artists in the circus describe how they pick up ideas from all kinds of different types of performances, not just circus performances. They then can apply new ideas in their own performances and reap the benefits: "When you can feel, hear and see the audience's reaction to an act. Or the energy on stage. That is a kicker."

Back-Burner Ideas

A third type of idea was the "Hmmmmm, let's put that on the back burner" type. Several people mentioned that their groups or organizations have ideas that are not (yet) feasible. Interestingly, a CEO, a coach, and others mentioned that, ultimately, they find use for more than 80 percent of the ideas that come up. Ideas morph, or change over time, but the organization can "find a way" to use most of the ideas that come up. A challenge for these organizations is finding ways to store ideas and inspire the people that come up with them to stay and realize them later. Some organizations have methods for storing those "hmmmmm" ideas, such as BMW's process we mentioned in chapter 2.

Idea Waves

Different sizes of ideas show up in different parts and places of an organization. In one organization, members consistently said the CEO had the "big innovative ideas; we do small creative ideas every day." The top manager had repeatedly over the years come up with what appeared to be big ideas that took not only the organization, but the industry, in new directions. He was an example of what we call in chapter 8 "Idea Central." The result was a double-wave approach to ideas (see Figure 5.7). Like the waves that pass through geologic material, they tend be "high frequency, low amplitude (the smaller, daily creative ideas) or "low frequency, high altitude" (the bigger, shake-up ideas).

Once we noted this, the organization's senior management acknowledged that model was likely accurate, or at least the perception was true. With more discussion, we learned that in fact, the main idea generator was constantly generating ideas, but that another senior manager acted as a filter—sorting out ones that had likely sustainable viability from those that were probably too far-fetched for the near term. So in essence, the Idea Central person was also carrying out "high frequency" waves of ideas, but most were invisible to the rest of the organization. Because the only "visible" ones were perceived as less frequent and big, the assumption was that his pattern was few, but big, ideas.

Figure 5.7. Idea Waves

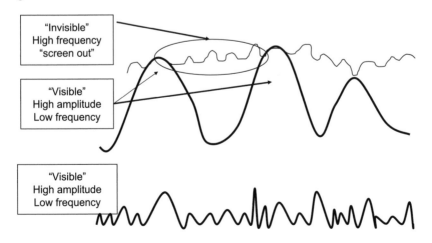

"Invisible"
High frequency
"screen out"

"Visible"
High amplitude
Low frequency

"Visible"
High amplitude
Low frequency

Instead, he did what many inventors say is necessary to find good ideas: he generated and discarded a lot of (bad) ideas.

Throughout the organizations, it was often CEOs or founders that came up with ideas, or had historically. As the organizations developed, ideas increasingly came from a number of different sources. What remained was the challenge of managing and synchronizing these big and small ideas in a way that allowed the organization to adopt ideas when both the idea and the organization were ready. As we touched upon in chapter 2, these creative organizations are under development themselves and need to find mechanisms to temper the impact of novelty across the organization. This can take many forms—as filters, gatekeepers, or prioritization through the process of allocating resources.

COLLABORATION: FROM STARS TO FIREWORKS

When you want to see the cluster of stars in the Pleiades group, it helps to squint or turn your head slightly sideways. We can see several stars when we don't directly look for them, but they disappear when we try to look straight on.

We found the same challenge when we tried to understand how organizations' creative and innovative processes work. Looking head-on, we see people in meetings, e-mailing, or writing reports and memos. But those actions don't always give a picture of the guts of how ideas start, or who controls them, or how they move.

So as we squinted, images emerged that we had not expected. Also, because we could not "see" the collaboration process directly, we needed other ways to describe it. Metaphors offer one option.[10] Also, many people we talked to and watched in organizations used metaphors to describe their collaboration.

In this next section, we'll describe forms of creative collaboration and innovation that emerged from the case organizations.[11] Creative collaboration rests on joint interest or a partnership that seeks to create a particular outcome or solve a problem. It is usually goal-driven—from writing software or producing a play to preparing for a sports event. Also, the people and groups involved may try to set routines so they can replicate the process that works for them.

When we squinted hard enough, we found at least four modes of collaboration within organizations: star, pyramid, amoeba, and fireworks. We'll describe each below.[12]

Star Collaboration: "There's a Reason the Title Is Director"

As theatre audience members, we may think actors are the stars. In fact, the director is "the star," at least when it comes to the creative process.

As we have suggested, creative collaboration in theatre, during the production of a play, happens among two main groups: (1) between director and designers; and (2) between director and actors or groups of actors (see Figure 5.8a). The director acts as a central point, almost a switchboard or star, in a very clear hierarchy, among the artists—designers and actors.

Figure 5.8a. Theatre Collaboration

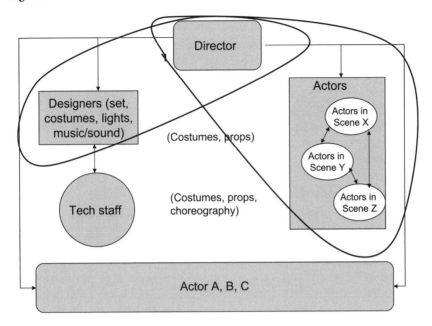

Figure 5.8b. Star Collaboration

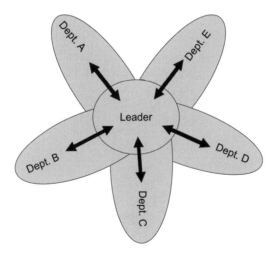

During the initial phase of the production, for example, designers and directors work in tandem, with the director setting an overall tone and vision for a play. If a director decides that *King Lear* will be set in modern-day China, that drives the decisions for designers of costumes, set, music, and other props. Designers work in parallel and sometimes interactively, but still the director is the core—the director gives final approval for all ideas and resolves differences, if they exist, across different groups

Designers, once they have agreement from the director, give technicians the designs for sets or costumes, for example. Those technicians, then, determine how to construct them. While there is creativity in the problem solving, technicians are unlikely to be involved in the generation of the main creative ideas driving the production, which is why they are not included in the creative collaboration process in this discussion.

Later, during rehearsals with actors, the director again plays a central coordinating role and makes final decisions. If, for example, an actor has ideas of how to change his approach to a character, the actor will discuss those changes individually with the director, not with other actors. Also, one actor does not give suggestions for changes to any other actors. Instead, if they have ideas for other actors, they go to the director, who may choose or not choose to pass along a suggestion. Actors say that this avoids misunderstandings and friction between them.

So, collaboration between the director and designers and the director and actors is bidirectional, but essentially hierarchical. The director is the center, the point from which creative activity begins and through which collaboration takes place. Figure 5.8b illustrates this central focus, which, as a metaphor, we saw as a star. In this case, collaboration is primarily between one person and several groups of people. That person has oversight, understanding, and decision-making power for the entire project, and thus becomes the focus for collaboration.

Pyramid Collaboration: He's the Coach

A second form of collaboration, but quite different from the "star" form, comes from another organization with a strict hierarchy: a sports team. A football program structure and collaboration pattern looks like a pyramid. The head coach sits at the top, with the next layer of key stones, positions coaches, just below. They are supported by players, some of whom (such as the quarterbacks or highly experienced offensive or defensive players) may also collaborate in creating the outcome, a game plan.

Although hierarchical, football differs from theatre, where the director "directs." In football, the head coach often plays a role of coordinator, who reviews, but does not typically override or change, decisions made at lower levels. In this case, clusters of key groups (position coaches) collaborate within the group, and a coordinator (head coach) does a final review for "balance" of the overall game plan.

In football, most creative collaboration happens within the coaching groups and among coaching groups and the head coach. Other interaction—between coaches and players, among players, between strength-conditioning coaches, trainers, and players—tends to focus more on problem solving than on generating new ideas.

Offensive and defensive coaches collaborate to develop play options within their position groups, but not across position groups, because their tasks are quite separate. Since players from each group (offensive and defensive) are not on the field at the same time, coordination among them is less essential (see Figure 5.9a).

The special teams coaching staff, which oversees kicking, punting, and receiving players, interacts and must creatively collaborate with the other position groups, since their players act on both sides, offensive and defensive.

A head coach typically does not direct or coordinate the creative collaboration, but may give input within the area of his expertise. In the case of Boise State University, the most recent head coaches—Dan Hawkins and Chris Petersen—were both offensive coordinators (head of the position coaches on the offensive side), so they do provide input in that area.

Creative collaboration among coaches appears very symmetrical, organized, and inclusive at the top of the organization, with little input coming from the bottom, and thus looks like a pyramid at the top (see Figure 5.9b).

Amoeba Collaboration: Up and Down and Throughout

To stay ahead of customers, technology, or market expectations, the software firm's leaders recognize and stress the importance that people at all levels are involved in innovative collaboration (see Figure 5.10a). Senior managers want the organization to become more "bottom-centric," with most idea generation coming from the lower levels, not the top. This stems from a view that development team members are likely to have more touch points—or contacts within a network—within and outside of the firm. Since touch points may provide input for ideas, people at all levels can learn from and possibly collaborate more with customers, other programmers/developers, technical journals, or blogs.

When an organization needs to be nimble, operates in a volatile environment, and changes creative groups, it needs a more fluid collaboration approach that stretches up and down and within the firm. In some ways, as we tried squinting, amoebas or "worms" emerged, running through the organization (see Figure 5.10b). In this creative collaboration approach, managers urge and encourage creativity at all levels, and as project groups change over time, the shape of the amoebas of collaboration change. Compared to the star or pyramid approaches, the amoeba creative collaboration is more dispersed, across several levels, with no single coordinator or overseer of the process.

In the amoeba pattern, ideas seem to filter both up and down as collaboration forms around them. Overall vision may come primarily from the senior managers, such as what problems may face customers in the future, but some may come from lower levels, for example, specific solution ideas or product features.

Figure 5.9a. Football Collaboration

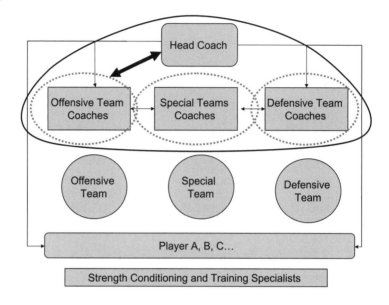

Figure 5.9b. Pyramid Collaboration

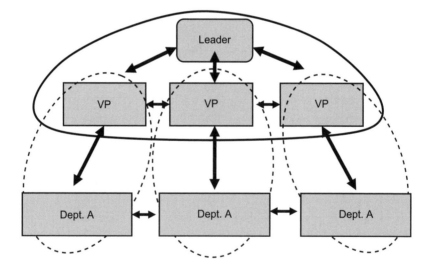

Fireworks Collaboration: When Bursts of Creativity Work Together

On the Fourth of July, fireworks from China explode in skies all over the United States. Many explode in a flash and fizzle right away. Some explode, and then shoot off smaller explosions that spark more light and shoot out; some even have a series of sparkler explosions trailing down the sky. At each

Figure 5.10a. Software Collaboration

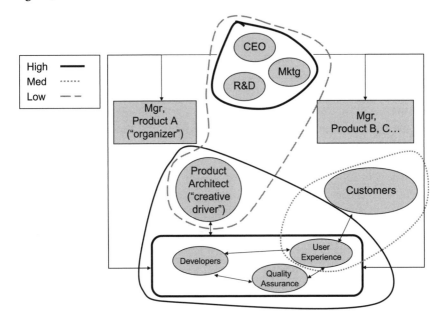

Figure 5.10b. Amoeba Collaboration

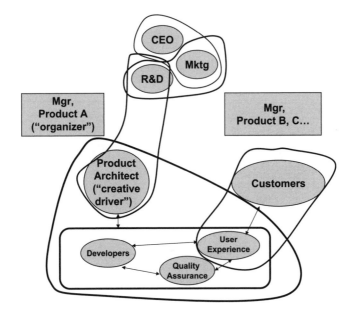

stage, it seems that a small explosion of energy and creativity happens—almost like one explosion generates another and yet another.

In the health-information organization, such a pattern of creative explosion and collaboration appeared as sparklers: multiple bursts of ideas that generated collaboration within smaller units (see Figure 5.11a). This happened in part because of a reorganization, which created one part of the organization to focus on existing products, and another part, somewhat more interdisciplinary, to emphasize new product areas. Firework collaboration can include sparks that start from a core, that jump from unit to unit, or that happen within a unit (see Figure 5.11b).

In some situations, the person who generates sparks not only sends them to other units, but works with the unit on the idea. More frequently, however, the idea generator may shoot off ideas, hoping that they will find a landing spot that is safe and people within a unit work on them. The simple attitude of letting smaller ideas have the chance to grow is critical. We talk more about this in chapter 8.

DEVELOPING A DISCIPLINED CREATIVE PROCESS

In this chapter our focus has been on the process and routines that are at the heart of these creative organizations. As you think back to the ideas and how your organization does and could work, consider:

- *What is your framework?* Guidelines in the creative process help you focus more on the creative process without being distracted by other issues; structure helps save time and energy. How do the four stages of the creative process—Preparation, Incubation, Illumination, and Verification—match your organization? They will be iterative and each step should have your hallmark and be designed to support your organization. How can you choose what fits your situation best? Starting with seriously reflecting on what you do today can be a start.
- *Process matters.* Theaters, circuses, software companies—the steps they use to generate and develop ideas are different. But, a clear process enhances creativity. What is your structure? What can you learn from these industries? What routines are required to manage and balance different aspects of your creative process?
- *Where is time well spent?* The degree of novelty and type of creative outcome, the complexity of human interaction, and whether you will be able to prototype or need to deliver through a performance determines how much effort to put into the process and where to focus (front end vs. back end). Analyze what outcome you develop, what is your process, and how much is new in what you do. Then make a plan that seriously considers how you should allocate resources and time to ensure you get the creativity and innovation you expect.

Figure 5.11a. Health Information

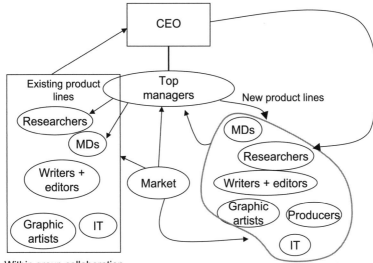

Within group collaboration
Some cross group collaboration

Figure 5.11b. Fireworks

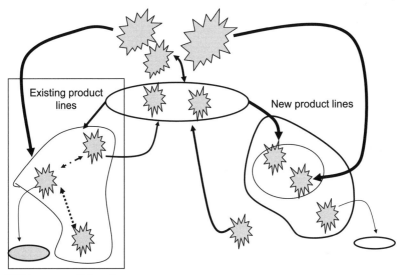

Within group collaboration
Some cross group collaboration

- *Synchronize and temper your ideas.* The type of creative outcome impacts idea shapes and sizes: Big ideas are great and not-so-common breakthroughs; tweaking ideas means improving other ideas; "hmmmmm" or back-burner ideas are those that are not yet feasible, but worth keeping for the future. Ideas can come in big and small waves from different parts of the organization across time. How do you balance and encourage people in your organization to come up with ideas, to support those that should be done now and store the ones you will need for later (and that is many). How can you temper those people (and the ideas) that can get the entire organization to oscillate by introducing many new big ideas and have the power to get people moving?

How does your creative team work?

- *Star collaboration*: Someone is the central point from which the creative activity begins and through which collaboration takes place, like a theatre director.
- *Pyramid collaboration*: There is someone who, like the coach of a football team, coordinates and reviews ideas coming from lower levels of the organization.
- *Amoeba collaboration*: A fluid collaboration approach emerges, where the shape of collaboration changes often. Ideas come from multiple, dispersed sources, and run across the organization.
- *Fireworks collaboration*: There are sparks of creativity and multiple bursts of ideas that land in different places of the organization; this creative explosion and collaboration lets small ideas have a chance to grow.

That takes us to part III, and the three "aces."

NOTES

1. Graham Wallas (1858–1932) was an early student of creativity and its process. A socialist and educational psychologist, Wallas's writings ranged from politics to biography to psychology. See Graham Wallas. 1926. *The Art of Thought.* New York: Harcourt Brace.

2. Harvard creativity expert Teresa Amabile suggests four creative cognitive processes for individuals: identification of a problem or task, preparation, generating responses, and validating and communicating the responses. See Amabile. 1996. *Creativity in Context.* Boulder, CO: Westview Press.

3. A review of the literature that outlines different types of processes for product development, is Shona L. Brown and Kathleen M. Eisenhardt. 1995. "Product Development: Past Research, Present Findings, and Future Directions," *Academy of*

Management Review (vol. 20, no. 2): 343–378. Similarly, innovation policy used to describe the innovation process as starting with ideas and creative insight at the universities and in the laboratories, which was then pushed onto a market. This view has also changed as research has shown the complex interaction between stages and types of knowledge along the process, as well as the importance of new manufacturing technology, new business models, and new routines for service and product delivery for innovation. This means creativity and innovation cannot just be understood as a linear process. See, for example, Eric Von Hippel. 1988. *The Sources of Innovation.* New York: Oxford University Press, and Gary P. Pisano. 1997. *The Development Factory.* Boston: Harvard Business School Press.

4. See Jeff DeGraff and Katherine A. Lawrence. 2002. *Creativity at Work: Developing the Right Practices to Make Innovation Happen.* San Francisco: Jossey-Bass.

5. Much of this section comes from an earlier publication: N. K. Napier. 2007. "3-D Creativity," in A. Davila, M. Epstein, and R. Shelton, *The Creative Enterprise,* 2:37–70. Westport, CT: Praeger.

6. See Mark D. Cannon and Amy C. Edmondson. 2005. "Failing to Learn and Learning to Fail (Intelligently): How Great Organizations Put Failure to Work to Innovate and Improve," *Long Range Planning* 38:299–319.

7. A process called *agile development* has helped the software industry decrease the amount of final testing time because it "builds it in" along the development path. Before the agile process, firms tended to create, write, and then test an entire software product. Agile development breaks the development process into monthly increments, during which a team creates fewer features or chunks of a product. During the month, developers create, write, and test those smaller pieces or chunks. The pieces could be used—or not—in a final product. With the prior approach, product development and testing took six months, and in the end, if the product did not fly in the marketplace, six months of effort was wasted. The agile process allows teams to develop smaller pieces of a product and test them along the way. So rather than have 30 percent of the six months used for final testing, the firm can reduce that time because it has been built in along the way. See Ken Schwaber and Mike Beedle. 2002. *Agile Software Development with Scrum.* Upper Saddle River, NJ: Prentice Hall; and Hirotaka Takeuchi and Ikujiro Nonaka. 1986. "The New New Product Development Game." *Harvard Business Review* (January–February): 2–11.

8. It might be worthwhile to note that while they do many things to evolve and develop their position and the market for contemporary circus, they still put up performances and shows. In 2006 they performed 157 times for approximately 56,000 people, despite a slower year to develop other parts of the circus. In 2005, the numbers were: 374 performances and 148,525 people in the audience.

9. DeGraff and Lawrence. 2002. *Creativity at Work.*

10. Metaphors have a history in scholarly research. Interestingly, they've gained more attention recently as the focus on analytical, quantitative explanations abounds. Yet for a process that is hard to describe in words, sometimes pictures and metaphors help.

11. A number of scholars have discussed collaboration and the importance of routines or patterns in a process. See, for example, A. Hargadon. 2003. *How Breakthroughs Happen: The Surprising Truth about How Companies Innovate.* Boston:

Harvard Business School Press; E. von Hippel. 1988. *The Sources of Innovation*. New York: Oxford University Press; R. R. Nelson and S. G. Winter. 1982. *An Evolutionary Theory of Economic Change*. Cambridge, MA: Belknap Press/Harvard University Press; J. S. Brown and P. Duguid. 1991. "Organizational Learning and Communities of Practice: Toward a Unified View of Working, Learning, and Innovation," *Organization Science* 2 (1): 40–57; C. K. Prahalad and V. Ramaswamy. 2004. *The Future of Competition: Co-creating Unique Value with Customers*. Boston: Harvard Business School Publishing; Vera John-Steiner. 2000. *Creative Collaboration*. New York: Oxford University Press; R. W. Woodman, J. E. Sawyer, and R. W. Griffin. 1993. "Toward a Theory of Organizational Creativity," *Academy of Management Review* 18:293–321.

12. Many of the ideas for this section began with an article in creativity and innovation management. See Nancy K. Napier and Mikael Nilsson. 2006. "The Development of Creative Capabilities In and Out of Creative Organizations: Three Case Studies," in *Creativity and Innovation Management* 15 (3, September): 268–278.

Part III

THE THREE "ACES"

In part III, we examine three "aces," or factors within an organization's context that can enhance or inhibit the creative and innovative process. These three elements form the circle of our framework (see Figure 2.1). In chapter 6, we discuss three "faces," or roles that are essential for organizations seeking to pursue innovative endeavors. Those three roles include the creative entrepreneur, the creative leader, and the creative team. Individuals may be involved in more than one role, or their roles may change over time and situation, but each role is critical for creative activities to thrive. The chapter discusses how these roles support the disciplined work covered in chapters 3–5.

Chapter 7 examines the organizational and physical infrastructure—the social and spatial architecture, or "places"—that supports innovation and creativity. Such elements include office and building design, as well as the organizational arrangements that support interaction among groups in and out of organizations.

Chapter 8 looks at what we call "traces," as in trace elements. Trace elements are a metaphor, taken from science, to illustrate examples of catalysts in an organization that enhance and support creativity and innovation. The catalytic elements can be understated yet quite significant. The chapter covers three types of trace elements: (1) trace elements for practice (human resource policies); (2) trace elements for environment (culture); and (3) trace elements for connection (networks in and out of organizations).

To end the book, chapter 9 goes back to the framework from chapter 2 and discusses the discipline required to make creativity and innovation a competitive advantage. It reminds us that, to stay ahead, an organization and all its members need to focus on the art and science of the creative discipline.

Chapter 6

FACES: THE AGENTS WHO MAKE CREATIVITY HAPPEN

If [James] Watson had been killed by a tennis ball, I am reasonably sure
I would not have solved the [DNA] structure alone, but who would?
Francis Crick, 1962 Nobel Laureate

By the end of the first few pages of *The Soul of the New Machine*, Tracy
Kidder has introduced us to Tom West, a "good man in a storm": the
only one of a crew of experienced sailors who, during a severe north-
easter, does not allow himself to become seasick, who goes four days without
sleeping, who has a child's awe every time he sees a sunrise or storm break,
and who refuses to say much about his work.[1] Essentially, he comes across as a
wild man and sailor with a near death wish. As readers, we are breathless, in
adrenaline overload, and thankful that Tom West isn't our boss. Yet, this man
accomplished one of the most challenging tasks of the twentieth century—
pulling together a group of engineers to build one of the world's fastest computers. His vision, leadership, and ability to protect the group's efforts despite
repeated onslaughts from management and other nonbelievers set him apart,
just as his performance as a sailor did.

Such creative agents, the best of whom combine many unusual characteristics, are the faces of creative energy and outcome in organizations and groups.
Like Francis Crick, they do not pretend to achieve extraordinary outputs alone.[2]
Yet such agents set the tone, create the setting, and drive the process that can
lead to extraordinarily creative ideas that have value. They are faces, not faceless
organization men—rather, a diverse selection of individuals bringing skills,
knowledge, hope, and a complex mix of experiences that motivate and drive
them to be creative. As Kidder's story divulges, these are long, hard processes to
achieve great results through a number of people and roles, at all levels of an
organization. The Eureka moments are few. As one entrepreneur told us, "It's
10 percent strategy and 90 percent execution." Strategic insight and direction
emerge over time and through a process of learning and development.

In this chapter, we'll talk about the various types of people and roles who
engage in innovative activities and guide and develop ideas through teams and
organizations to creative greatness. In their book, *Organizing Genius*, Warren

Bennis and Patricia Ward Biederman claim that creative leaders are able to find and guide the right people, allow and encourage enough friction to spark ideas, and when needed, protect the group from invasion of naysayers or "resource skimmers."[3] Sometimes such characteristics exist in a single person—like Tom West at Data General Corporation. Sometimes multiple people play different roles. Over time, an organization will come to rely on both to excel.[4]

However designed, creative organizations need at least three types of creative agents: creative entrepreneurs, creative leaders, and creative team members. The first two tend to be people who are able to find and exploit an opportunity in the environment and/or turn a creative vision into reality. Team members should have a bit of both—able to understand a vision and help turn it into something feasible. People make creativity and innovation happen.

Creative entrepreneurs straddle the border between the internal and external worlds of their organizations.[5] They identify opportunities, often from outside an organization, take risks, and find resources to exploit those opportunities. In the process, they build relationships and exploit market-based assets (externally), while setting an overall spark to start the creative collaboration processes (internally).[6]

Creative leaders, who may (or may not) also be entrepreneurs, have as a key task to turn the creative vision into reality for others to "see," understand, and implement/execute. As part of that task, they often need to scan and choose feasible ideas, form teams, and buffer groups and people to give them the room to develop the ideas. Some creative entrepreneurs and leaders do both, as creative integrators.

Finally, organizations need creative teams filled with people who execute and carry out the vision in very concrete ways, working with others both in and often outside of the organization. How do we attract and stimulate these people? What do we need to do to ensure that they succeed and what functions are required to make it real? The rest of the chapter will cover these issues.

CREATIVE ENTREPRENEURS

U.S. Highway 20 hugs Montana's eastern border with Wyoming and Yellowstone National Park, where at times the animal population of mountain lions, black bears, and wolves may outnumber humans. Just north of the town of West Yellowstone, population 2,000, drivers see the first of a dozen bright yellow warning signs:

Animals on road, next 10 miles.

Nice for the tourists. Maybe they'll see a deer or two.

Deer on the highway can be like squirrels in town. They stand motionless on the side of the road, startled and dazed, and a driver never quite knows what to expect. A deer can leap onto the road just as well as leap off to the side, bounding back into the woods. While a squirrel that leaps into the road may be squashed and give a driver a nasty feeling, a deer leaping onto the road and into a car can wreak much more damage to car, driver, and deer. But in Idaho and Montana, deer are only one of the animals that venture onto Highway 20.

Two miles on, another blinking sign appears:

Bison on road. Be prepared to stop.

Bison are another story. Some can be over six feet (two meters) tall, ten feet (three meters) long, and up to 2,000 pounds (900 kilos). Buffalo tend to mosey, sauntering across a highway like a slow moving tide. They ignore cars and plod. In a bison-versus-car contest, the winner is rarely the car.

As the sun sets on Highway 20, anything with reflective glazing or bright eyes stands out as brilliant points of light in the darkness. For the next twenty-five miles, what seem like holiday lights on the posts litter both sides of the road. Each post, which stands about ten yards from the next, has three reflective glazing buttons, lined vertically. The glazing makes the night road seem lit by fireflies, startling the driver more because lightning bugs are not indigenous to the dry western rangeland.

In the dark polka-dot road, good night vision is critical. Anyone driving Highway 20 in the dark needs antennae that won't quit—tracing the world outside the car, scanning for deer or bison or even those pesky squirrels that may venture onto the road.

Creative entrepreneurs are like drivers with night vision. They track their environments with a vengeance, looking for what others may not see, anticipating what the rest of us might not see, and reseeing—remembering past patterns of behavior that might be useful in the present and future. Often they can seem to be a step ahead, because of their mind sets (remember Naisbitt from chapter 3).

Like the roads near Yellowstone Park, organizational environments may be hard to see clearly, across sectors or even for organizations within similar sectors. To avoid danger and forge a path, creative entrepreneurs need deep knowledge of their environments, and they need to interpret that knowledge for implications, which should ultimately create competitive advantage for their organizations.

So how do creative entrepreneurs develop night vision to find those opportunities in the environment? They seem to have three ways of "seeing." Some simply "see what others don't," the factors that other people miss or don't fully recognize as being important. Especially talented creative entrepreneurs may also have a sense of what *may* be coming, what trends are emerging in the market place and what they might mean. This is more a talent to "foresee" opportunities—spot gaps in a marketplace that no one has seen, or even more daring, create new areas completely unseen by others.[7]

Finally, some creative entrepreneurs dismiss the thought that they can see or foresee new ideas. Rather, they claim instead to find something that exists and tweak it—through reseeing and rediscovering or reframing ideas that others have forgotten, or perhaps never seen in the past.

To understand the context of seeing, think again about the road winding through the beautiful, yet dark, landscape. To keep the car moving, you engage in a number of different activities: turn the wheel to the right and left as you go; brake and accelerate based on, for example, the actions or presence of other drivers, the character of the specific stretch of the road, or the need to stop to get gas. In the same way, creative entrepreneurs in organizations are undertaking a large number of daily activities, going this way and that way, learning how to best drive this stretch of the road, calling friends for assistance, and so forth. This makes up the work that moves the organization ahead. As Karl Weick, in *Managing as Designing*, puts it in relation to designing:

> Design is usually portrayed as forethought that leads to intention. But on closer inspection, design may be less original than it looks. One reason is because beginnings and endings are rare, middles are common. People, whether designers or clients, are always in the middle of something, which means designing is as much about re-design, interruption, resumption, continuity, and re-contextualizing, as it is about design, creation, invention, initiation, and contextualizing.[8]

Seeing What Others Don't

Vietnam's Boom: Reading the Environment Wrong ... and Then Right

As a child, Vuong Quan Hoang lived on the Vietnamese side of the Chinese border in the last years of the American War. He returned to his parents in Hanoi after the war. As did most Vietnamese in the 1980s, his family lived on food rations, which they could not trade or give away, under penalty of law. Vuong not only survived, he overcame his early life's constraints and has thrived.

Smart and ambitious, he aced school, attended university, and then earned a masters in business administration from an American university.

"I just thought of it as a piece of paper. Nothing more," he said.

In Asia, where credentials count as much as personal relationships can, Vuong pursued the degree to add it to his resume. But then he spent a summer in the United States, working as an intern in a university's Small

Business Development Center. He consulted with several dozen companies, watching as owners started and built their business firms; he even saw some failures. The experience was a turning point.

"I learned only one thing in America. And it's the most important of my career. That one thing is a word and an idea—entrepreneurship."

And learn he did.

After receiving his MBA degree, Vuong worked for the World Bank's International Finance Corporation, helping small businesses in Vietnam. He then earned a doctorate from the University of Brussels and has since started four firms, including a consulting firm to help investors enter Vietnam's budding stock market, do financial planning, and learn about doing business on line.

Vuong's approach reflects Vietnam today: scrappy, determined to do well, in a country that has struggled to join the regional and now global economic scene. His latest venture is Vietnam's first online business educational and informational Web site, Saga.vn (in English, http://en.saga.vn). He's written a book about business, opened offices in Hanoi and Saigon, and joined the less than 1 percent of Vietnamese who own their own vehicles. Vuong scanned the environment in Vietnam and beyond, built his knowledge of business, and understood the implications of the changes that Vietnam is experiencing, as its private and state owned enterprises move into regional and global business.

But like the American business owners he worked with so many years before, he also experienced failure. Vuong's first business was an investment service, started in 2000. He and a partner opened an office in one of Hanoi's most prestigious office buildings, and crammed two other employees and loads of technology into a room the size of a small bedroom. The firm closed a year later. At that time, not enough Vietnamese understood the concept of investment, and so the market was negligible.

Since then, however, Vuong's reading of the environment has been nearly pitch perfect. He's seeing opportunities that others are just beginning to recognize and thus is ahead of competitors.

The Alliance No One Tried ... Until Now

When Charlie Fee, producing artistic director of the Idaho Shakespeare Festival, was recruited to become the artistic director of the Great Lakes Shakespeare Festival in Cleveland, Ohio, 2,000 thousand miles away, he proposed doing both jobs, splitting time between the two cities. The theatre in Idaho was in strong shape: financially and artistically stable, having opened a new outdoor theatre that was fully paid for, with a strong administrative structure and a widespread donor base. The Cleveland theatre, in contrast, had problems.

Little seemed to be going right. Cleveland, a city once known as having more Fortune 500 headquarters than any other city in the United States, is increasingly perceived as unsafe and unattractive for visitors and theatre patrons. The theatre's artistic director had announced his resignation, the theatre faced serious financial difficulties, and there was talk of a merger with a significant, stronger, competitor. Fee was brought in to manage the merger process. And then, the merger talks collapsed, and Fee was left to manage the turnaround of a failing organization.

Fee's first task was cost cutting in Cleveland, which he did within the first few months, slowing the financial hemorrhaging. Yet, as he learned more about the Cleveland theatre environment, he began to envision an opportunity that, to date, no other regional theatres in the United States have pursued: an alliance between the theatres, in Idaho and Ohio. The two theatres offered similar content (i.e., Shakespeare plays, one musical, and one or two other classical plays per season). But they had roughly opposite seasons: Idaho's was June through September; Cleveland's was September through May. And they had different areas of administrative strength (e.g., fundraising in Idaho; educational outreach in Cleveland). The complementary seasons meant Fee could hire high quality directors, designers, and actors for longer seasons, who work for both organizations. They, in turn, could receive benefits (unusual in the theatre world), which made those jobs more attractive to the best artists in the country. Finally, the theatres were geographically separate, and thus noncompeting.

The alliance, which has now operated for several years, is unique in U.S. regional professional theatres. Essentially a new business model, it allows each theatre to develop and mount two plays and then transfer them to the other. The result is economies of scale, savings, and long-term loyalty of directors, actors, and designers.

Interestingly, as successful as the alliance has been, other theatres have not (yet) adopted anything similar. The advantages would be to create synergies from their strengths, save production costs, and become more attractive to artists. In fact, Fee has approached other directors in the western part of the United States. None wants to pursue such an alliance. He speculates that the Idaho-Ohio alliance succeeds in large part because he is the director of both. Rather than two directors needing to compromise or worry about losing some control, they prefer not to pursue an alliance and hence forego the benefits from such a model.

As creative entrepreneurs, Fee and Vuong have remarkable senses of what their environments mean for their organizations, how to interpret those implications, and how to find the resources to turn some of those trends into potential opportunities. In doing so, each has been able to create advantages over competitors, whether in remote Idaho or remote Vietnam. Such understanding might include the ability to better "read" customers, understand competitors more thoroughly, or anticipate implications of trends. They have taken action, by setting up several ventures as Vuong has, or by creating a platform for continued development and to experiment from, as Fee has.

Foreseeing Opportunities

> He gets an abstract idea and then puts a word to it.
>
> a manager, reflecting on a creative entrepreneur

An ability to see something that is not yet "there" and "put a word to it" separates visionary forward-seeing entrepreneurs from others. Especially for organizations that are remote, their creative entrepreneurs need to be active in their search for trends and anticipating them.

Knowing What the Market Needs before It Knows

Healthwise's CEO Don Kemper heard a speech by a leading health-policy expert over thirty years ago that triggered his notion of how to encourage patients to take more responsibility for their own health care. He founded his organization on that fundamental, simple, yet profoundly different perspective in the health field. Healthwise's mission is to help people make better health decisions. It has driven all strategic moves since. One manager puts it this way: "[It may be] contrary to what everybody might think, but [he sees] the direction we should be going. And he's done a very good job.... And we [see it] over and over and over again."

An example of an abstract idea that Kemper "put a word to" more than five years ago is "information therapy" (Ix).[9] Just as a physician writes a prescription for medication, she can write one for information, to be given and used at specific times, for specific purposes. Ix is becoming increasingly known and accepted within the industry; the founder and creative entrepreneur has spoken about it both inside and outside of North America as well.[10] An idea that patients may not even know they may need, Information Therapy could well become as commonplace as the medical prescription.

Kemper's almost eerie ability to foresee trends and their implications has kept his organization at the leading edge of health-care information support for patients. And, it has set a tone inside the organization that it is able to lead the industry, rather than worry about what competition might do. In large part, that comes from the CEO's ability to create a new market, rather than compete with existing products or services. One employee explains: "[In] other companies I have worked for, a lot of time was spent worrying about what the competition was doing and making sure that we have every feature [they do.] We don't worry about that so much here. We spend some time [on it] but we are very true to our mission and vision. And [the CEO] is the visionary." Instead of focusing on the competition, Kemper's vision has created new areas, or "blue ocean strategies," for the organization to move to new, untapped market areas.[11] Finding those new opportunities is driven by pursuing the organization's mission of helping people make better health decisions.

Tilde Björfors got her revelation when traveling. Seeing and experiencing contemporary circus gave her the idea to bring it back to Sweden. But it was a long journey from that insight—making others see the novelty, setting up and selling performances in a number of settings, engaging people in circus, and more. Now the market wants more, and the circus is better at knowing what it wants, making the long journey and development pay off as its artists come out on top. It is foresight turned into opportunity.

Reseeing Opportunities

In some organizations or sectors, new ideas or ways of operating may appear to be relatively scarce. In sports, some claim that major innovations come rarely, and then most often from individuals. Olympian Dick Fosbury's backward flip high-jump technique revolutionized the sport. Instead of leaping with one arm and leg leading the jump, facedown, his jump was upside down, with his chest pointing skyward. Standard procedure today but completely novel then, Fosbury's technique has allowed jumpers to reach much higher levels—literally and figuratively. Shot-put champion Parry O'Brien studied physics and body mechanics to improve his shot-put technique, allowing him to win two Olympic gold medals and shatter records.[12]

But some team sports coaches look less for the dramatic novel idea than ways to improve and tweak what exists. Football coaches at Boise State University often claim "there's nothing new in football," and yet, to some observers (especially during the 2006 season), the team blossomed with fresh approaches during games.[13] And they paid off, with a fifth place ranking at the end of the 2006 season.

Rather than talk of creative plays or training, though, head coach Chris Petersen says they often reuse or resee ideas that come from studying football history, and years of videos from long-past games. The "hook and lateral," called "Circus" at Boise State, and an adapted version of the "Statue of Liberty play," two of football's oldest and most difficult to pull off successfully, helped turn the tide of the January 2007 Fiesta Bowl game and ultimately win it for Boise State. One coach claims that "What may be called 'innovative' right now was something that was being used 15 years ago. It's just resurfaced.... [The plays] kind of come back."

Coaches and players spend hours reviewing videotapes of opponents' previous games to see what plays they used in various situations. Coaches also mine historical tapes, some many decades old, to re-see plays that they can tweak and reuse, which often look "new" to opponents. That knowledge and the coaches' ability to weave it into a game plan that takes advantage of opponent weaknesses, can be a major creative competitive advantage.

In 2005, New Wave Group bought one of Sweden's famous glass companies, Orrefors Kosta Boda. This hallmark of creative glass making, based on solid mastery, was then in deep financial trouble. By reseeing what could be done, New Wave managers have turned the company around, though it meant that they had to reduce the workforce by 50 percent. How? By seeing that the opportunity lay not just within the company, but in creating a number of activities and business opportunities around the myth and story of Swedish glass making. The glass company today sells glass boats for $46,000. Customers who buy one get to fly to the place of origin and meet the artist. It also sells champagne flutes for $4,600, created by a designer determined to make them look "sexy." This has led to a large increase in the number of visitors, providing new jobs to those who were let go earlier. New Wave Group saw that by investing in both internal and external development, they could create new companies and opportunities outside the organization that could turn the company around. Through skills, passion, luck, and a keen interest in knowing who they are and who their customers are, they created an opportunity. The CEO says: "When people ask me what is the biggest difference now compared to three years ago, I always answer 'people are whistling in the factory again.'"[14]

In sum, creative entrepreneurs have a knack for reading their external environments and finding ways to exploit what they see, foresee or resee. The next step, of course, is implementing this vision of what is possible. And that's where creative leaders—in the same person, or in others—come into play.

CREATIVE LEADERS: TURNING VISION INTO REALITY

The world hates change, yet it is the only thing that has brought progress.

Charles Kettering

Whereas creative entrepreneurs are the principal finders or formers of opportunities and vision, creative leaders are the people who turn them into reality. Creative leaders take on at least four roles: (1) translating a creative vision into an idea that others can "see"; (2) forming teams to carry out the vision; (3) guiding teams; and (4) buffering teams from potential obstacles. They create the work conditions and have the executive abilities to get ideas implemented and bear fruit.[15] These efforts will be described in the rest of the chapter.

Translating Vision into an Idea Others Can See

Two examples—from theatre and from the jungles and rice fields of emerging countries—show how creative leaders can turn an idea into a vision that all can see.

An Indoor "Outdoor Theatre"

It's one thing to have the notion of what will bring an audience to a theatre in a decayed inner city. It's quite something else to make it happen.

The Great Lakes Theatre Festival in Cleveland, Ohio, sits in downtown Cleveland, which is deserted after 7 P.M.; there are no people strolling, no restaurants open, and no bustling crowds. Even the hundred yards from the theatre to a nearby hotel, within eyesight of each other, is a stretch rife with pickpockets and muggers. Anyone attending the theatre or a concert parks in an attached garage and scurries through glassed-in second floor tunnels to the theatre. They see the play, return to their cars, and leave. One restaurant in the theatre complex stays open for a few brave patrons and actors still wound up from the play.

The Ohio Theatre, where the Great Lakes Shakespeare Festival company plays, is a grand 1,100-seat theatre, a renovated and much-loved art deco space that thrived in the city's bustling center in the 1920s. But in the last decades festival performances packed in only 600 people, so the theatre space always seemed empty and a bit lifeless.

Having come from the outdoor Shakespeare Festival theatre in Idaho, Charlie Fee knew what a lively theatre could be. The outdoor theatre is the same size as the Globe Theatre in England, seats 600, and is 90 percent full for its four-month season, bringing in more than 50,000 people every year. Theatre goers range from babies to 80+ year olds; family nights, a gala dinner, pretheatre talks by directors, and preshow comedic skits, make for a bustling season all summer long. Seating ranges from picnic style on the lawn to tables for four or six, to chairs or blankets on the berm, fitting any budget or leg length. Visitors bring dinner and wine or buy it at the theatre, chat with friends during the play if they like, and joke with the Green Show actors before the play begins. The dry, warm weather helps as well; with temperatures of 90 degrees Fahrenheit at 7 P.M., theatre goers come in sunglasses and hats, but by 10 P.M., they yank sweaters from their picnic baskets and cradle cups of coffee in their hands against the cooling night air.

The physical infrastructure and feeling within each theatre space could not have been more different. When Fee joined the Cleveland group, he sought to alter the basic culture of the audience, staff, and board, but knew it would be tough going, in a world of "old money, old culture, and old traditions."

So he began with small feasible changes, creative ideas designed for Cleveland, not for Idaho—actions that could lay the groundwork for a future bigger vision. He started with "curtain talks." Before a production begins, Fee walks onto a lighted stage in front of the curtains to welcome patrons, explain a little about the play, and thank sponsors.

Common practice in Idaho, heresy in Ohio.

Theatre goers in Idaho were used to bringing food and wine into the theatre—not so in Ohio, where the traditional intermission meant a hasty glass of wine, gulped in ten minutes. So one evening, Fee told the Ohio house staff to allow patrons to bring wineglasses into the theatre after intermission. The response from audience members was immediate and positive. The somewhat skeptical board supported the move once Fee explained the reasoning.

Common practice in Idaho, heresy in Ohio.

Fee brought staff and board members to the Idaho theatre to experience the informal outdoor atmosphere and interactions between the actors and theatre goers, even sometimes during the play, when the weather or a major mistake wreaked havoc and the only sensible reaction was humor and engaging the audience.

Common practice in Idaho, heresy in Ohio.

All of these steps were tiny compared to Fee's bigger and longer-term vision: a new and different type of theatre space for the Ohio company. Essentially, he is seeking to create an indoor theatre space in the old-moneyed center of Cleveland, Ohio, with the atmosphere and feel of the informal outside space of upstart remote Boise in the U.S. Mountain West. The architects and designers he works with claim that, to date, no such facility exists in the United States. If it works, it could be a model for other theatres trying to create more of a creative experience for their audiences.

Fee has started the design process and anticipates a newly renovated, unique theatre by September 2008. The outlook is good, given that the audience has increased by 36 percent over the last three years, even in the old site. Just imagine what the new one will bring.

A process of seeing what works, starting small while using probes to learn, having a benchmark to compare to, and making sense of what is emerging are components of the leadership in this creative organization.[16]

Computers, Bare Feet, and an Open World

Anyone who complains about students in North America or Europe should try to teach sixth graders in a developing country—forty-five of them, packed three to a desk, in a cement-floor room, with no teaching materials other than a blackboard and a smile.

One summer, Nancy and her son worked as volunteers in a small fishing village in Ghana, on the equator. If you squint hard, Prampram looks like a tropical paradise—palm trees, balmy winds, soft sand beaches, twinkling single light bulbs and small fires outside huts at night. But in the daytime, eyes wide open, it's clear this is a "hollow village," populated mostly with grandparents and children. Younger, able, energetic people leave for the capital, Accra, in search of work.

The sixth-grade children come to school in shifts, mornings or afternoons, because the room lacks enough desks, even though three children share each desk in the jammed room. The school district buys pens and chalk; the children bring their own notebooks, covered with newspaper to keep them from falling apart. Their uniforms—peach-colored shirts, dark-brown shorts or skirts—are torn, worn, and passed down. Some children come barefoot, many wear flip-flops, and only a few have shoes, usually much too large and with no shoelaces. Not even the principal has a computer, and Prampram certainly is not a hot destination for Internet cafes. Yet some dreamers think a village like Prampram is ripe for technology. But only a creative entrepreneur and leader could make it happen.

Nicholas Negroponte, founder of the MIT Media Lab, creative entrepreneur and now creative leader, developed a vision that has shattered beliefs about limitations in some of the world's poorest countries.[17] To facilitate education and help reduce the "digital divide," Negroponte (and now some competitors) found ways to bring computers to villages at reasonable costs—an opportunity unthinkable before his technology emerged. His One Laptop per Child (OLPC) research has developed technology for a $188 laptop that is affordable for children worldwide. His vision is clear—this is an education project. And the way to carry it out is also clear—by building and distributing laptops that are "ultra-low cost, power efficient, responsive, and durable," that are child-powered, through a yellow crank, and which are functional, as well as interesting from a design standpoint.

Negroponte's idea is visual, concrete, and big. The idea was so ambitious that at first few could envision it would ever happen. It's taken four decades to reach a point where it can become reality, but it has taken his entrepreneurial and leadership guidance. At last he is attracting both funders and school programs in selected countries to give the idea a try.

In completely different sectors, downtown Cleveland and poor developing countries, Fee and Negroponte exhibited the key characteristic of creative entrepreneurs who are also creative leaders. Both have an ability to read the environment and anticipate what that meant for their organizations, and then translate their visions into something feasible and real for others, both inside and out of their organizations. Then they used their relationships to move the ideas forward. Fee managed his internal staff and the artists, as well as his board and the audience, to help implement his ideas. Negroponte's Media Lab worked the internal technological development; he also had to convince external stakeholders, from funders to users.

Both men exhibit the ability to translate visions into something doable. Individuals like Negroponte and Fee ensure they get attention and the power required to push an idea forward. In many cases, however, these individuals and leaders that are so important are happy to keep a low profile and to work in stealth mode, and this often makes them more effective. For those lesser-known "faces," creative entrepreneurs and leaders also need to ensure they get the attention and backup they require and deserve. In all these organizations there is a balance of sorts between creative development and profitability and efficiency. Maintaining it is a continuous managerial process, as we have seen. Michael M. Kaiser, president of the John F. Kennedy Center of Performing Arts in Washington, DC, frames it like this: "You can't just address costs. You must address revenue. If you have a good product, that will help turn things around."[18]

Next, we'll look at the forming and directing of creative teams to carry out the vision.

FORMING AND DIRECTING CREATIVE TEAMS: MOVING TARGETS

In an American comedy series from the 1960s, *The Dick Van Dyke Show*, three writers meet daily to hammer out sketches for a weekly show. Rosemary, Buddy, and Rob spin ideas, type them up, toss them out, and generate new ones. We have the impression they've worked together for years and plan to retire together. A long-standing creative team, they share personal lives and know one another's strengths and weaknesses in ways that come only from years of time spent together.

But how many creative teams stay together these days for years, regardless of industry sector? Increased turnover comes from, for example, an increasing number of temporary workers and use of consultants. In cases where short-term contracts are in place, our case organizations often work to make them longer, full-time engagements, to allow for prolonged development and cocreated knowledge. Also, creative high performers are well aware of their worth and are sometimes skeptical of employers unless they see leaders taking them on responsibly. Creative teams form temporary organizations, requiring management attention to ensure knowledge, processes, and skills are also kept alive as new ventures form. So for a number of obvious reasons, few teams stay together long.

Regional theatres have budgets that limit preparation of plays to six to eight months: the director and designer creative team work together for four months; the director and actor creative team rehearse for four to six weeks. In software, employees may stay with a company for years, but frequently change teams, as projects change. Football coaches see a predictable 25–30 percent annual turnover in their players, regularly shifting the mix of talent. Movie production brings experts together for a set time and budget, and then they disperse when the project is completed. Forest fire fighters from Australia may join groups from Florida or Oregon for days or weeks, then move on to assist other fire-fighting teams. People change organizations; organizations change people; projects change teams; and teams move on. Team members need to come together as a team fast, work efficiently, and then move on when the project is finished.

Thus, one challenge for a creative leader is to find ways to select and manage team members. Two aspects come into play: forming teams and managing diversity.

Perhaps as many approaches to forming teams exist as creative leaders. Three common approaches emerged in our cases in terms of selecting team members: (1) directive selection; (2) selective shuffling; and (3) drafting and accepting.[19] In addition, creative leaders must manage diversity within teams.

The case organizations had more or less structured ways to decide which members joined which teams. Questions you might start with as you determine your approach are: What are you trying to achieve? Could creativity be impacted or hampered depending on how far you try to predetermine the capabilities required? And lastly, what motivates people? We start with the more directive approach and move towards those where the team members have greater leeway.

Directive Selection

As we have mentioned, the theatre world is quite hierarchical. A theatre's producing artistic director hires external directors for most of its plays, who in turn hire most of the designers (e.g., set, lighting, music/sound, costume) for a given play. The producing artistic director may also hire most or all of the support personnel—technicians (people who build sets, sew costumes, or run the lights)—who in turn work with the designers and director on a particular play. The teams of artistic and technical staff are, by their very nature, temporary. They work on a given play, which is constrained by time, budget, and place.[20] Thus, the director, actors, designers, and technicians remain in a given location for the life of their respective responsibilities.

For a play, the director, sometimes with input from the theatre's artistic director, chooses actors and designers who become the creative team. The selection process, then, is quite directed and directive—the producing artistic director and play director choose key participants, with little input from the participants themselves.

While auditions are common, the director typically uses long-standing relationships with other artists to choose who will play which role. Since several professional actors could conceivably fill a role, directors often select people they know will act well. But another factor comes into play. Many say they choose people they know will be good team members and easy to work with. In theatre, where emotions can run high, being able to work with the director and with other creative team members may make the difference between having a job or not. Interestingly, the same idea of being "easy to work with" arises in other sectors. A small high-tech firm CEO also commented that "being easy to deal with" had become a "competitive advantage" for his company. Thus, directors select members, give them the roles they are to play, and coordinate efforts of all of the members. While some directors may seek input from other artists, ultimately, decisions and responsibility for the quality and performance of the play rests with that person.

Another example of directive selection comes from a setting where latitude and expected involvement of a variety of members is the norm—a university. And yet one manager took an approach that was contrary to traditional practice.

When a university began a new executive program, the senior administration asked for something that would be unique, generate regional visibility, and be profitable. The creative leader and head of the graduate program, Kirk Smith, faced a challenge in picking a team, because universities and faculty governance differs dramatically from expectations in private companies. In universities, committees and task forces typically are representative: one member from each discipline, such as finance, production, or marketing, sits on the committee. In this case, Smith's deliberate selection focused on choosing faculty members with critical characteristics, ones that are not common among faculty ranks. Once members joined, they shifted perspectives and positions over time. As he describes it:

> Two things were important: [members'] ability to think creatively and their ability to think beyond their own functions or disciplines. That limited the pool. So, I picked one person who is the most far out, creative person in our school—at one end of the continuum. Then I wanted to balance that person with someone who's really practical and will bring us down to earth. From that point, I worked "inward": picked another person who's creative but a little closer to being practical, a fourth person who's really practical but a little more toward the creative end. And then someone in the middle who had strong expertise within the key discipline for the program. Finally, I wanted someone with expertise in executive education—someone who had already taught in the type of program we planned to develop.

Picking selectively can get you the variety and character you want, as long as directive picking does not limit diversity.

Selective Shuffling

Another approach to forming a team might be called "selective shuffling," which is common in football.

Somewhat like theatre, university football programs have three main groups involved in "producing" a game: coaches, players, and support personnel (e.g., strength-conditioning coaches who help players become stronger and trainers who work with injured players). These groups become a type of creative team and subteams.

The head coach runs the football sports program. As we suggested earlier, the head coach sets a vision for the program and the team—from living certain types of values (e.g., integrity, professionalism) to being winners. If we stretch the analogy, he must also be a creative leader and help turn that vision into reality. He manages expectations—of investors (donors), competitors (opposing teams), and customers (fans, in this case) on the outside. He also manages the organization on the inside.

Three groups of position coaches handle specific tasks to turn vision into reality. Offensive coaches focus on moving the football down field, when their team has control. The movement comes from a series of plays, where the ball moves (usually) down the field through a run or pass/throw by one or more players. The defensive players try to stop the opposing team's forward movement of the ball. Defensive coaches and players, then, try to anticipate the opposing team's play and seek to prevent its success. In the lucky situation where the defensive side gains control of the ball, its players must be prepared to run toward their own goal. The special teams group comprises players who kick the ball at various points in the game, such as at the beginning of significant plays, and those who receive and run with the ball when it has been kicked by the opposing team.

The three groups of coaches work with players within those clusters of positions. The Boise State University team is somewhat different because they use a sort of "selective shuffling" to create the various player groupings and subteams they want. In other words, they may shuffle players across various positions during spring training. They may want to see if an offensive player could also play in a defensive position, for example. A few professional coaches, such as Bill Belichick, head coach of the New England Patriots, use a similar selective-shuffling approach—moving players to different positions. This can be disconcerting to the opposing team, which cannot readily anticipate which personnel will be in which positions on the field.

Thus, unlike most teams that use one or two players in critical positions, Boise State University's team may have several players who are able to do the task. It not only gives players more chances to play, it reduces reliance on any one or two players. If one person is injured, there are more in reserve. Similar approaches can be found in, for example, management trainee programs where most use some kind of rotation through which one gets exposure to many facets of an organization before being placed later on.

Drafting and Self-Selection

In our case software firm, members were generally assigned to project teams, and shuffled according to the nature of the product. But some programmers and developers have wanted more opportunity to choose which projects they participated on, rather than being assigned and moved. Thus, the firm tried a more fluid method for forming teams.

The firm uses a sort of "drafting" process. Potential team members rank order the project they would like to join; potential project managers review which team members want to work on the different projects. Typically, there is overlap between which people a project manager would select and those who want to work on a project. In this tough, "prove yourself every day" atmosphere, developers and managers learn they need to be at the top of their expertise and management games to be attractive to potential "recruits." Those technical engineers who are rarely listed as being ones that managers want, or managers whose projects are less desirable, will theoretically be sparked to improve their skills.

In some organizations, employees can choose how and where to spend their time, which becomes an indicator of how important an idea is. The thinking is that if an idea does not capture the excitement and heads of coworkers, it probably isn't worth doing.

Paradox, a game-development company, takes this idea of letting employees, users, and developers "vote with their feet" to a extreme. It has gathered a large online community of people from both inside and outside of the firm to provide input, write code, and develop their product. Community members participate solely based on their own initiative. Members of the community then buy the final product. In a market where the first quarter after a launch is the period where you will make all the earnings, using these creative team members increases the likelihood you deliver to requirements.[21]

Managing Diversity in Creative Teams

As teams form, a creative leader manages the strengths and diversity of team members and finds ways to take advantage of each. Part of that involves recognizing whether and how to use diversity in group members. Diane Mutz found in her research on how people interact on politics that it is acceptable to disagree, but only to a point. If you go too far, the person you are discussing politics with will withdraw, as your opinions could be construed as too far apart to engage in discussion. So diversity requires that you find common ground to start interacting on, and then move forward.[22]

Three ways of looking at and managing diversity appeared in the organizations we worked with: invisible, conscious, and "playing the cards that were dealt."

"Invisible" Diversity

An almost unquestioned assumption about creative teams is that they need diversity of members, which allows perspectives to clash at times, and, from that friction, comes new ideas and methods for operating. Some creative leaders, however, have a love-hate relationship with diversity, for the tension that it can cause, as one senior manager explained: "I want diversity but I don't want diversity. I want there to be some common themes that are very much the same [for all of us]. Now, outside of that, I love it when people are different ... but there need to be some things we genuinely care about."

Within the various cases we examined, one of our early surprises was how lacking in diversity some of the groups seemed. In the football case, for example, the coaches seemed to vary only slightly. True, ethnic backgrounds varied somewhat—some African Americans, one from the Pacific Islands, but the rest were white, male, and in their thirties or early forties. Many had prior experience at the same program, the University of California at Davis. Others had worked together at the same universities. In some sense, they seemed to move in hives from university program to university program.

For the Boise State University group, "He's a 'Davis guy'" seemed almost a code for "He's one of us; we understand each other; we're part of the same group." A major point of connection for many, they commented that they all understood and valued the "system" they had learned at UC–Davis. To an outsider, diversity seemed negligible. But diversity comes in different forms.

A psychologist who conducted personality tests on the coaches revealed remarkable differences, which surprised one coach: "Each coach was quite distinct—some were extremely analytical, some had desks that are a mess, and some were very rigid and a lot more structured. I thought, 'Interesting that none of us are the same.' And that might be a reason we have a really good combination and balance." So even when diversity appears negligible, it can exist and be drawn out.

Conscious Diversity

Other organizations proactively seek out widely diverse group members, especially when it comes to solving certain problems. ProClarity's Clay Young recognized the need for balance in diversity of creativity: "We [aren't] constrained by much, which is a good problem. We have people who are way out there on the [high creativity] end. And we've got to have people … who are sort of right in the middle. That's what you need for product managers. They need to have a nice balance between unconstrained thinking and discipline." Likewise, Healthwise forms groups with the intent of mixing people

> to first build a good creative team that works well.… People that have different ideas, different backgrounds and ways of living their lives every day so that we grow to appreciate each other. So that we have a good team that feels really good about each other and safe about giving out any ideas because anything goes. Then we will invite other people in from the organization who may not have anything to do with this project or rarely have an opportunity to sit in on a creative brainstorming session.

Playing the Cards That Are Dealt to You

At a circus, uniqueness is what customers are paying for. Diversity is what leaders want from the members of these extended teams—the company. Yet, as the performance unfolds, the diverse skills and experiences, and their performances, and the expression of the artist are interlaced into a story or a theme. Complementarity combined with a base in individual expression as an artist make the creative director, artists, and the whole team working on costumes and décor come together.

Playing the cards refers to the fact that an organization such as a circus starts with the expectation that members will be diverse. It is a baseline—not something to build in. Management instead must focus on how to integrate that diverse group of people, their performances, their experiences, and creative expression into a final product.

A Second Take on the Functions of the "Aces"

A couple of key faces in our organizations helped us understand how they develop and stay creative: the creative entrepreneur, the creative leader, and the creative team members. Let us now continue with the functions of the faces and how one can keep making faces in the creative organization.

Integration

Creative teams help move an idea through the steps in a development process. A team may change its makeup and focus of activities to adapt to the demands at the time. A software team may, for example, adapt by having different members, roles, and linkages to complete a set of features in software. Since not all members may have all the skills or experience to complete a particular feature, the team may bring in new members, reach out to experts in other parts of the firm, or call in other partners. In other situations, the team may make more jolting shifts to achieve a goal. This process is less one of step by step, but more dramatic, with giant steps and then periods of slower progress. In biological evolution, the term *punctuated equilibrium* refers to such jumps or dramatic steps in evolution; likewise, teams can experience instances where the equilibrium becomes unbalanced (is punctuated), and such a jump occurs.[23] Also, how this process looks over time can vary.

In addition to the sometimes smooth, sometimes jerky process of turning ideas into action, another theme emerged: how teams and their work integrate and bridge—inside as well as outside an organization—with a community. It happens often at Cirkus Cirkör.

The company is located in a suburb outside of Stockholm, Sweden. During the past few years, its members have worked with several municipalities and regions to develop circus performances, training camps, and interaction with schools. They are called, for example, Cirkör C/O Landskrona. C/O indicates that it is Cirkör staying in the community, and the name is the community (Landskrona), the host. A number of roles and different forms for working together are needed to generate alternatives for action and moving these alternatives forward.

These initiatives rely on a number of roles and people to work. A few of these are:

- *Local liaison officers and decision makers* who can integrate the circus ideas into school curricula, find performance stages, and find

organizations that should be involved to work together and which
might be able to financially support the venture.

- *Coproducers* who come from Cirkör manage the collaboration, discuss
  how they can participate, work with the municipalities to implement
  ideas, and clarify roles, based on experiences from previous
  engagements.

- *Artists and pedagogical experts* who bring the circus into the theatres and
  stages, the schools, and the everyday lives of teachers and students. Producers from Cirkör and municipalities coproduce the shows. Pedagogical project managers from Cirkör ensure quality.

Mobility of people—that is, moving between geographical places, between
different types of organizations, such as between academia and industry, and
across knowledge areas—is one way to develop the ability to integrate and
bridge. This can be done systematically, in which incentives and career paths
may support such people who are bridges. A danger is that organizations may
miss such people, because often their cross-disciplinary nature makes them fall
"in between the cracks," and they disappear from view.

Different roles, played by various members, are necessary in a creative team.
Over time the makeup of a team is also likely to change, partly to provide
members new opportunities, but also to maintain efficiency in getting work
done. As we have discussed, within-discipline knowledge and practices provide a
common platform and language for team members to continue working and
maintain interaction as they move in and out of teams and roles. In addition,
the creative process, in its various shapes in different firms, provides the discipline and agreed-upon practices that enable efficiency. In the circus, the basis
for practices is the artistic process. In the software firm, it is the scrum approach.
In the football team, it is the set schedule for the week and the specific setup of
practices and activities during that week. These allow members to move between
roles, yet understand what is expected of them and how they fit in.[24]

Practices are a mechanism for integration, as they allow for a shared understanding of how work should be carried out, who does what, and how different members of teams and the surrounding organization connect and interact.

In addition to integration and bridging, the organization and creative teams
need buffering and protecting, which we turn to next.

Buffer and Protector

It took 22 years to develop the ulcer medicine Losec. More than 150
researchers, technicians, and experts participated in developing the
project. It was threatened by termination five times, of which four during the time when I was managing it. Losec has been used for more than
150 million treatments in more than 90 countries. No serious side-
effects have been proven to come from Losec.

Ivan Östholm

Creative leaders also protect and buffer, as Östholm did for Losec.[25] Indeed, they protect embryonic ideas from likely dampeners within an organization, something we discuss further in chapter 8. But they buffer in other unexpected ways as well. Two ways that surprised us emerged from our case organizations: (1) protecting the creative entrepreneur from himself; and (2) protecting a creative team from the creative entrepreneur!

Protecting the Creative Entrepreneur from Himself

Because creative entrepreneurs are often the founders and initial leaders of their organizations, they can easily become mired in management and other daily tasks. Several mentioned the need to withdraw, to pull themselves out of management to do more of what they do best: seeing opportunities. Two CEOs in Vietnam—one in construction and manufacturing, another in the ceramics business—commented on how they had discovered how much "better" they were at seeing and creating opportunities for their firms than at management or implementation of ideas. They both talked about finding ways to buffer and protect themselves from tasks that were less interesting for them and for which they had less competence. One said he had begun implementing steps to buffer or protect himself, as idea generator, from the administration and leadership activities of his firm as it grows. His company works with some foreign firms to provide the local knowledge of such topics as soil and construction conditions and labor management, which the CEO feels is the firm's competitive advantage. The other CEO is currently scaling back the time he spends leading the firm to focus on creative entrepreneurship activities. His goal is to spend 60 percent of his time on coming up with new ideas. In both cases, they recognized they needed a creative leader, which each is mentoring within their firms, to take more responsibility for implementing visionary ideas.

This gets back to our idea of tempering ideas (chapter 5). To do this truthfully, you need to relinquish some of the tasks and let others into the idea generation and creation process. This can be very hard to do since part of getting to your position is that you have been very successful at what you do. Now is the time to keep this competitiveness in reins to allow others to grow. Knowing you should do this is one thing; doing it is completely different.

Protecting a Creative Team from the Creative Entrepreneur

Some creative entrepreneurs overwhelm their creative teams with ideas.

Extreme Arts and Sciences consultant and CEO Larry Harrington works for companies like Microsoft to help them anticipate trends in the environment and interpret what they might mean for their firms.

But he is also a man overflowing with ideas, to the point where his employees start meetings with the chant, "Larry, no new ideas."

Would that more organizations had that problem.

But Larry's firm is not alone. In some of the organizations we worked with as well, the creative entrepreneurs sometimes shower their organizational members with ideas, often without a screen for them. In chapter 5, we talked about Healthwise and how the CEO often comes up with many big ideas. Part of this organization's success is that creative leaders have helped to screen the overwhelming number of ideas so creative team members do not become inundated.

Another way that buffering from a creative entrepreneur overflowing with ideas may happen is an informal "self-screening" by the entrepreneur. In one organization, the CEO sends ideas along to team members or leaders, but instead of signing them with a real name, the CEO uses an alternative name. It is code for, "when I sign it like this, it's more an idea to consider, not one to pursue with vigor." Thus, creative leaders and team members can understand which ideas the entrepreneur is serious about looking into, and which ideas could be "hmmmm" or back-burner ideas for a time.

Buffering versus Selecting

Fine-tuning the balance between allowing new ideas in and allowing the ideas that are coming up to continue to develop based on their own merit is an art. Protecting and buffering falls back on a process that throughout an idea's evolution needs to come into play: the process of selecting what ideas should and could continue to develop and managing the associated risks.[26] The leaders we talked with had several hints:

- Keep your purpose and direction in mind. With an entrepreneurial mindset, it is easy to see opportunities wherever you look. While many of these will bring you and your purpose forward, some components fall outside of your current scope. Over time it is important to look back at opportunities, and consider to what extent this keeps you on or off track.
- Break the ideas down. Failure is part of the process. So, initiate several approaches to a problem, talk to different people and organizations about collaboration, and design your work as smaller packages and modules that can be reused.
- Think broader. As examples here have shown, it is seldom wise to have only one person pick what should and should not be developed. Instead, a broader set of perspectives and ideas should be taken into account, and used to sift through potential ideas and projects.

Making Faces

The creative organizations we have studied all work to match teams with objectives, drawing upon people with certain roles, skills, and capabilities.

They have also learned how to balance the need to achieve outcomes with the need to develop individuals so they will continue to be creative and entrepreneurial even as their teams achieve specific goals.

An example of this is the effort by both the theatre and the circus to keep people over longer periods of time. By providing longer seasons, the artists avoid having to search for new jobs and thus are able to enjoy a longer period of interaction and artistic exchange. But this does not fit all artists and company members. You need to identify people for which this is attractive, for whom stability and a longer commitment is interesting. While some artists appreciate the chance to work for one or a few organizations for longer periods, others prefer the ability to move between opportunities, of not being tied down by future commitments. So, picking and designing a development path for the individual is important.

An interesting by-product of keeping people on board at the circus for longer periods is that the normal process and contractual rules do not apply. Instead, new contracts, routines for insuring them, and for how agreements should be settled have had to be developed. This has been done in an effort to give the artists peace of mind and to create the company stability and compliance with rules.

We have presented several ideas in this chapter on how faces work in creative organizations. They are:

- *Creative agents* are the faces of creative energy and outcome in organizations and groups; they are, like Tom West, the "good man in the storm." Every organization needs them. They do not act alone, yet drive the creative process by finding and motivating the right people and creating an environment where ideas and innovation can spark.
- *Creative entrepreneurs* are drivers with night vision: they look at the border between the internal and external worlds of their organizations, and once opportunities are found, they take risks and find resources to start the innovative process. They identify potential by seeing what others don't, by foreseeing what may be coming, and by reseeing or rediscovering ideas others have forgotten.
- *Creative leaders* turn the creative vision into reality for others to understand and implement. They translate the creative vision into an idea that others can see, form teams to implement the idea, guide the teams, and buffer teams from potential obstacles.
- *Creative teams* carry out the vision and are the creative brain and brawn. Diversity is crucial since it allows clashes and frictions between different perspectives. Look at where your diversity comes from, see that you have enough, and manage what you have.
- *Integration and bridging* relies on faces. Getting ideas through a complex development process, getting different organizations and people

to interact and contribute, and integrating new and old units and knowledge areas to see mutual benefit of novelty require that perspectives and stakes are integrated and bridged. Certain people and roles do that. Value them.

This takes us to the next chapter, where we will discuss the physical structures in which creative people meet, interact, and develop innovative products and concepts.

NOTES

1. Kidder's books often highlight a seemingly normal character who is capable of extraordinary achievements. West is one of the first. He epitomizes the characteristics of an entrepreneur and leader, within a major organization. See Tracy Kidder. 1981. *The Soul of a New Machine.* New York: Avon Books.

2. Francis Crick and James Watson, along with colleagues Maurice Wilkins and Rosalind Franklin, and competitor Linus Pauling, were days and weeks apart in their race to solve the DNA structure puzzle. Crick and Watson's partnership and creative collaboration as a team is legend, as his comment suggests. See Matt Ridley. 2006. *Francis Crick: Discoverer of the Genetic Code.* New York: Atlas Books.

3. See Warren Bennis and Patricia Ward Biederman. 1997. *Organizing Genius: The Secrets of Creative Collaboration.* Reading, MA: Addison-Wesley.

4. A recent great read is Thomas Kelley with Jonathan Littman. 2005. *The Ten Faces of Innovation: IDEO's Strategies for Defeating the Devil's Advocate and Driving Creativity Throughout Your Organization.* Strawberry Hills, Australia: Currency Press. The book outlines ten types of roles that are important to consider in a process of taking a creative idea through its different stages. They all have their focus and might play a more or less prominent role in a certain project, but by thinking clearly about the roles, you open up venues for what is useful at different stages.

5. The main focus of this research has been on smaller, entrepreneurial organizations that have done a great job at developing and being successful over a longer period of time. In these organizations the founders and early members of the organization come to take a big role in shaping their agenda and early development process. Thus, these leaders come to the fore in our story. That is also partly why we name them creative entrepreneurs; they could also be named intrapreneurs, or something else that describes people doing this hard work within larger organizations. As we noted in chapter 2, these organizations are under development, and most likely we will see a new set of people across levels and functional areas take on these roles and drive the organizations forward. That is why we think the roles are key.

6. For a fuller discussion of entrepreneurs see Scott Shane. 2003. *A General Theory of Entrepreneurship: The Individual-Opportunity Nexus.* Cheltenham, UK: Edward Elgar. For more on market-based assets and routines as competitive advantage, see R. R. Nelson and S. G. Winter. 1982. *An Evolutionary Theory of Economic Change.* Cambridge, MA: Belknap Press/Harvard University Press; M. Zolla and S. G. Winter. 2002. "Deliberate Learning and the Evolution of Dynamic Capabilities," *Organization Science* 13 (3): 339–352. With regard to how creative entrepreneurs use relationships

to exploit market-based assets and creative routines, see Nancy K. Napier and Mikael Nilsson. 2006. "The Development of Creative Capabilities In and Out of Creative Organizations: Three Case Studies," in *Creativity and Innovation Management* 15 (3, September): 268–278.

7. Academics and practitioners have commented on the importance of seeing what's not there or tapping into market gaps. See, for example, Clayton M. Christiansen. 1997. *The Innovator's Dilemma.* Boston: Harvard Business School Press; W. Chan Kim and Renee Mauborgne. 2005. *Blue Ocean Strategy.* Boston: Harvard Business School Press; Peter Gloor and Scott Cooper. 2007. *Coolhunting.* New York: AMACOM.

8. Karl E. Weick. 2004. "Designing for Thrownness," in Richard J. Boland, Jr. and Fred Collopy. *Managing as Designing.* Stanford, CA: Stanford Business Books: 74.

9. Ix is a trademark of the Center for Information Therapy.

10. Several white papers and articles on information therapy are available on the Web at: http://www.ixcenter.org.

11. See W. Chan Kim and Renee Mauborgne. 2005. *Blue Ocean Strategy.* Boston: Harvard Business School Press. Red ocean strategies refer to conditions when firms seek to compete in markets filled with thirsty and hungry competitors. Like sharks, they bloody the waters trying to find prey and markets. More successful are organizations that seek out "blue waters," open spaces where no or few competitors exist and where the pickings are easier. Classic examples include Southwest Airlines and FEDEX early in their histories, and Cirque du Soleil, the blend of circus and theater that began as a street show in Montreal.

12. A radio program highlighted O'Brien's process of studying and adapting his technique. To hear it, go to "The Man Who Reshaped the Shot Put," April 23, 2007, All Things Considered, www.npr.org.

13. See, for example, Josh Levin. 2007. "Boise Fallout: The Fiesta Bowl Shows That College Football Is More Innovative than the NFL." January 2, Slate.com; Matt Zemek. 2007. "Fiesta Bowl Fallout: Lessons from a Classic." January 3, scout.com.

14. The story about Orrefors Kosta Boda was told by Magnus Andersson, the CEO, at the seminar "Creative, Cultural and Experience Industry—Is This the New Growth Factor of the EU?" in Brussels, December 6, 2007. More information at www.itps.se.

15. Compare to the individuals in Thomas H. Davenport, Laurence Prusak, and H. James Wilson. 2003. "Who Is Bringing You Hot Ideas (and How Are You Responding)?" *Harvard Business Review,* February: 58–65. Ivan Östholm, the manager responsible for developing Losec, one of the most successful ulcer treatments, sums up creative leadership like this: "Project management is an art. It can be compared to the job of a conductor. He needs to stimulate each individual musician in the orchestra to perform to the best of his or her abilities. He is also to lead the entire orchestra so that all musicians do a maximum performance. Skilled project managers are a company's most important asset. It is crucial to take well care of them." (p. 187, own translation) in Ivan Östholm et al. 1996. *Nya skapelser—Losec entreprenörens recept. (New creations—the prescription of the Losec entrepreneur),* Stockholm: T. Fischer & Co. (In Swedish.).

16. Clemens Thornquist found, while researching creative leadership at Vivienne Westwood, and with Robert Wilson, that leadership in these organizations are

performance/artistic processes in themselves. "One could view the image of the organization at each moment as a piece of art." Clemens Thornquist. 2005. "The Savage and the Design." Dissertation at Stockholm University.

17. One Laptop per Child Web site: http://laptop.org; The news program *60 Minutes* had a segment on Negreponte and the project, which aired August 26, 2007 on CBS.

18. Interview in the school's alumni magazine, *MIT Sloan Magazine*, Spring–Summer 2006: 8.

19. Many of these ideas come from Napier and Nilsson. 2006. "Development of Creative Capabilities In and Out of Creative Organizations."

20. See Lawrence P. Goodman and Richard A. Goodman. 1972. "Theater as a Temporary System," *California Management Review* 15 (2): 103–107.

21. Based on a talk by the CEO at a seminar in November 2007.

22. Diane Mutz. 2006. *Hearing the Other Side: Deliberate versus Participatory Democracy.* Cambridge: Cambridge University Press.

23. Connie J. G. Gersick. 1988. "Time and Transition in Work Teams: Toward a New Model of Group Development," *Academy of Management Journal* 31 (1): 9–41.

24. The interaction and coexistence of roles and practices has been addressed in, for example, Lucy L. Gilson et al. 2005. "Creativity and Standardization: Complementary or Conflicting Drivers of Team Effectiveness?" *Academy of Management Journal* 48 (3): 521–531; Mitch McCrimmon. 1995. "Teams without Roles: Empowering Teams for Greater Creativity," *Journal of Management Development* 14 (6): 35–41; Douglass J. Wilde. 2004. "Team Creativity." Paper presented at Education That Works: The NCIIA 8th Annual Meeting, March 18–20, 2004.

25. Ivan Östholm et al. 1996. *Nya Skapelser—Losec Entreprenörens Recept* [New creations—the prescription of the Losec entrepreneur]. Stockholm: T. Fischer & Co.: 96 (translated by the authors).

26. See Donald N. Sull. 2004. "Disciplined Entrepreneurship," *MIT Sloan Management Review,* Fall: 71–77.

Chapter 7

PLACES: SPATIAL AND SOCIAL ARCHITECTURES

We embrace responsibility in order to implement vision.... The implementation of good ideas demands as much, if not more, creativity than their conceptualization. Increasingly reluctant to assume liability, architects have retreated from the accountability (and productivity) of Master Builders to the safety (and impotence) of stylists.

Joshua Prince-Ramus

The challenges of the future are so much more complex and systems-based than the object culture architecture currently embraces. We need a new culture of responsibility and comprehensive engagement with long-term implications that can only come from *broadening the base of architecture to include the design of business models* that generate more of the qualities we live with in our cities. [emphasis added]

Bruce Mau

In the summer of 2003, the doors opened to the Interactive Institute's research studio in Åre, a small but prosperous community in the middle of Sweden. An early contender for MIT Media Lab Europe, the Institute instead evolved to a distributed model of studios located across Sweden. The Institute is a Swedish nonprofit organization, focusing on experimental information technology (IT) research. It challenges traditional perspectives by combining art, design, and technology in research projects and strategic initiatives. Through exploring and integrating these three areas, the institute contributes to innovation, creativity, and sustainable development.

The studio in Åre was the latest addition to the organization and would focus on trends and the impact of IT on society. Designers worked late in the last few days to get the rooms and furniture to look exactly right. The open conference room with Eames chairs and a large, dark-brown rug became a media center for interaction and Internet-based conferencing. The next room, filled with guests on opening day, had a wall-mounted sofa, background-lit glass walls to post images on, and a second media center, for showing videos and for lounging. Wall art in the form of plastic ribbons hung in sections of the space. The office in Åre became symbolic of a place where creative research happened.

About six months after the opening, the designers were back to fix some things. Oddly, it was the first time the designers and researchers who worked in the place had talked in any depth. The researchers told the designers about the functions of the office and how they used the space. The designers told the researchers about some of the design intentions, many of which were cut because of budget limitations. The designers said, for example, that they had wanted to design the space to bring together people from all walks of life— that they had intended for the office to be opened up to nature. They had hoped to put images of animals in the wild on the walls, but they got cut with the budget, so instead snowboard posters went up. And because the designers' intentions were unclear to the researchers at the beginning, none of the people using the office knew or implemented the ideas.

Three key groups had ideas about the place, but did not discuss them together. First, the people working in the workplace made use of the studio in their own ways. Management also had ideas to serve its purposes. And the designers certainly had ideas. But they weren't discussed explicitly in relation to the work and performance that was expected of the studio.

Such lack of discussion reflects what Joshua Prince-Ramus and Bruce Mau talk about in the quotations at the beginning of this chapter.[1] Broadening the base of architecture to include both design and business needs has rarely been achieved. But just think if they were: What might result?

We find that many creative and innovative organizations do indeed manage place with the same discipline as they do other parts of their business. While they may not always consciously manage every piece of the complex relationship between work spaces and work processes, they do manage those parts that make a difference and shape their ability to be creative.

The best ones manage both spatial and social architecture to encourage creativity and innovation. For such organizations, the spatial architecture, which includes the building, the layout, and the systems in the buildings, is in sync with the social architecture, or how individuals and groups work together within the spaces. In particular, the organizations start with what we call architectural intent, or understanding the purpose that physical and social architecture plays in encouraging creativity and innovation.

ARCHITECTURAL INTENT: BUILDINGS AND BEYOND

In 1999, Mr. [Peter B.] Lewis donated $36.9 million to the Weatherhead School for the building that bears his name—the most recent gift in a series of contributions to Case Western Reserve University honoring four generations of the Lewis family who have attended the University.

Web site of the Weatherhead School of Management

For American universities, the potential for a substantial donation from private funds, a corporation, or local and regional authorities is much greater if the funding focus is a building rather than "architecture for human interaction." A building is tangible, while human interaction is not.

Yet, human interaction is just what a building can encourage—or inhibit. Those that encourage it may, in the long run, find it a significant business advantage. Think about a building project you were part of. How much did people talk about how the building would help develop new ways of working, or permit workers to use their skills more efficiently and effectively, or how to enable fuller utilization of the space's potential? If your experience is typical, such discussions happened seldom, if ever. While we think of buildings as being places of production for tangible goods, we rarely think of them as places to create product ideas. But increasingly, in a knowledge and creative economy, that is what they become. So why not think of them in ways like we might with a traditional production facility? Who would consider putting up a production facility without thinking through how work teams will carry out their jobs, how the production line should be laid out, or how six sigma or kanban systems could be incorporated? So why not think of the workplace or space for "knowledge" production and use, which deserves as much thought?

Organizations that use place as a strategic asset manage space and other aspects with intent. Such *strategic intent* suggests overall purpose and direction of the underlying business.[2] We use the term *architectural intent* to describe how three factors come together to generate positive transformation. Those factors are space, the human and social processes at work in that space over time, and the goals of the organization.[3]

Researcher Franklin Becker thinks of the workplace as a form of organizational ecology because it captures the interdependence of social and physical systems.[4] And just how are those social and physical systems related? Several researchers have surveyed employees to find out what they perceive those links to be.[5] At least three themes emerge in how employees view their work spaces, creativity, and performance.[6] First, work today is different than in the past. As we move to a knowledge-based economy, employees spend more time in offices, at desks, and working with others. They report: (1) 72 percent of their work time is spent at a desk; (2) 74 percent of their workweek is spent in an office; and (3) 67 percent feel they are more efficient when working closely with coworkers. A second finding is that employees think space can enhance creativity. Results suggest that:

- 89 percent think the workplace design is important for their work performance
- 21 percent feel they could do more work in better-designed work environments
- 50 percent believe their current workplace design encourages innovation and creativity

- 50 percent claim physical layout is the main way their work environment could be improved, by having more personal work space, more privacy, and more storage space.

Finally, despite employees' perception that their place of work is important to their performance, many feel that their organizations do not take advantage of or design work places well. The Gensler Survey suggests that only 5 percent of U.S. corporations appear to use the work place as a tool for improving organizational performance, and a third of employees believe that creating a productive work place is a priority at their company.

Such employee reactions suggest a "gap in … understanding how the environment impacts innovation performance and how this performance matches the underlying strategic intentions of the organization."[7] So what might organizations do to enhance the links between architecture, defined both in terms of the spaces and the social processes that occur, and creativity and innovation? We will start with how spatial architecture plays a role in place.

Spatial Architecture

If we consider offices, buildings, and labs as places for production, then the notion of inputs and outputs emerges, with place as a location for transformation to occur. Designers may use inputs, like the physical layout or materials to influence output—production or performance of people who work in the spaces. Understanding the elements of those design inputs can help designers and users better understand what might result.[8]

Individual Buildings and Intent

Healthwise offers one example of how an organization may link architectural intent to its physical spaces. The organization's building sits just next to a large natural area, easily accessible for employees who wish to walk and think (with their dogs!). The location alone, with its access to the outdoors, and the organization's strong health-focused mission, encourages well-being among employees. The building's design includes interior colors that reflect nature in the intermountain U.S. West. Further, its many conference rooms and glass-fronted offices provide privacy from noise, but openness for light. A meditation room offers a getaway spot for thinking or napping; a small fitness room includes workout equipment and machines. Also interesting is the artwork on the building's three floors. It emphasizes the outdoors from various elevations. On the ground floor, the paintings comprise mostly rivers and forest scenes; on the middle floor, the emphasis is on the foothills and lower elevations of the mountains; finally, the top floor's art works are of snow capped mountains, which in Idaho can be up to 10,000 feet (3,000 meters). In its design, then, the building seeks to integrate the organization's intent and mission—"helping people make better health decisions," and encouraging people to take responsibility for their own health.

Such building designs make sense in anecdotal terms. Yet some researchers are seeking to take the idea of architectural intent further. Kevin Kampschroer and colleagues from the U.S. General Service Administration's Public Buildings Service have developed an approach that integrates three dimensions: (1) organizational performance (business metrics), (2) the attributes of the physical environment (building design), and (3) the changes in work processes, perceptions, and attitudes that result from changes to this physical space (employee behavior). They have developed a way to measure the contribution of the building to business success and employee behavior change. As they say, unless and until success can be evaluated, "we are forced to treat real estate as a unit of overhead whose value is created through reduction of cost."[9]

Such a shift in perspective—that a building could facilitate organizational performance and behavior—requires that we think about causes and effects when it comes to creating and utilizing spaces. For alignment to happen, managers need to be able to shape and change the relationships between organizational context, work processes, and place over time. Rather than consider the building as a status quo, we need to start viewing buildings in a creative organization as places for producing creativity and innovation—and mirror that work in the design process.

Clusters of Buildings and Intent

Individual buildings are one type of space that can be designed and developed to support business success. But some spaces go beyond a physical building to include groups of buildings.[10] Science parks, distributed offices, colocated offices, and living labs are geographical terms for groups of buildings that can also enhance and be sources for creativity and innovation. Many universities, for example, work with cities to create science parks with the intent to transform ideas into new companies, which may in turn help with community renewal and growth. In a world in which communities seek to attract the creative class, building clusters or parks or labs that offer interesting work for such people makes sense.

Yet, Anthony Townsend of the Institute of the Future thinks this approach may be a paradox. On one hand, R&D labs are moving into towns, to be physically closer to users and markets. But on the other hand, as globalized R&D emerges, including a growing and substantive relationship with R&D labs in China and India, that may conflict with localization in R&D labs.[11] In the face of such developments, Townsend wonders, how can a science park in one city create spontaneous meetings and collaboration spaces in a global environment? Essentially, such a paradox raises questions about how organizations will develop and use place, which will likely increasingly be physical and local as well as virtual and global. For example, how will organizations connect global innovation networks, and accommodate and enable new forms of R&D? Also, how will organizations create more places for casual encounters and digitally enhanced collaboration? At a very basic level, such questions raise the issue of how place can adapt to the ongoing changes in business. Does place have a role in solving such challenges? Some architects would argue that now more than ever, place helps define the identity of what an organization wants to be and how it wants its inhabitants to behave.

Developing places that are adjusted and adjustable appears to be more common, especially as architects work with customers more explicitly during design. In 2004, the Massachusetts Institute of Technology opened a new space, the MIT Stata Center for Computer, Information and Intelligence Science. The so-called "Geek Palace" was designed by architect Frank Gehry and his team.[12] In an interview, Mr. Gehry described how throughout the design process, his team talked with people who would inhabit the building to get their input on how the building should be designed, just as he had done during the design of the Case Western Weatherhead business building.[13] The wishes of the MIT researchers, professors, and administrators reflected in great detail how their buildings and office layout had been in the past—more individual or smaller research areas. The design was different from what Gehry had originally wanted to do. In the MIT building, for example, rather than the more traditional single-office arrangement, 40 percent of floor space is dedicated to collaborative work, including meeting rooms, labs, and spaces for creative endeavor among several people. The resulting design reflected, and pushed somewhat, the boundaries for who and what the institution saw itself becoming, an identity of collaborative research. And as the human element takes a greater role in what the physical space should look like, it also influences the social architecture.

Community and Intent

During the research and writing of this book, we have seen surveys that describe creative cities, organizations, regions, and countries.[14] Rankings have started to influence actions, but can also can make people and organizations complacent. They believe they are doing enough and "are creative." Instead, rankings should be a trigger to deepen the discussion on how a region, organization, or community should continue working to develop capabilities and just what the intent for change should be.[15]

Some cities have the intent to pursue the next level, and use spatial architecture as a lever.[16] Cities and regions such as Milan, Italy, Toronto, Canada, and the Nordic countries are developing strategies for enhancing creativity and innovation.[17] We take a look at one Nordic city.

Malmö, Sweden's third largest city, is on a mission. Being a part of the Öresund region, together with Copenhagen, Denmark, it has great potential.[18]

The city center and the seaside close by are shaped by a history of shipbuilding. To revitalize the city center, the city council and the regional authorities agreed to develop the portion of the city that is situated on the old docks of the shipyards, opening up the city to the sea. In the emerging center, a cluster of organizations and companies is gathering, including the Swedish state-owned television company SVT, many smaller as well as some larger multimedia companies, an incubator, and Malmö University. On its way to becoming a creative industry hub, the city and the region invested strategically in Media Mötesplats Malmö, one of eight cross-boundary arenas in the network for the experience industry focused on multimedia. In nearby Lund, Sony Ericsson, a leading developer of mobile phones and multimedia products, has established a major R&D center.

It started with creating an energetic city, with a high quality of life, full of people and things to do. In 2001, Malmö hosted the Swedish housing fair (Bo01), which provided an opportunity to invite many international architects to submit designs and suggestions for buildings. Rather than choose one master architect, the city built a small number of each chosen architect's buildings, which has given a "quilty" feel to the area closest to the sea. The buildings and their designs reflect a mix of creative ideas in the design of the city—creativity, the city, and the creative people are interwoven.

Malmö is matching spatial architecture with community intent by developing the city and the region. A gathering point for companies large and small, the city focuses on connecting. Members of firms meet in joint work spaces, share experiences and knowledge, and start collaborating—something likely to increase over time. Companies developing and selling media and information-technology products and services, regional economic developers, creative people, the university—all are part of developing Malmö as a city with competitive advantage.

Social Architecture

Social architecture is a term that captures the processes and procedures that affect how work is performed. It appears at the individual, group, and organizational level, and can influence productivity as well as creativity and innovation.

In the case of the MIT Stata Center and others, like the Googleplex in California, creative and innovative shapes, forms, and locations have changed over time.[19] We are now more aware that the spaces should encourage and reflect creative processes.[20] Indeed, architects like Frank Gehry and Rem Koolhaas—"starchitects"—are increasingly able to express their opinions on many levels when it comes to architecture's influence on individuals, regions, or nations.

For some firms, the social architecture is increasingly built into the expectation for the spatial architecture. One example of this is SANAA, a Tokyo-based architecture firm that worked on the design of the New Museum of Contemporary Art in New York City. At a presentation about the museum design, the speaker talked extensively about how the buildings had evolved based on finding constructions and materials that pushed the envelope. But when asked why he did not talk explicitly about how people flow and move in the spaces, the speaker said: "Because that is what Kazuyo Sejima and Ryue Nishizawa [principals of SANAA] always talk about." In essence, those questions were always considered, even by the materials and construction experts, as they designed a building. In a way, the people and work flow aspects were such an integral part of the design, they were "givens," and in this talk, needed no specific attention.

Social architecture can come into play in several ways: the disciplined process that organizations use to develop creative and innovative ideas, how people within organizations play different roles to drive the creativity and innovation forward, and the culture and practices organizations use to sustain it. As we have noted, such practices are not a simple blueprint that one organization can copy from another, but rather involve change and adaptation over time.

The buzz about space comes from several sources. Cities and regions have taken Richard Florida's ideas to redesign physical spaces in their downtown areas. Others look to "virtual spaces" like MySpace, Facebook or LinkedIn as ways for people to meet and express themselves. While there has been lots of talk, tangible illustrations and evidence of the links between physical and social architecture have been more limited. We offer some examples, though, of organizations seeking to close the gap.

A Walk around Cisco

On any ordinary morning in the Bay area of California, roads are jammed with commuters heading to meetings in this Mecca of technology and innovation. One new office being used as proof of this concept is Cisco's Building 14 in San José.[21]

Having used traditional cubicle and office structures for a long time, Cisco's management made a change in 2004. After learning that employees spent 30 percent of their time out of the office, an obvious question arose: "Would a firm have a plant that runs at only 70 percent capacity? Then why should an office be run that way?" Cisco's new office building has open and closed spaces, with smaller quiet areas, as well as meeting rooms and team areas. Advances in technology give employees mobility to move from their workspace office, to a home office, and to move around the Cisco campus. The layouts and systems were explicitly designed to be flexible and accommodating to different employee needs.

Cisco has reaped economic benefits as well as exciting employee reactions. The firm gained in lower costs on rent, construction, workplace services, furniture, IT capital spent, and equipment room space. In addition, informal feedback from employees reflects they are happy with the layout. But the firm would like to know more. Thus, a potentially controversial question is whether it could (or should) seek to understand more about how people use the space, by using radio frequency identification (RFID) technology to track flow patterns of how and where people move. Understanding more about how people in different roles use such spaces could help in future designs.

WHAT CAN PLACE DO FOR ORGANIZATIONS?

We have suggested that the workplace is a new place of production. The products coming out of the workplace are increasingly intangible, and many stem from creativity and innovation. So the types and functions of work space may be different to accommodate the different type of production output. Specifically, places can help organizations achieve several types of outcomes that are important in creative production. First, they can become nodes for internal interaction and collaboration, as well as competition. Second, places can support an organization's expression of its culture and values, which can help attract talent and knowledge.[22] A close third is the role that temporary space can play in the values of an organization: if the place changes, does that instill openness and expectation of change within members? Finally, place can help generate experiences that may in turn enhance creativity and innovation in a community. We will discuss each outcome in the following sections.

Place as a Node for Interaction, Collaboration, and Competition

Picture a large room filled with acrobats and circus artists warming up, training, and testing new tricks and forms of expression. They are young as well as professional artists working side by side, testing their new skills and urging others to do the same, giving small hints on what to improve, and practicing the tools to increase performance. The large room becomes a space where they meet and develop the core of the circus—the skills, the knowledge, and the tricks that make them extraordinary. But the open space also fosters competition, as we discussed in chapter 3 on within-discipline expertise. The competitive spirit combines with camaraderie to build a company. Pushing the boundaries of the performance depends on their having a physical space to see and experience one another's skills and expertise. Through interaction and competition they are developing both the talent and the performances of tomorrow.

Such a space also allows for cocreation. As we have mentioned previously, the popular image of creativity is that of a creative individual, or sometimes a designated group, like a research-and-development department. Yet increasingly, creativity happens in groups, often within the same organization, but also among groups of people who cross organizational boundaries. Such cocreation, as we have discussed, is a new formula for value creation, and demands places where people can meet, interact, and develop ideas. And those spaces have a number of dimensions relating to interaction, in particular degree and type of interaction, and ability to reach outside to bring new players in.

Degree of Interaction

The degree of desired interaction is one dimension on which to develop organizational space. Simple physical location and proximity of groups to one another can spur interaction and communication and presumably creativity. MIT's Tom Allen identified communication among organizational members as having three key purposes: coordination, information, and inspiration. He suggests that there is a drastic reduction of interaction when the distance between groups exceeds 50 meters (164 feet).[23] So, for cocreation to happen, certain groups may need to be close to one another.

But, according to Allen, sometimes proximity is not enough. An organizational culture of internal entrepreneurship and independence may work against cocreation. In organizations with strong cultures of independence among members, the culture can actually create barriers for interaction and exchange. For all practical purposes, members went their separate ways and avoided contact, regardless of how close to one another they were located.[24] So even when groups are near one another, lone wolves who protect rather than share ideas may thwart the best physical place efforts.

Type of Interaction

A second dimension that is critical for cocreation to occur is the type of work that happens within a space. Cocreation is more likely in places where cross functional work occurs among a mix of engineers and sales people or customers. Interaction could range over a number of topics from innovation to how different functions work together (or could better work together), including sales, product development, manufacturing, and services. Such interaction sparks the out-of-discipline thinking that we talked about in chapter 4, which can help generate new ideas for products, services, and other outcomes.

Cambridge (U.K.) offers an example of a community that fully embraces degree and type of interaction as well as competition. Cambridge is a Mecca for very smart people, that exceptional scientists say is "an island that you want to swim to, not from." They like being with other smart people and challenging themselves with them. More than seventy Nobel Prize winners attribute part of their work success to having spent time in the Cambridge environment.[25] Through the eyes of the laureates, Cambridge is a place where the interaction of experts in a number of different fields inspires and challenges each of them to be better than they were and to come up with new ideas.

Reaching Outside to Bring New Players In

In some cases a meeting place pulls external organizations into interaction and acts as a nexus for collaboration or competition. In Sweden, the Knowledge Foundation established five cross-boundary arenas for the experience industry across the country. Each hub was created to bring together experts from at least two fields within the experience industry.[26] The members come from society at large, creative industries, business, and academia.

These physical places offer sites for interaction, but also help to shape regional competitive advantage within the experience industry in Sweden. First, the arenas are where individuals and groups interact to share knowledge and ultimately become stronger because of the competition that exists among some of the organizations. Interaction among competing organizations "sharpens the saw," based on each organization's starting point. Second, the arenas help strengthen the interaction among organizations in the private, public, and related experience industry sectors. In an industry with a majority of small companies, interaction and cocreation would have been hard to do were it not for the physical space that allowed members to meet.[27] In addition, the space is especially important for their interaction with government agencies. For these agencies to invest and start programs that promote the creative industry, they need a counterpart—someone that they can design the program with, negotiate its progress, and measure to ensure they are improving Sweden's competitiveness. These arenas become these interaction points and can be used as leverage when lobbying and persuading the government and other large organizations that they should invest in the creative industry's development. Critical mass is a final dimension to consider, when interaction and competition is on the agenda.

Place as an Expression of Culture: "This Is Who We Are"

The Idaho Shakespeare Festival theatre's site is physically the same size as the Globe Theatre in England. And like at the Globe, the stage and performances are outside, in the open. The theatre sits close to the Boise River. During performances, frequent visits by hawks and cranes flying overhead and even the odd skunk moseying onto the stage are not uncommon. For actors unused to being on stage for several hours as the light fades and the air cools, it can be daunting at first. Watching audience members watching themselves, some actors admit that they feel the audience participates more in the play than they sense in the typical "black box" indoor theatre.

Visitors bring dinner and wine, set up picnics on the lawn, at tables, or on the back berm. They get up during the play when they need to, check the aisles to be sure Lear or Benedict is not speeding down en route to the stage, and then get more wine or desert. The atmosphere is informal, yet highly respective of the actors and the work presented. As one *New York Times* reporter mentioned years ago, the Idaho audience knows its Shakespeare and knows how to enjoy the evening.

When board members and staff from the partner theatre in Cleveland, Ohio, come to visit, they finally understand and "get it." Only when they experience it do they realize the power that the overwhelming, open-air setting has on the production, and how it defines for the organization "who it is." The culture of the organization in Idaho, from the artists who come during the summer, to staff members who are in town year round, is one of discipline and high-quality performance, yet embracing the openness of the western United States. The performances just would not be the same indoors. Some patrons claim they will never see Shakespeare plays indoors again.

In contrast, a software firm, perhaps like many in the Silicon Valley, uses basic—not very ergonomically sound—furniture and workstations that cluster developers within yards of one another, and has the requisite ping-pong table when employees need a break. And for a longer break, there is a company refrigerator with a beer keg. Interestingly, when the firm's top managers talk about the company, it's the beer keg that reporters and outsiders remember most. The office space is Spartan, devoid of splashy paint or art work. The conference room fits a table that could squeeze eight people in a pinch, with a single large and well-used white board on one wall. The auditorium seats fifty or so, on folding chairs. Yet, employees and managers alike are proud of the spare look. As one says, it works wonders to tell venture capitalists that the firm "puts its money into brains, not chairs."

Both organizations, the theatre and the software firm, made some explicit decisions about place and what it would say about the organizations' cultures. Such examples illustrate how a work space can express the culture of the organization inhabiting it: what it values and emphasizes. It also can project an image to visitors who enter the space. Ultimately, then, creative organizations need to consider what direction the organization may take with its design of the work space. And specifically, what might be the consequences on people's beliefs, attitudes, and behaviors given different designs?

TEMPORARY PLACES: WHEN CHANGE IS A PART OF SPACE

> Artists that work with us are more comfortable living in a caravan and moving around all the time. They are terrified of the burden and risk of mortgages and rent involved in getting your own apartment or house.
>
> Tilde Björfors, Manager, Cirkus Cirkör

Several organizations we looked at, such as the circus and the theatre, operate in spaces that are temporary in the sense that they are built and rebuilt again and again to accommodate new performances or work processes. A circus moves from city to city and brings its stage with it. The theatre group moves sets across country, from an outdoor stage to an indoor stage (or vice versa), and finds ways to adjust to the different size and nature of the available space. Such places reflect the temporal nature of the work that takes place, and a culture of change that remains at the core of these organizations. But it occurs in organizations that are more traditional, as well.

SEI Investments and Oticon, a leader in hearing aids, are two examples of "ordinary" organizations that have created both office layouts and systems to communicate the culture of change to everyone in the company.[28] Moveable and modular furniture allow for frequent and rapid rearrangement of people and teams. The Interactive Institute of Sweden also has at its core research units that host industry, academia, and art in an open space where tangible items can be built, tested, and displayed—like a gallery or an art studio. The research units, called studios, are very open and "nondesigned." Each studio has a life span, or theme focus, of five years, to reflect the transitory nature of the research and work in a studio.

Three of our core examples—theatre, circus, and football team—base their work on temporary spaces. They are temporary in several ways. As mentioned previously, the theatre and circus change stage sets between performances. All three groups may change locations where they perform. In an outdoor theatre and football field, the environment may change. The theatre setting may experience a range of weather, noise of birds or other animals, or lighting, depending upon cloud cover. For a football team, the environment changes as well, from the humid heat of Hawaii to the frigid bite of northern Idaho to the damp cold of Seattle. The sports fields themselves clearly matter as well. The University of Oregon's Autzen Stadium, for example, is known as one of the toughest for a visiting team to play in; it has no track ring between the stands and the field, so players comment that they feel the fans are right next to, or nearly on top of, the field, making the noise level intimidating. The audience or fans for each organization change with every performance; players and artists alike comment on the role that the audience or crowd can play in their ability to perform well. Finally, the people involved with the production may change, whether planned or unplanned. Again, the University of Oregon, ranked in the top ten U.S. college football teams in fall 2007, lost its potential Heisman Trophy-candidate quarterback midway through the season. Shifting to the second-, third-, and finally fourth-string quarterbacks ended the team's chances for a bowl game.

In these cases, the organization leaders acknowledge that change and novelty can be an advantage—to keep a performance fresh, to force constant within-discipline focus, to encourage an out-of-discipline look for new ideas. But even if novelty is key, how much is "enough?" Even if various types of discipline drive and nurture creativity, how does an organization use place to capture and build upon organizational history and knowledge to enhance that sense of creativity? Despite the various types of change, organization members often comment that a base of stability provided the springboard from which change could occur. So, as we'll discuss in chapter 8, key elements emerge as being important for instilling a sense of change as acceptable, especially when place is perceived as temporary.

Place as a Spark for Community

In the Open Lab, the circus has set up a place where employees work on new ideas with other creative people, with people from other companies and with consumers/audiences. Ideas emerge and are scrutinized by all participants, who learn from the reactions and modify the ideas. The experience of cocreation happens both for those who are developing new ideas and products and those who will "prosume" them, or produce and consume them.

So what happens when the idea of an Open Lab takes place at the community level?

In 2004, one of us was involved in a project that focused on developing social arenas of the future.[29] The premise was that communities could develop places that would bring people from different walks of life together, generate news ways of interaction, and ultimately new forms of economic viability.

At the core was the notion that social areas could be the spark for developing spectacular and interesting experiences for community members and customers. Examples of arenas are shopping malls, sports arenas, city and regional centers, and concert halls. They are social in the sense that they are places for social interaction. But they are also commercial areas. The experiences could be in the form of events in the arenas.

Increasingly, these social arenas became places where likeminded people met to learn, experience nature, and get adrenalin thrills! As the project evolved, it became clear that part of its outcome was to help people spend more time with their friends and families on fun and rich experiences at an arena. In return, more time would mean that their spending could increase and that new products, services, and experiences could be developed and marketed. In essence, the experiences helped to build a greater sense of community and commitment to community.

The project focused on how these social arenas could develop new offerings and themselves as places to experience new things. Three approaches were suggested: (1) cocreation of content, experiences, and events; (2) interaction among participants through multidimensional experiences; and (3) engaging with "new families," groups and subcultures in society that would attract others to the arena. Cocreation involved getting community members to put their passion and creativity into building a successful social arena experience. Interaction through multidimensional experiences involved finding ways for audiences in events to interact before, during, and after getting together at a social meeting place. As the number and types of interaction increased, community members returned for new ones. Finally, the idea of new families grew out of the recognition that existing and emerging networks and groups of people provide the social structures to which many people turn. If they could be an attractor and a channel for interaction—much in the same way they are for spreading new trends—the arenas could be nodes of interaction and gathering places for these new families. Examples of such emerging groups that communities wanted to tap were gay partnerships, the affluent creative class (many of whom were postponing marriage and childbirth, a concern in many European countries), increasing numbers of unemployed youths, and social groups that some might feel were fringe groups, such as skaters, punk rockers, or hip hoppers. By using a variety of community places and involving all groups in developing new experiences, several communities were able to retain young people and build stronger social capital and, ultimately, economic vitality.

At a city level, the spark for community and connection can also occur. One example comes from northern Italy. In Italy and the world, Milan is renowned for its design houses and creative sectors. The province of Milan is Italy's most important economic region, hosting world-renowned creative as well as high-tech companies. Approximately one third of Italy's high-tech workers work in the region in both manufacturing and service firms.[30] So, Milan's leaders should have no worries, right? Perhaps, but rather than resting on the creative laurels of the past, several organizations, private and public, have started projects that are changing the city's appearance and self-awareness.

The province of Milan and the Chamber of Commerce have established a portal for creative enterprises to be a driving force for local development. The region of Lombardy has initiated a project called *Paralleli* to compare best practices in the Milanese region with those of other regions and to build lasting relationships especially with other creative and strong economic regions, such as Bavaria (southern Germany) and Catalonia (eastern Spain). The Creativity Group Europe, founded by creative class gurus Richard Florida and Irene Tinagli, has its headquarters in Milan. Finally, in 2004 Assolombarda (Milan's Association of Industrialists) started a project called "Scena Creativa: Un Progetto per Milano" (Creative Scene: A Project for Milan) to spark different institutions and economic leaders to focus on Milan's creativity and innovation power.[31] Ultimately, Milan's success in pushing its edge as a community and creative front runner rests on its ability to pursue key initiatives, find resources, and generate collaborative processes within the region and around the globe, with partners in Korea, China, and Germany.

In sum, place as a source for experience goes far beyond the stage or sports field. It can reach into any space—organizational or community—that is designed to evoke the strong emotions and involvement of a range of people, to encourage creativity and innovation.

These questions open up new approaches for both the design and development of new spaces, as well as the many roles and functions involved in running the space and the experiences within it—what training is required to keep in contact and facilitate the experiences, what tools and processes, what types of spaces and transitions between them, and what interaction among the organizations/companies/departments that inhabit the space? This notion stretches the spaces to the outside community as well, which is where we go next.

Place as a Magnet for Talent

Because entrepreneurs gain many of the resources necessary for entrepreneurship from existing organizations and because entrepreneurs' networks geographically constrain their options for starting new companies, the companies already doing business within a given community are likely the best sources for new entrepreneurs and, by extension, new companies.

Pino G. Audia and Christopher I. Rider

Place can be part of a community, as we suggested in the previous discussion about social arenas.[32] And community can draw people for events, and for work and life. We next talk about place's role as an attractor of people and how organizations can leverage from it.[33]

Unexpected Attraction

While Malmö, Sweden, focused on specific industry areas to develop, such as information technology, New York City discovered that another approach could yield unexpected benefits for the city and its companies. A 2007 study sought to gauge the city's opportunities in the information technology industry.[34] While many studies focus on mapping existing or starting high-tech companies to show that a city is creative, innovative, and has a (great) potential for growth, New York City turned the question slightly around. Instead, the study suggested that the city might not be a leader in the narrow cross section of the (IT) economy. However, if you consider the people with advanced degrees and skill sets of interest in today's economy, specifically in information technology, New York City has a large number of those people, in new as well as traditional and existing organizations. It turns out that the city has two-and-a-half times as many such creative people as Silicon Valley does. But New York City still lags in venture funding and its image—it is not seen as a hub with critical mass for technology-driven growth. But this perception may be turning. Viewed differently, it could inspire potential entrepreneurs who are currently employed by the large, traditional, or existing organizations to spin off.[35] So changing the perception and description of the city as a supportive place for entrepreneurs could create a potential for growth in New York City.

Location as an Attractor and Fringe Benefit

In chapter 1, we made the point that one of the interesting features of our organizations is that they operate on the fringe—of their industries and in communities that would not typically be considered front runners and hotbeds of creativity and innovation. Yet, as many of the managers and employees in the case-study organizations we examined have said, being on the fringe allows them leeway to take a different tack and approach. They can operate "behind a mountain," as one CEO in Boise said, without others in the industry seeing what his firm is doing until it is ready to do it more publicly. Another CEO commented that being in a remote site allows fewer distractions than might a large, bustling city. Quality of life, wonderful surroundings with close proximity to nature, allow people to combine work with play—from skiing to mountain biking to cultural outdoors activities.

But not everyone knows that or believes it. Remote locations may face challenges in attracting talent. Early in the Idaho theatre's life, artists from New York City, Chicago, or San Francisco scoffed at the idea of being banished to a small summer theatre in Idaho. Later, after they spent one glorious, sunfilled summer at the site, they clamored to return. But getting highly talented and creative people to come the first time was a challenge.

Further, and not surprisingly, organizations in remote locations may not always be taken seriously. One senior manager commented that his major competition is in California, Israel, Canada, and France. "Why would a global corporation come to a tiny firm in a city and state it has never heard of?" But cutting through the pros and cons, a critical element emerges that relates directly to place as a factor encouraging creativity and innovation: access to and cooperation with key movers and shakers. Some community members, from different sectors and fields, have been able to work closely together to support notions of building economic vitality and enhance creativity and innovation. An emerging example is a small project in Idaho called the WaterCooler.

Communal Entrepreneurship for Development

At times, place can spark entrepreneurship and development, whether in the developed or developing worlds. We offer two examples of how individuals and communities work together to spur entrepreneurship, in India and in Idaho.

Pioneers in Developing Countries

Despite the plethora of articles and reports of India's tremendous growth, information technology power, and drive, it remains a country of serious poverty and economic challenge. Aid organizations have long tried to help solve some of the basic problems common in developing countries, ranging from providing food to safe water, health care to schooling. Yet, years of work in many countries yields minimal results. The problems require ingenuity, and several entrepreneurs within those countries have begun to tackle those challenges. As we suggested in chapter 1, developing economies, although poor, are becoming a place for pioneers, especially in social entrepreneurship.[36] Rather than solutions coming from the experts in developed countries, local entrepreneurs found answers to some of the challenging problems.[37] Many adapt business methods to develop approaches that can subsequently be used or exported elsewhere. A classic example is the Grameen Bank in Bangladesh, founded by 2006 Nobel Peace Prize winner Muhammad Yunus to make economic change "from below." The bank's use of microfinance loans to rural businesspeople (very often women) has helped the poor develop some level of economic independence. By being creative in approaching the problems, social entrepreneurs, and now increasingly some aid organizations, are helping communities to develop.[38]

In remote locations in the western United States, the spirit of pioneers remains under the surface, popping up on a regular basis. Pioneers, which may have a negative connotation outside of North America, represent an image that is fundamental to American culture and identity. Adventurers who moved from the eastern part of North America to the West, pioneers in the 1800s and today are independent people willing to move toward an unknown destination—geographic or otherwise—and let the situation evolve as it happens. They are comfortable having no clear plan; they are willing to risk and fail and risk again. Typically, as well, they seek to build something themselves, rather than to rely on others, whether a government or large organization.

That captures the situation with a downtown creative incubator in Boise, Idaho. As part of a course requirement, Boise State University Executive MBA students developed plans for making the city a world-class creative and competitive site. One idea from several groups was a downtown incubator with a focus on creative industries. When the teams presented their ideas to city council members, business executives, the city's downtown development agency, as well as several private real estate developers, one developer jumped on the idea and ran with it. He is succeeding in part because the city is relatively small and entrepreneurial. Within two months, he found a site in town. The Capital City Development Corporation has leased space to the developer to renovate a former headquarters building of a heating and air conditioning company. In nine months, he secured most of the funding from both public and private sources. He recruited six resident firms as well as university and technology transfer experts to join in the WaterCooler project. A major technology company in town has donated workstations and furniture; another will offer the Wi-Fi hookup.

The WaterCooler is not only a physical place, but also a place for creative sparks to fly. Members, as well as the university partners, will provide mentoring support for resident organizations. They will have the opportunity to interact with each other and the community. The intent is that the Water-Cooler will help spark creativity and economic vitality among the tenant firms, will attract more creative people and firms into the city's inner core, and that organizations already in the downtown core will support WaterCooler residents. Thus, place at the community level can also help to spur creativity and innovation in a broader sense.[39]

Place: Sources for Spatial and Social Interaction

We have suggested in this chapter that organizations need to consider place as a way to enhance creativity and innovation. To get the most out of place, they need to consider several aspects:

- *Consider the architectural intent.* Mindful organizational leaders can use spatial and social architecture to clarify how they would like to motivate and support employees who work together. Keys are to recognize that place can in fact support such notions and that the physical and social architectures need to work together. Alone, they are unlikely to encourage creativity and innovation.
- *Think of place as an investment, not just a cost.* Although knowledge and approaches to using the social and spatial architectures to encourage interaction do exist, they are neither formulaic, nor easy to assess. Organizations will likely need trials and tests to learn what works for their conditions. To that end, in addition, organizations will need to consider business metrics to justify investments in place that are aimed at improving performance.
- *Place can express organizational values.* The spaces that organizations develop may express culture, values of interaction and competition, and the types of experience that leaders want to encourage among people within and out of organizations.
- *If done well, places can knit together organizations and communities beyond them.* As some countries like Sweden are finding, when interaction and linkages between community and organization occur, they can help spur economic development. Place can help create a sense of communal entrepreneurship.

NOTES

1. Joshua Prince-Ramus. 2007. "Manifesto No. 31," *ICON*, issue 50, August: 85; Bruce Mau. 2007. "Manifesto No. 08," *ICON*, issue 50, August: 78.

2. *Strategic intent* as a term was made popular through the work of Gary Hamel and C. K. Prahalad. 1989. "Strategic Intent," *Harvard Business Review* 1989 (67): 63–76, and also in their book *Competing for the Future*, Boston: Harvard Business School Press, 1996.

3. See John A. Seiler. 1984. "Architecture at Work," *Harvard Business Review* (September-October): 111–120.

4. See Franklin Becker. 2007. "Organizational Ecology and Knowledge Networks," *California Management Review* 49 (2):42–61.

5. M. Bell and M. Joroff, 2000. "The Agile Workplace: Supporting People and Their Work," report published by the Gartner Group and the Massachusetts Institute of Technology, as mentioned in Kevin Kampschroer, Judith Heerwagen, and Kevin Powell. 2007. "Creating and Testing Workplace Strategy," *California Management Review* 49 (2): 119–137.

6. See *The Gensler Design + Performance Index: The U.S. Workplace Survey*. 2006, published by architecture firm Gensler (www.gensler.com). The study is based on more than 8,000 workers that were initially solicited, with a final qualified respondent sample of 2,013. The survey took place in March 2006.

7. See James Moultrie, Mikael Nilsson, Marcel Dissel, Udo-Ernst Haner, Sebastiaan Janssen, and Remko Van der Lugt. 2007. "Innovation Spaces: Towards a Framework for Understanding the Role of the Physical Environment in Innovation," *Creativity and Innovation Management Journal* 16 (1): 54.

8. A group that has contributed to a lot of this thinking is the "Space Group" from Oxford, U.K. See Moultrie et al. (op cit): 53–65.

9. Kevin Kampschroer, Judith Heerwagen, and Kevin Powell, Kevin. 2007. "Creating and Testing Workplace Strategy," *California Management Review* 49 (2): 120.

10. See Anthony Townsend. 2007. "Tectonic Shifts in the Geography of R&D—The Next Fifty Years, Institute of the Future." Talk at the International Association of Science Parks Conference, Barcelona, July 2–4.

11. For an inspiring study, look at the think-tank Demos's project *The Atlas of Ideas* (http://www.demos.co.uk/publications/atlasofideas, last accessed January 9, 2008), which focuses on the relationship between the United Kingdom, and India and China. Final report: Charles Leadbeater and James Wilsdon. 2007. *The Atlas of Ideas: How Asian Innovation Can Benefit Us All*, London: Demos.

12. The building is formally known as the Ray and Maria Stata Center for Computer, Information, and Intelligence Sciences. Spencer Reiss. 2004. "Frank Gehry's Geek Palace," *Wired* 5: 194.

13. Interview/discussions found in chapter 2, "Reflection on Designing and Architectural Practice," in R. J. Boland and F. Collopy (Eds.). 2004. *Managing as Designing*. Stanford, CA: Stanford Business Books.

14. Examples of surveys and rankings include: *Business Week*, in collaboration with Boston Consulting Group (see, for example, Jena McGregor. 2007. "The World's Most Innovative Companies," *BusinessWeek*, May 14); *Fast Company's* rankings (see, for example, Andrew Park. 2007. "Fast Cities 2007," *Fast Company*, July–August: 90–102); and Richard Florida's studies (see, for example, Richard Florida. 2005. *The Flight of the Creative Class*. New York: HarperCollins).

15. An article suggesting that rankings do not speak the whole truth is Tac Anderson. 2007. "The Emperor's New Clothes, Idaho's Technology Fable," *IQ Idaho* 5 (6): 22–24. The article should be seen in relation to Boise Idaho's ranking as one of three "High-Tech Hot Spots in Fast Cities" in *Fast Company* (op cit). Kairos Future Group, a Swedish consultancy, did a simple yet interesting comparison. They did a correlation

analysis between Richard Florida's Euro-creativity index and the Global Entrepreneurship Monitor (data from 2002). The analysis showed that while Sweden, in this case, ranked very high on the creativity index, there was a lack of entrepreneurial activity. They went on to say that it is not enough to have creative people; they need to do something with that creativity. A panel study they had done with Swedish decision makers suggested similar doubts about future competitiveness. See Mats Lindgren and Anna Kiefer. 2006. "The Recipe for Growth—Creativity v/s Entrepreneurship," Stockholm: Kairos Future Group.

16. Thank you to Serena Bergonzi for providing data to this section, allowing for a broader analysis.

17. In the Nordic countries, a recent example outlining a strategic intent is the Nordic Innovation Centre's Green paper: Tom Fleming. 2007. *A Creative Economy Green Paper for the Nordic Region.* Oslo: Nordic Innovation Centre. The Nordic Innovation Centre is an institution under the Nordic Council of Ministers. It initiates and finances activities that enhance innovation collaboration and develop and maintain a smoothly functioning market in the Nordic region. A similar example from the United Kingdom is: Work Foundation. 2007. *Staying Ahead: The Economic Performance of the UK's Creative Industries.* London: Department for Culture, Media, and Sport.

18. Copenhagen is another place that has been identified as a future cool city, by Charles Landry.

19. Information on the Googleplex: http://valleywag.com/tech/google/25-things-to-see-at-the-googleplex-before-you-die-234103.php.

20. See Udo-Ernst Haner. 2005. "Spaces for Creativity and Innovation in Two Established Organizations," *Creativity and Innovation Management* 14 (3): 289–98.

21. Mikael Nilsson visited during summer of 2004 and also used background material from Cisco case studies and video footage, as well as information available on the Web, such as http://www.cisco.com/web/about/ciscoitatwork/case_studies/real_estate_dl2.html. See also more about the office in Thomas H. Davenport. 2005. *Thinking for a Living: How to Get Better Performances and Results from Knowledge Workers,* Boston: Harvard Business School Press.

22. See, for example, Anders Malmberg and Peter Maskell. 2002. "The Elusive Concept of Localisation Economies: Towards a Knowledge-based Theory of Spatial Clustering," *Environment and Planning* 34: 429–49; Bruce Kogut and Udo Zander. 1996. "What Firms Do? Coordination Identity and Learning," *Organisation Science* 7 (5): 502–18.

23. See Thomas J. Allen. 1984. *Managing the Flow of Technology: Technology Transfer and the Dissemination of Technological Information within the R&D Organization.* Cambridge, MA: MIT Press.

24. See Thomas J. Allen. 2007. "Architecture and Communication among Product Development Engineers," *California Management Review* 49 (2): 23–41.

25. Ulf Larsson (Ed.). 2006. *Cultures of Creativity: The Centennial Exhibition of the Nobel Prize.* Sagamore Beach, MA: Science History Publications.

26. Stina Algotson and Carin Daal. 2007. *Mötesplatser för Upplevelseindustrin. Metoder för Samproduktion av Kunskaps och Kompetensutveckling* [Cross-boundary arenas for the experience industry: Methods for coproduction of knowledge and competence development]. Stockholm: The Knowledge Foundation.

27. Micro-organizations typically have 1–10 employees who often split their time between different companies and sources of income. A person could have a portion of his or her livelihood and type of work in one company and other types in another. Well-known examples are designers like Tom Ford who has different collections and labels with different styles at different companies and manufacturers of fine goods.

28. Alfred P. West, Jr., and Yoram Wind. 2007. "Putting the Organization on Wheels: Workplace Design at SEI," *California Management Review* 49 (2): 138–153.

29. Kudos should go to Daniel Spikol, Ante Jämtlid, and Lene Dalsjö-Bull, as well as our Norwegian friends Elisabeth Frydenlund and Atle Hauge. Some of these ideas are described in Daniel Spikol and Mikael Nilsson. 2004. *Arenas of the Future: Changing Social Meeting Places and Innovation Opportunities; A trend newsletter.* Spring 2004, Interactive Institute, Sense Studio. For further reading, see B. Joseph Pine II and James H. Gilmore. 1999. *The Experience Economy.* Boston: Harvard Business School Press; C. K. Prahalad and Venkatram Ramaswamy. 2003. "The New Frontier of Experience Innovation," *MIT Sloan Management Review*; Martin Raymond. 2004. "Theater of the Senses," *Viewpoint,* (No. 15, Spring).

30. For more, see the Web site on Innovating Regions in Europe, available at: http://www.innovating-regions.org/network/whoswho/regions_search.cfm?region_id=62 (last accessed January 6, 2008). Copenhagen is another place that has been identified as a future cool city. See Erich Follath and Gerhard Spörl. 2007. "An Inside Look at Europe's Coolest Cities," Spiegel Online (www.spiegel.de/international/europe/0,1518,502297,00.html, last accessed September 4, 2007). Also read the interview with Charles Landry, one of the early speakers of the potential and importance of the creative city (www.spiegel.de/international/europe/0,1518,503211,00.html, last accessed September 4, 2007).

31. The portal is named www.impresecreative.it. The Lombardy report can be found at http://www.polidesign.net/paralleli/default.htm (in Italian); Richard Florida and Irene Tinagli previously worked on a report on Europe's creative class: Richard Florida and Irene Tinagli. 2004. *Europe in the Creative Age.* London: Demos. Assolombarda is a membership organization for companies in the province of Milan. Assolombarda is part of Confindustria (Italian Entrepreneurial Association). For more see www.assolombarda.it. Also see the article Silvia Pavoni. 2007. "Creative Powers," Foreign Direct Investment (www.fdimagazine.com/news/printpage.php/aid/1908/Creative_powers.html, last accessed July 24, 2007)

32. The quotation above is from Pino G. Audia and Christopher I. Rider. 2005. "A Garage and an Idea: What More Does an Entrepreneur Need?" *California Management Review* 48 (1): 21.

33. See Graham Drake. 2003. "'This Place Gives Me Space': Place and Creativity in the Creative Industries," *Geoforum* (34): 511–524.

34. "While technology contributes heavily to our economy and to the city's status as a high-powered research and development (R&D) center, it isn't recognized as such. This, we hypothesized, was due to the fact that the sector itself was far too complex and disaggregated to be sufficiently defined. Current measures of economic activity do not accurately reflect its nature, size or depth." This quotation is from p. iv of: Industrial and Technology Assistance Corporation (ITAC), with the help of Mt. Auburn Associates and Bayer Consulting, Inc. 2007. *Buried Treasure: New York City's Hidden Technology Sector.* New York: ITAC.

35. Audia and Rider. 2005. "A Garage and an Idea."

36. Wikipedia's definition: "Social entrepreneurship is the work of a social entrepreneur. A social entrepreneur is someone who recognizes a social problem and uses entrepreneurial principles to organize, create, and manage a venture to make social change. Whereas business entrepreneurs typically measure performance in profit and return, social entrepreneurs assess their success in terms of the impact they have on society. While social entrepreneurs often work through nonprofits and citizen groups, many work in the private and governmental sectors." (http://en.wikipedia.org/wiki/Social_entrepreneurship, last accessed January 6, 2008.)

37. For a discussion of reverse learning, when "learners" teach the "experts" in developing countries, see N. K. Napier. 2006. "Cross-Cultural Learning and the Role of Reverse Knowledge Flows in Vietnam," *International Journal of Cross-Cultural Management* 6 (1): 47–64.

38. One initiative on social entrepreneurship is taken by Klaus Schwab, executive chairman and founder of the World Economic Forum, who each year delivers the Indian Social Entrepreneur Award together with the United Nations Development Programme and the Confederation of Indian Industry, described in Murali Krishnan. 2006. "India Has the Most Innovative Social Entrepreneurs: Schwab," *Hindustan News*, New Delhi, October 31, 2006. Other examples can be found in, for example, the *Stanford Social Innovation Review* (www.ssireview.org) or *Fast Company*; see, for example, the Fast Company/Monitor Group Social Capitalist Awards in the December 2007 issue.

39. An interesting analysis of New York City as a community with thriving technology sector organizations highlights the interaction between private and public initiatives necessary to grow; see Industrial and Technology Assistance Corporation. 2007. *Buried Treasure.*

Chapter 8

TRACES: CREATING MAGIC IN ORGANIZATIONS

I had the authority and freedom and a week to do what I wanted to....
In other companies, you can't get that magic to work on your idea.

a software programmer

"The magic to work on your idea"—isn't that what any organization would want its employees to feel they have?

But what is that "magic"? The programmer's comment suggests some sort of boost or spark that he gets from his organization that is unlike what he experienced elsewhere. He had authority, freedom, and time to work on an idea. By authority, he meant that he had a position within his organization that provided him the decision-making power and political ability to pursue an idea. In other words, he had freedom to work on an idea, which for him meant several things. First, he could pursue an idea in his own way, at his own speed, using his own methods. He was encouraged to try, allowed to fail and learn from the failure, but then find a way to move forward and make the idea reality. Next, he worked alone, but also had and could draw upon a network of people in and out of his organization—to generate and experiment with ideas. Finally, he "had a week," or "dabble time," to pursue an idea. His team leader buffered him from other activities and obligations.[1]

Many employees do not feel as lucky as the software engineer with "magic."[2] The Fairfax County Virginia Economic Development Authority commissioned a study, conducted during the summer of 2007, with over 500 adults in the United States, to find out how much creativity workers have in their jobs. The survey found that 88 percent of American workers think they are creative, but that only 63 percent were in positions that allowed them to use their creativity. The implications could be serious for firms that do not fill the "creativity gap" between workers wanting to use their creativity and having the chance to use their creativity in their jobs. In fact, one in five workers reported they would change jobs to find ones that allowed more creativity. Even more striking, 37 percent of the eighteen to thirty-four year olds surveyed said they would move between cities to become part of a more creative community.

In previous chapters, we described how organizations that embed creativity and innovation in their ongoing activities rely on creative faces and places to support and provide a context for these activities. A less-tangible, but critical, third component to the "aces" circle is what we call *traces*.

The notion of traces comes from *trace elements*, a concept in biology and physiology. Trace elements are essential for certain functions in the body, but are needed in only very small amounts, measured in micro parts per million. For humans, they include elements such as iodine, chromium, and zinc, which act as catalysts to encourage more efficient and effective chemical reactions, which in turn support healthy growth and development. Interestingly, research over the last thirty years has identified additional trace elements, so new ones seem to appear periodically.

We use trace elements as a metaphor for several reasons. First, their purpose is catalytic in the human body, encouraging efficient and effective chemical reactions to support needed functions. In an organization, the trace elements discussed in this chapter encourage efficient and effective reactions that support creativity and innovation. Second, while there are about a dozen known trace elements critical for human biochemistry, researchers continue to "discover" new ones. Likewise, organizations may have several key elements that encourage innovation, but also discover new catalysts over time. Third, in the body, the amount of essential trace elements needed is small, but their impact is powerful. Again, in organizations, some trace elements may be nearly invisible, and perhaps as a result, easy to ignore or forego nurturing; but if they are acknowledged and fostered, they can have a large impact.

Trace elements, while being a distinct part of creative organizations' milieu, rely on several things mentioned in previous chapters for traction and development. Practices and culture together ensure that we reach mastery and are in turn shaped by the disciplined process. Faces set the tone in many organizations, and places provide the structure and self-image for creatives. Traces develop and stand out in the interaction with the other elements of our model (see Figure 2.1).

The rest of this chapter talks about trace elements in organizations that have creativity and innovation as part of what they do. As with human bodies, we cannot identify all trace elements that support creativity, but we can share several that appear to be important in the organizations we know well. Similar to their role in a human body, they appear to spark reactions for optimal performance within organizations. Also, just as the human body uses different trace elements to generate different types of chemical reactions, we suggest that different types of trace elements in organizations may generate different sparks of creativity: specifically, we include trace elements of practice, trace elements of culture, and trace elements beyond the boundaries of the organization.

TRACE ELEMENTS OF PRACTICE

You know what really keeps me up at night? Hiring the right people, finding who will fit our organization. People with low ego, high output.

Chris Petersen

When Boise State University's former head football coach, Dan Hawkins, left for the University of Colorado program in 2006, he took six coaches with him. The new head coach, Chris Petersen, and three others stayed behind, and so Petersen went looking for new coaches to fill in the roster. Finding the right people who had the talent, the right fit and ability to work well with players was his first challenge. Once he had those people in place, he knew he could make sparks fly. Interestingly, the coaches use the same criteria when choosing players.

Petersen is not alone. Ask a CEO, an artistic director of a theatre, or a vice president of research and development what worries them most in running a successful organization, and the answer is often whether they have the right "faces," or people. In his landmark book, *Good to Great,* Jim Collins uses the phrase "getting the right people on the bus."[3] Once the right people are on the bus, they need to be in the right "seats," and then the organization can head in the direction it needs or wants to go.

As key trace elements of practice, activities relating to recruiting and staffing an organization can help encourage creativity and innovation throughout an organization. We saw three elements of practice in the organizations we looked at closely: (1) trace elements of fit: finding employees who will fit the culture and organization and be catalysts for innovative activity; (2) trace elements of expectations: being clear that creativity and innovation are not just "nice" to have, but expected characteristics employees bring to the job; and (3) trace elements of reward: ways to recognize employees for being creative and innovative.

Trace Elements of Fit: Finding Employees

Several leaders talk about a contradiction between fit and diversity. One manager we talked about in chapter 5 illustrated this dilemma when he said, "I want diversity, but I don't." Diversity promotes a range of ideas and perspectives, but too much or the "wrong type" may generate conflict within the organization in meeting its vision and supporting its culture.

Members of the organizations we worked with are well aware of, talk about, and try to shape their cultures, which in each case was robust. Part of that shaping includes having people who fit in ways that matter. The practice of staffing, for example, is one way to ensure that trace elements for creativity and innovation are present.

Organizations with strong missions and cultures often have quite demanding practices for choosing people. Healthwise is rabid about fit and has an elaborate, multiple-day process for candidates they are serious about. One manager said it seems as though "fifteen people look at an applicant." As an organization that values complementarity in employees, it tries to balance fit and ability with diversity. But mostly, managers seem to seek people who are passionate about what the organization does and can fit the culture. One manager exemplified that attitude: "I look for a person who will appreciate differences in people and who loves our mission.... I think when you have those things—a passion for the mission or the culture—I think then you will feel real comfortable about giving new ideas and accepting people's ideas."

In addition to fit with culture, organizations seeking to spark creativity look for fit with a specific team or group. The Boise State University football coaches, for instance, look at fit on the coaching team, as well as on the player team. For the coaches, similar background experiences at certain schools are clues or traces that a person might be a good fit, as one describes: "[When people say,] 'Oh, so you're a [UC] Davis guy,' they know what that means.... It's this appreciation of other things in life than football. There's a balance ... it's being able to talk with a kid about [something other than football] and enjoy that just as much as talking about cover two inside of the red zone. We don't like myopic guys." In addition, for this group, fit means the ability to "check your ego at the door." In recent years, some coaches at the professional sports level have sought to downplay stars and focus on the team as a whole.[4] Boise State's program has followed suit. It focuses on the team as a family or group, rather than a collection of star players. This rubs off in many ways. During the 2007 season, for instance, the Boise State team removed player names from the backs of their jerseys as a gesture toward team focus, rather than individual player focus.

Further, as part of the building-a-team approach, Boise State football players themselves try to help new players understand what it means to fit into the system. According to a former offensive lineman, who now plays professional football, "[Recruits have to] buy into being a family.... This is a 'family' that works together ... as a unit. That's why we get it done every year. We're family and we don't try to point fingers at each other—we just try to get better as a unit."

But sports is not the only place where fit in teams matters and helps spark creative efforts. Some people think of software engineers as nerds, geeks, and loners. Indeed, some engineers pride themselves on being out of the mainstream. Yet, at some firms, fitting into and working with a team is critical. As software manager Bob Keiser frames it, "So, a core philosophy for creativity [means we] need really good people that work together in teams. You don't need a great person who likes to work alone. It's like they're wasting your time."

In addition, when teams work together well, the creativity can surge. Elaine Anderson at ProClarity urges collaboration and teamwork as a way to reduce fear of criticism and become a catalyst for creative ideas: "As we work more as a team to release a product, and no one has ownership, I think [we will be more] willing to accept criticism and more open to creative ideas and collaboration. I believe that's where we're headed. Putting people together."

Trace Elements of Expectations: Making It Happen

It's August, 90 degrees Fahrenheit, and the eighteen-year-old, first-year football players are antsy. A coach drills them, goes through the main points over and over, and asks them to show they understand. The repetition is grueling, and sometimes reaches the point where players roll their eyes—oh no, here goes the coach … again.

But Boise State's Chris Petersen isn't putting players through drills on the field. He's talking, again, about the program's values, expected behaviors, and goals. Using a triangle visual, filled with critical phrases to express those values, expected behaviors, and outcomes, the coaches and senior players want to drill into the younger ones the expectations that should become second nature.

Instilling those behaviors is critical to making things happen on the field. Young players learn that these expectations, such as having a competitive spirit, having no fear of failure, as well as key outcomes, such as high grade-point averages and winning the conference games, are just as critical on the field and in their workouts as they are in life.

Software engineers, some ten to twenty years older than those freshmen players, face a similar environment, where expected behaviors and outcomes drive performance. Russ Whitney, head of R&D at ProClarity, describes how the firm tries to instill expectations of making things happen: "We were trying to articulate [creative activities] as outcomes, [rather than] 'responsibilities.' You don't want to say what they're supposed to do when they come to work. What you want to say is, 'What do you want to have happen when it's all done?' … We're trying to create a culture with a minimum amount of mandated process [and tasks] but is mostly articulated in terms of desired outcomes." This translates into a focus on trace elements of practice to show expectations—expectations of creativity. It's one thing to talk about being creative or innovative; it's another to show and live it. Organizations may have symbols that show their commitment, but ultimately what convinces employees that creativity and innovation are part of their daily jobs are the consistent actions that support the talk.

At the front door of Boise-based Healthwise's headquarters on Bogus Basin Road, the first thing a visitor sees is a huge sculpture at the building's entry. It's a 25-foot-tall, bronze windmill. The sculpture itself is beautiful, but so is its title: *Relentless Innovation*. Yes, it is a symbol, but the organization carries the notion further, in several ways. Innovation is a key value, appearing on the Circle of Values posted on the building walls, on its Web site and on wallet-sized cards given to each employee. The CEO speaks about the need for all, not just some, employees to be innovative. He comes up with many ideas and encourages others to do the same. The organization hosts speakers and sends employees to workshops and other organizations known to be creative. Of course, like all of the organizations we studied, the action of allowing outside researchers inside to examine what the organizations do is itself a trace element or catalyst that helped foster more discussion.

In a similar vein, the circus company is starting training and an internal development program focused on the origins and core values of circus. The initiative goes back to expectations about how to work, and what and when one can contribute to a long tradition and history of circus art. These are the overarching ideas and principles that guide work and interaction with others—and are key to the context in which acts and performances are shown.

Simply by frequently asking, "How can we do it better?"—and by being willing to listen hard to the answers—leaders' actions can be catalysts to urge employees to think more openly and creatively. In Boise State's football program, players complete annual questionnaires and spend time talking with coaches about how to improve the program. And the coaches listen to these ideas, from how to improve the food, to bus rides, to game plays. The sports marketing unit also asks and takes action to find new ways to draw fans to programs other than football. As one manager said, "All we need for inspiration is to look at that blue field. It's our excuse to try new things."[5]

Trace Elements of Recognition: Rewarding Creative Activity

Congratulations, Miss Hang! You've just won the Golden Butterfly Award for the month! And you, Mr. Trung, you are our Golden Bird award winner for the month!

Vietnam is a country that sometimes seems quaint to North American eyes and ears. Yet, the CEO of Mobicom, one of the country's fastest-growing mobile communications firms, knows how to encourage creativity and ideas within his firm. And he's doing it in ways that are far outside the norm in this collective, group-oriented society.

Mobicom starts by seeking out and hiring some of the country's best programmers by finding those who have won national and international awards in software development. Then, the firm recognizes individuals—almost unheard of in a collective culture—for coming up with ideas. His firm gives the Golden Bird or Butterfly monthly awards, one to a male, one to a female, for the most ideas generated per month that will improve the firm. The firm uses an award system for new text games that can be played on mobile phones. Employees also receive points for organizing and attending employee development seminars. And apparently, it's working. Of the hundreds of ideas that come in each month, two or three might be "good ideas." As the CEO says, though, that's two or three more good ideas than the firm otherwise might have had.

Cirkus Cirkör has set up ways to finance and show their affiliation with new, smaller companies that are developing their own acts. By providing this public affirmation, they give these groups recognition and the ability to continue with their artistic work. It also means that they announce that new forms and performances are required to develop circus art. Whether inside their own organization or by people they like and admire, it should be recognized and given a chance to develop.

TRACE ELEMENTS OF CULTURE

One July night in Hanoi, Vietnam, Nancy stood in front of 40 Vietnamese MBA students in a cramped room, alternately dripping from heat and then freezing when a blast of air shot out of the sputtering air conditioner.

That night she faced a delicate question—illustrating the frustration that comes from differences between professed and actual culture, albeit this time within a country rather than an organization.

In their twenties, these young people worked in small business firms, foreign multinational firms, and state-owned, government organizations. They were too young to have experienced the American War, which ended in 1975, and also too young to have remembered the lack of food and resources their country faced as the Soviet Union began to crumble in the late 1980s. Instead, they had grown up hearing about the courageous and valiant Vietnamese who defeated the cowardly French or Americans. They lived through the 1990s and early 2000s, when Vietnam's economic growth rate blistered along at nearly 10 percent per year, when the stock market started, and when the country was touted as the "next little tiger."

"Our government says we are strong. Our economy grows fast. We can buy televisions and computers. We can compete anywhere in the world. Many have houses and power and water. But our population grows too fast. My parents live in the countryside and grow rice like their parents did. Village people are poor. We have sick people and not good care for them. The government is wrong. Things are not changing fast enough. What do you think?" asked one of the men in the back row.

Instead of whether the government was right or wrong, the discussion shifted to how the hopes of the young, ambitious Vietnamese did not match what they heard from the government: the professed state versus their perceptions of the economy, the culture, the growth. The mismatch appeared to be a lag between the professed condition and the perceived actual position. The MBAs' frustration emerged perhaps partly because of their youthful impatience, and perhaps also because of their own views of what should happen.

A similar situation can emerge in organizations where professed support for innovation and actual culture supporting it diverge. Culture generally refers to a pattern of assumptions and behaviors that a group of people share, which may be within an organization, profession, geographic location, or ethnic group. In Vietnam's context, it means encouraging entrepreneurial behavior without rocking the political boat, protecting new businesses while providing needed social services. In the context of the organizations trying to urge creative and innovative endeavors, it means shaping an environment that supports the generation of ideas from a wide range of organizational members, and nurtures and protects ideas, once they emerge.[6]

As the young Vietnamese made clear that steamy night, professing growth and entrepreneurial spirit and actualizing it is difficult. Likewise, professing an organizational culture that promotes creativity and innovation, and actually having one, may be different. Any employee will know it.

So what are the characteristics of firms that know and show cultures that encourage creativity and innovation? In our investigations and from many other researchers' findings as well, several common aspects emerge. They start with simply making creativity and innovation a stated—and actual—part of the culture, even part of the mission of an organization: to know it and show it.

Shaping an organization's culture to create and protect ideas demands at least three elements. First, organizations need to broaden the pool of people from which they draw ideas. Rather than designating or depending upon a few people, organizations need to expand the periphery of ideas.

Next, the culture or environment needs to be open to and protective of ideas. Think of the last time you had a "great idea," and how vulnerable it was. All too often, other individuals and organizational obstacles squelch ideas at their earliest stages. So organization members need to understand how the culture can encourage or hamper ideas. Finally, ideas may jump, crawl, or just simmer—and organizations need to be aware of whether and how ideas may flow within the culture.

The Danger of "Idea Central": When Too Many Depend upon Too Few

Healthwise founder Don Kemper is considered within, and outside, of his organization to be an extraordinary creative entrepreneur. He is "idea central" for his organization, and in some ways, for patient-focused health care more broadly. He's identified several trends in the health-care industry that have changed the industry's perspectives and direction. Starting with the notion of patients as active participants in their health care, he has introduced ideas that continue to shape the industry's future, ranging from providing a handbook for use at home, to Internet information, to information therapy—information delivered at the right time, place, and manner for patients. Even his employees say that "Don does the big innovations; we do the smaller creative stuff."

Now in his early sixties, Kemper shows no signs of slowing down. Yet, his board, his managers, and his employees—let alone industry colleagues—are irresponsible if they do not ask: "What if he weren't here? What would we do?" Partly because of this, Kemper and Healthwise have begun an earnest attempt to push the responsibility of coming up with ideas to other levels of the organization. Healthwise is seeking to avoid the trap that some organizations fall into of identifying, explicitly or not, a key person or persons who are seen as the main idea generators.

Falling into the danger of relying on "idea central" can be risky for several reasons. First, as an organization's environment changes, it will likely need more brainpower and ideas. Russ Whitney, ProClarity's R&D manager, was concerned that his company, especially in its early years, limited itself by depending too much on too few, and needed to expand who was involved: "[A startup company] can ride solo in the market [for a while]. Then it proves there's a viable market. And guess what? You've just invited lots of competition. The problem is that in our firm, [just] a few people were trying to figure out what to do [next] and how to do it. And [we're] only going to be able to do so much with limited brain power." ProClarity sought to avoid narrowness by having a creative entrepreneurial team of three people. In software, the environment changes rapidly, includes multiple global competitors, and faces trends that shift daily. As a small, remotely located business intelligence analysis firm, that has meant understanding customers, technology trends, and financial markets better than other firms in their markets. For that organization, a three-pronged team of top executives watched externally, with a focus on each of the three areas: market and customer trends, financial markets, and technology.

But it didn't work as planned. The CEO explained that he and his two colleagues scoured the environment for trends, and then identified what types of solutions the firm should create for the problems they found. They became, in essence, idea central. Over the longer run, that approach failed for at least two reasons. The developers saw their work becoming more "carry out what they tell us to do" rather than having any creative input. The creative entrepreneurial team recognized that they had been trying to "give the solution" rather than to provide the problem. When they thought in terms of problems, the developers generated multiple solutions, and more variety led to better solutions. And it created an environment in which people can grow. It also emphasizes, as noted in chapter 5, that the process includes multiple steps and iterations between an idea and its realization.

A second danger is that with an idea central, other organizational members become complacent. When organizations depend upon a few people for ideas, or worse, allow structural inefficiency, like ingrained hierarchy, to limit ideas, employees feel reluctant or apathetic about speaking up. If they refrain from offering ideas, communication fails, and firms may ultimately limit their ability to compete.[7] Employees withdraw from feeling a part of the organization and making it succeed. In addition, depending only upon top creative entrepreneurs and leaders may relieve others in the organization from the responsibility, expectation, and fun of being part of the idea-finding process. Further, without building a pool of others who can do the task, the organization as a whole may not gain the confidence it needs to take on the responsibility when the creative entrepreneur relinquishes it.

Third, depending upon one or a few idea generators can also mean dangers from long tails and "twitches": "Our CEO is an idea guy—he's always got a new idea. [But] he's at the head of something with a very long tail. From an R&D standpoint, any idea takes six, eight, twelve months to actually end up in the product. If you keep changing the mind all the time at the head, it's pretty difficult to actually ship a new product." As an organization grows, the "tail" from idea central to those implementing it may be too long. As the employee in our example suggests, it may take a long time for an idea to go from the center to the area of the organization where it will be carried out. In addition, if the idea generator "twitches"—revises or changes an idea—the implementers can feel they are being asked to change direction and purpose too often.

Fourth and finally, a reliance on idea central might start a process through which a few people think and act like they have (all) the answers. Strategy research indicates that an organization's capabilities and unique position emerges as the result of many small and large decisions and work.[8] Seldom are great strategic decisions the singular reason for success and competitive advantage. Making an organization creative requires creative decisions and actions across levels and units within the organization. One way to herald the importance of the many is to separate roles, power, and resources. Remember that we spoke in chapter 5 of how the circus had separated the executive management from the founder (creative entrepreneur). This is one way to temper involvement and to encourage more people to contribute.

Expanding the Periphery of Idea Generators

Given the dangers of depending upon idea central, some organizations have adopted ways to increase the numbers of idea generators by expanding the periphery or area from which to attract ideas. In a *Wall Street Journal* interview, the top three executives from Target, a high-performing U.S. retail firm, argued that being innovative in all areas, not just a few, is critical for their firm: "You can't be unique in one category. You can't be really mundane in small electrics if you're trying to be innovative in textiles.... You have to ... get more consistency across the board."[9] To achieve consistent and widespread innovation, more people from more parts of the organization need to be involved. As one high-tech firm manager says, the further down you go in the organization, the more people there are; the more people, the more touch points to the outside—they are where the action is.

Going where the action is in football means tapping people other than coaches for ideas. But the notion of creativity in sports, let alone by players, strikes some people as odd. During our interviews, several people, including former football players, commented that players do what they are told by coaches, period—no creativity, no going outside of the set expectations.

Yet some Boise State players mentioned that they "improvised" on the field. One offensive player described how, from one year to the next, he adjusted his running angle to block an oncoming defensive back from a team; he had not talked with his coaches about it, but rather, as he said, "I just improvised to make things work." Another commented that the team sometimes slightly adjusted a play to better fit what they read on the field; finally, a receiver used what his teammates called a "personal dance" as he took extra steps to move around a defensive block.

When former players and current coaches heard that players felt they improvised, some blanched. One former player (from a dozen years earlier) shook his head and commented that players were just supposed to do what they were told, not come up with new ideas. But some coaches smiled. One said," Of course [they improvise]. We *want* them to think. They're not puppets, just doing what we say. They are out on the field, *they see things the coaches can't ... and we've got to be willing to take some chances in what we do to be creative* [emphasis added]. You've got to be able to get your players to buy into taking some chances. To be creative, you have to be willing to deal with the fact that it is not going to be successful all the time."

Some firms expand their periphery of ideas by looking outside their own walls. They may seek ideas from people who they perceive to be close to the market or who see trends that might create new markets. Target's top marketing and other executives hire people from around the United States and beyond to feed ideas back to the company. Such trend spotters can be in the movie world, advertising, or other fields where they are likely to pick up ideas. A recent "stack" of ideas was on sustainability and green issues. Others relate to architecture or merchandising or technology. These networks of people provide input to the creative process. Encouraging ideas from the periphery helps the firm stay ahead of competition and take advantage of innovation.

Finally, some organizations encourage "stealth creativity," which happens when employees far down the organization pursue ideas without the senior managers' knowledge. Best Buy's "smashing the clock" was classic stealth creativity.[10] Two managers recognized the toll that the company's time-focused culture had begun taking on employees. The firm's culture drove productivity by insisting on disciplined time management. For years, employees had to sign out at lunch, give their estimated return time, and track their work every fifteen minutes. Such focus led to unexpected outcomes: employees felt they needed to sneak into their buildings if they were late, or discover ways to appear to be "in the office" when they weren't. Two managers saw a need for change.

Without senior management's knowledge, or approval, two middle-level managers developed and implemented a new approach: "the results-only work environment," or ROWE. It focused on end results, not time spent in the office. The managers, and the other employees who used it, developed and applied ROWE as a "stealth innovation," without the CEO's knowledge. He found out about it only two years after it had begun—and then he lauded their efforts and initiative. Many new developments in companies depend on people who take the initiative and chisel out resources to work on their idea. They often do not come from management. John Seely Brown, based on his long history of technology and organizational development, says that "the best products are often the product of 'renegades' on the periphery of the company."[11]

Interestingly, some organizations formally acknowledge such stealth innovation. One software firm has a Jesse James award for an employee who comes up with and implements an idea that is "under the radar," and yet turns out to be valuable. Yet, one former employee who won the award found it ironic that the company talked innovation and yet the biggest award an employee could gain was one that was for an unsanctioned idea!

Shaping Culture: Nurturing and Protecting Ideas

> A new idea is delicate. It can be killed by a sneer or a yawn; it can be stabbed to death by a quip and worried to death by a frown on the right man's brow.
>
> Charles Brower, advertising executive

Years ago, a German colleague asked how Americans nurture friendships. For a man to ask such a question was a shock in itself—typically it's women who consider how to care for relationships. But *nurture* is an appropriate word for friendships, which need care and time for long-term survival and growth.[12]

In a different vein, the remarkable nature series Planet Earth shows example after example of animals nurturing and protecting their young. Baby elephants defy logic by running almost underneath their lumbering mothers; penguins lift their soft bulk up and over the bodies of chicks unable to walk.

Just as friendships and baby animals need to be nurtured and protected, so too with ideas. Without it, they, like the species, will be extinct. Organizations that shape their cultures and environments to nurture and care for ideas are likely to succeed in generating and keeping some good ones. We'll talk about several ways that organizations do just that: (1) cultural porosity and permeability; (2) "using the whole pigeon"; (3) "just say yes"; and (4) protection from "swamping out."

Cultural Porosity and Permeability: Helping Ideas Move

Geophysicists study the material that lies beneath the earth's surface to look for oil and other natural resources. They use a method called tomography, which is much like medical imaging. To learn what's underground, they drill boreholes, place senders and receivers in the boreholes, and transmit electromagnetic or seismic waves through the earth. A borehole is typically six to twelve inches in diameter, made from a pipe of steel or PVC, or no liner at all in consolidated materials. Geophysicists drill at least two boreholes, but can use as many as needed, depending upon the purpose of their investigation. A site outside of Boise, Idaho, for example, has six holes in a circle about one hundred feet in diameter. Borehole depth is a function of the geologic material the scientists want to investigate; for ground water, they may drill 200 feet, but for petroleum, many thousands of feet.

In one borehole, a sender initiates the waves, which move toward the borehole with receivers. The sender drops down the hole every foot or two, sends a wave, and then drops down another foot or two, repeating the wave-sending process as deep as the geophysicists need it. The waves go to borehole receivers, which are at one- to two-foot intervals down the depth of the receiving borehole (see Figure 8.1). Depending upon the frequency and velocity of the waves that pass from the senders to the receivers, geophysicists can tell what geologic material exists between boreholes. Because rock differs from soil, which differs from soil with water in it, which differs from oil, and so on, the waves passing through rock will differ from those passing through soil, or soil and water.

In this aspect of tomography, scientists are especially interested in two properties of the geologic material: porosity and permeability. According to Boise State University geophysicist Jack Pelton, porosity refers to the "void space" per unit volume; more void spaces within a given subsurface region means more porosity. The void spaces are important because they hold the material like oil or water. Of even greater importance, though, is whether void spaces are connected. When they are not, the material within them does not flow. When there are cracks or fractures connecting the void space, however, fluid materials can move more easily, making the subsurface more permeable.

When that happens, water or oil or gas can flow between and among void spaces. Thus, the more connections, or cracks and fractures in the earth's matter, the more permeable it is. Sometimes, the void spaces are connected naturally; other times, scientists introduce artificial fractures to induce flow of fluids (see Figure 8.2).

Figure 8.1. Boreholes

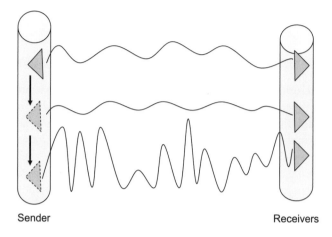

Sender   Receivers

The notions of porosity and permeability may be useful metaphors for an organization's culture as well. Porosity in a culture would mean having special void spaces, or units where ideas start, bubble, and simmer. In a high-tech firm, programmers may work independently but are physically nearby, exchange ideas within the group through "scrum meetings," and talk over e-mail or texts when they don't talk face to face. So within their "void space," ideas bubble. The spaces may be somewhat isolated, but in a sense, that can protect them when they are early stage.

Cultural permeability is important when ideas need to flow within the organization. For a high-tech firm, as the ideas simmer and become ones that

Figure 8.2. Porosity and Permeability

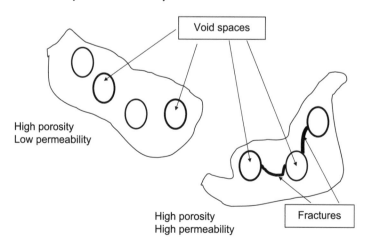

need more review and shaping, they need to be able to move from a small scrum group to others, whether in user experience or to people more involved with other customers. If a culture is full of obstacles and is hard to penetrate, ideas themselves may become set, unable to be nurtured and grow. When the organization's culture has fractures or cracks, or networks within (and without) to allow flow of ideas, then they move more freely.

Of course, the amount of idea flow differs between types of organizations. In football, the position coaches operate within their own void spaces, working out ideas for defensive or offensive plays. They have little incentive to move ideas from one to the other because the players do not interact on the field. Yet, the special teams void space does need to allow ideas of plays to flow between it and the other two position groups. The "cracks" in football planning and flow of ideas can be quite simple: in Boise, a large room covered with white boards becomes the focal point for coaches to come in, put play ideas on their boards, and review what is appearing from other coaches on other boards.

Thus, organizations may need to review both their porosity (void spaces) and permeability (flow) as possible trace elements of culture to act as catalysts that ideas can and do move as well as they might.

Using the Whole Pigeon

In Vietnam, "friendly dinners" to honor foreign guests happen regularly. One evening, an American banker visited old Vietnamese friends who wanted to treat him to a special dinner. The dozen people settled at a lakeside table, with a gentle breeze kicking up on the lake, and ordered beer. Gracious as ever, his friends asked what he might like for dinner.

"Fowl? Do you eat fowl?"

"Sure, just no fish, thanks."

More beer and at last the meal: vegetables, rice, soup, and several small birds, including head and feet, landed in the center of the table.

"Pigeon," one of the hosts said, his mouth nearly watering over the bird.

"I can handle this," thought the guest of honor, "but it doesn't seem to have a lot of meat on it."

As his hosts portioned out the bird thigh, wing, and breast, the guest waited, his bowl empty. Finally, his host stood and bowed toward him, chop sticks holding the pigeon head, as he placed it in his honored guest's bowl.

"In Vietnam, we use the whole pigeon. But the head is the best part and you are our guest."

A second way that organizations nurture ideas is by "using the whole pigeon"—to be open to all sorts of ideas and look beyond the obvious use of an idea. Many managers and employees we talked with commented that they gathered, and whenever possible used, all parts and types of ideas, even parts that didn't initially seem appealing. Sometimes, what may seem like an unappealing head or feet may turnout to be the "best part."

Healthwise, which some employees claim is too "meeting happy," strives to be open to ideas from anyone in the organization. People and ideas are not "shut out" and can attend meetings, give ideas, from any part of the organization. Interestingly, some people may suggest ideas they don't think are valuable, but discover others can nevertheless use them. Because the pattern of "crazy ideas that someone finds useful" has continued, organization members have learned to encourage and listen to all sorts of ideas. Healthwise's Geoff Moore puts it this way: "I am amazed at how ideas are thrown out [in a meeting]. Some people may not even think [their idea is] a good idea when they say it, but people hear things differently ... and it is all about how you use what you hear. Multiple people hear different things but the original person may not even mean it that way, but then you take it and then you combine those thoughts into a tangible product." Thus, openness to the whole pigeon may nurture unexpected idea rewards.

Just Say "Yes"

How many of us consistently embrace new ideas? When they mean we'll have to learn something new, behave in a different way, or change our patterns of thinking—the first response is, why change?

In his book *A Sense of Direction*, legendary theatre director William Ball commented that, alone, he could not possibly come up with the best ideas for a given play.[13] So, to encourage a creative environment and get the best from all involved, he tried to "say yes" to ideas or suggestions that came up from actors, designers, or anyone involved in a production. Imagine some of the conversation:

> *Actor:* Could I try saying this line while holding the apple on my head?
> *Ball:* Yes.
> *Actor:* Could I read the line faster and with a Jersey accent?
> *Ball:* Yes.
> *Marketing director:* Could we put a Nike logo on Julius Caesar's toga?
> *Ball:* Hmmmmm.

Of course, Ball had not said that he would accept and use each idea, just that he would be open to hearing and considering it. An idea might not be useful, but by simply "saying yes," the idea was public, the director modeled the behavior he wanted from his actors—that they would be willing to listen and try ideas he might propose that were foreign to them.

Some master idea nurturers, like Ball, have used a simple phrase as a way to open their own minds and ears to allow new ideas in. Granted, only two in a hundred ideas may succeed, but as one manager says, "you never know which ones those two might be."

Risa Brainin, a University of California professor and a theatre director, uses a process called "leading from behind." While she may have many of the ideas for a production settled in her mind, she seeks to remain open to theatre company member ideas throughout the process. She does so partly because actors do bring new ideas that are useful for the production, but almost more so to gain buy-in from those actors as they create and deliver the production: "Instead of me saying what I think should happen, I try to get the actor to find [out what to do], so they own it. I want everyone from the designers to technicians to actors feel they own a piece of this."

An example for how you can encourage ideas and suggestions for new concepts and offerings comes from the circus. As artists and creators show that they have an interesting idea and a suggestion for what they should set up, the artistic director or the head of production have a discussion with the person. While it is sometimes difficult to start right at that moment due to timing and resources, they see when it could be possible, discuss the person's role to take it forward, and, assuming they agree to do it, start looking for resources or schedule when they start doing it. In this way they say, "yes … but," to balance the initiative and resource requirements over time.

In addition to openness to ideas, no matter how unlikely, members of creative organizations have an unusually nondefensive attitude about considering ideas as well as accepting the notion that that not all ideas work.[14] Remarkably, when we talked to—and returned again to talk to—people in the cases we examined, they were nondefensive about trying ideas and using their own organizations as testing grounds. Members were willing to talk openly about their organization's desire to improve, and frequently willing to share failures. As we mentioned earlier, the business analysis software firm with the book group experiments with ideas in a unit for six weeks or so, and then decides whether to integrate it throughout the organization. If the idea works, they pursue it; if it does not, they drop it. There is no concern about having tried something and failed; rather, the focus is more to "just say yes" for a while and decide on the merits of a new product, process, or mode of operating.

Protection from Swamping Out

A method for protecting ideas in their early stages comes from evolutionary biology, a field that has long discussed the fate of new ideas—or in its case, new genetic variants.[15] Biological evolution is the genetic change that happens in a population when a new genetic variant becomes more prevalent in that population. However, the rate of evolution can actually be quite slow in a large population. This happens because of swamping out of a new genetic variant by the myriad of existing genetic variants in the population. Geneticist Sewell Wright first recognized that evolution proceeds more rapidly in smaller, isolated populations where adaptation to a particular environment can occur, where random genetic drift might happen, and where genes from the rest of the population are less common and thus less likely to "swamp out" the new genetic variant.

As a result, in a small and isolated population, the genetic variant is protected and nurtured, and may prevail in a local population. Then, if the variant is advantageous to the entire species, it can spread.

Just as populations in nature may evolve more quickly when new genetic variants avoid swamping out, organizations may likewise seek to reduce the chance of swamping out of emerging ideas. The notion is not new. The term *skunk works* has come to reflect a form of protection, in which a group works independently, sometimes secretively, on a project that may be unknown or unsanctioned by an organization's management.

The term's initial concept was a bit different. It began during World War II at the aircraft designer and manufacturer Lockheed. In June 1943, a group of Lockheed engineers began to work on the XP-80 airframe, for a new engine. The skunk works group began without an official contract for the job, which became fundamental to the idea. In fact, the group completed the project in less time than expected and about the time the formal contract was signed.

The legend of skunk works operations has thrived. Xerox's sequestered research group, Best Buy's "stealth innovation," and the quiet Jesse James award exemplify the spirit of nurturing and growing an idea in a smaller group or population, to avoid swamping out. Such groups tend to be small, somewhat separated from the main part of an organization, and often have a "protector," as we discussed in chapter 6 about one of the roles of creative leaders.

But skunk works, like other catalysts for creativity, may have drawbacks. While the concept of skunk works is exhilarating, it could also signal management failure. If skunk works groups are necessary for the production of new ideas, perhaps it signals that the rest of an organization lacks the practices, culture, and structure conducive to encourage innovative endeavors.[16] After all, wouldn't it be better if innovation were nurtured throughout an organization rather than in only a particular group? Thus, the advantages of skunk works may need to be considered in light of what else goes on in an organization. Also, Xerox for one has found the challenge of bringing the good ideas back into the larger organization daunting. Instead, the ideas—of which many are of great magnitude—have been acquired by others that have achieved great success with them.[17]

Evolutionary biology offers other metaphors when we examine small and isolated populations. As we've suggested, genetic change or ideas in isolated populations may result from adaptation to a local environment. If the group is not isolated, its members would face the scrutiny of a larger group as well as its rules and regulations. Genetic change can also occur as a result of genetic drift, which comes from random variation in the survival of genes. In other words, the genetic makeup of a population or group will tend to "drift" or change over time. Genetic drift may be similar to the way in which isolated groups come up with different solutions to the same problem. Finally, chance may play a role. In isolated groups within organizations, the right combination of individuals may generate chemistry and interaction to produce remarkable new innovations. In evolution, a genetic variant could be in the wrong place at the wrong time, and as a result, fizzle and die. In the case of an idea, it could be in the wrong place at the wrong time and suffer a similar fate.

Change = Culture

Change happens in all organizations, and sometimes it becomes a core value. In the formative work around an experimental IT research institute in Sweden in the early 1990s, the people from what later became the Interactive Institute met with MIT Media Lab. Media Lab was considering an expansion to Europe, and was in discussions with Sweden and other countries to determine the best site. The people from MIT clearly favored an institute located in central Stockholm, with its entire staff concentrated there. The parties disagreed, and MIT established themselves in Ireland.

Interactive Institute's model instead became almost the opposite. A number of studios were established across Sweden, each with a research theme. Each studio had a five-year lifespan. When the five years were up, the studio had to either close or find a new theme to research. This provided the impetus for continuous renewal and reexamination of the research and the constellations for doing the research.

When change is a constant, as it has been in many of the organizations we have studied, you need to create stability while organizational structures and processes change. One such stabilizer is keeping a management team or core leadership the same. Several of the organizations have done this. Such continuity gives consistency of purpose and also gives the management team time to develop experience and skills for managing turbulent development processes.

This brings us to the next section, suggesting that creativity resides with organizations, groups, and people in the world surrounding you.

TRACING BOUNDARIES: THE CREATIVITY SYSTEM

The culture in creative organizations is shaped through interaction with the broader networks and community in which the organization works. Organizations, individuals, authorities, and the general community of the company come to play a part in how it develops. We have seen this happen in different ways: through the blogs and communities in which the software developers interact and share tips and ideas; through the communities of artists both for the theatre and the circus, from which the people of a certain performance are chosen; in the interaction of the circus with local developers and working to get the community in which they are located to grow and change; and in the number of interactions between small/micro companies within the creative industries, working both to develop knowledge and competence, but also looking to identify common business opportunities. The list could go on.

Naturally some of this attention relates to online communities, which have surged with interest around social networks.

These creative ecosystems are important for an individual organization's ability to get resources, identify new ideas, exchange knowledge and competence, and find strength and a voice for large-scale community development. This goes beyond loosely coupled networks of people. More formal systems are those that exist between different cocreators of product, for example, suppliers, customers, and other companies within the value chain, of code that goes into a final product, and of user-generated content, products, and services.

In sports, both players and coaches acknowledge the importance of spending time away from work—off the field—as a way to build networks, understand one another, and perform better at work because of it. They encourage networks formally, through structure, and informally, by supporting outside work endeavors. One offensive-line football player made a point to get to know teammates who played other positions. The informal, off-the-field interactions helped him understand how the other players thought and worked: "So in the locker room and hanging out—you interact with everybody ... linemen, freshman, receivers, and offense and defense players. What it all comes down to is you're a team—you have to interact ... with your teammates."

One coach reflected the same sentiments in terms of how much the coaches interact with each other over years and different teams: "You have these long partnerships ... coaches move [to universities] together. I mean, it's 'in the trenches.' They spend a lot of hours together. They have to kind of like each other, but not always, because they do have some disagreements [but work them out]."

The point is that networks and the extended organization repeatedly play a role in finding, spreading, and building ideas to final delivery. Creative organizations should consider how informal networks can enable members to see beyond their own disciplines and areas, understand the organization's goals as a whole, and gain ideas from outside of their disciplines. Organizations can also get support from informal networks in idea generation.

TRACE ELEMENTS: THE MAGIC MAKERS

This chapter has focused on trace elements, the catalytic elements that encourage efficient and effective reactions that support creativity and innovation. Consider the following for your organization:

- *Find and create magic!* Employees crave magic at work—having the authority, freedom, and time to work on their ideas. When they find it, they seem more involved and committed.

- *Value trace elements:* These small, often overlooked elements of organizational practice, culture, and connection play a significant role in the success of a creative business. They are catalysts that increase the sparks of creativity and innovation in number, quality, and implementation potential.

- *Trace elements of practice:*
  1. Fit: There is a contradiction between fit and diversity, both are necessary to spark creativity. Managers look for people passionate about what the company does—passion overpowers fit and diversity as the real driver of creativity.
  2. Expectations: If creativity is expected from everyone, they need evidence that it is measured and leads to progress and recognition. Shared symbols and routines reinforce key values.
  3. Recognition: Rewarding those who come up with something new and publicly recognizing their merits boost innovation and commitment to the company.

- *Trace elements of culture:*
  1. Know it and show it: Put creativity and innovation at the heart of the culture.
  2. Expand the periphery of idea generators: Depending on "idea central" is dangerous and ineffective; more people from more parts of the organization need to be involved if the firm wants to achieve a consistent and widespread innovation.
  3. Maintain an open and protective culture for ideas: Allow for void spaces (porosity) where ideas can start and simmer, and for fractures (permeability) within the organization and with the outside, so that ideas can flow. Be open to hearing and considering—not necessarily accepting—each idea (just say yes) in all its aspects, even those that are less appealing at first (whole pigeon). Give ideas a chance to develop without being overwhelmed.

- *Tracing boundaries:* The creativity system relies on interaction with a number of people, organizations, and communities inside and outside the organization. Build your platform and approach to do this over time.

In the final chapter of the book, we will bring together some of these ideas, yet focus on the big picture again.

NOTES

1. J. Andrews. 1996. "Creative Ideas Take Time: Business Practices That Help Product Managers Cope with Time Pressure," *Journal of Product and Brand Management* 5 (1): 6–18.

2. As the focus on a creative economy increases, the emphasis on how and whether employees have the chance to be creative at work arises. The survey done during summer 2007 will likely be the start of many such surveys and more discussion. See Andrew R. McIlvaine. 2007. "Creativity and the Organization," *Human Resource Executive Online* September 27. See study at http://home.businesswire.com/portal/site/google/index.jsp?ndmViewId=news_view&newsId=20070921005064&newsLang=en.

3. Jim Collins. 2001. *Good to Great.* New York: HarperCollins.

4. Coaches in many sports and levels (college and professional) have talked of the challenges of focusing on a team, rather than the stars of the group. The Los Angeles Lakers have been among the most visible. See Phil Jackson and Michael Arkush. 2004. *The Last Season: A Team in Search of Its Soul.* New York: Penguin Group; Mark Heisler. 2004. *Madmen's Ball: The Inside Story of the Lakers' Dysfunctional Dynasties.* Chicago: Triumph Books.

5. The Boise State football field went from green to blue turf in 1986. To date, it remains the only royal blue college football Astroturf field in the United States. The team, the coaches, even some community members mention the "turf" as something that suggests a willingness to be different and creative.

6. Eric G. Flamholtz and Rangapriya Kannan-Narasimhan. 2007. "The Role of Effective Organizational Culture in Fostering Innovation and Entrepreneurship," in T. Davila, Marc J. Epstein, and Robert Shelton. *The Creative Enterprise: Managing Innovation Organizations and People.* Westport, CT: Praeger, 123–154.

7. Even the general press is focusing on such silence and complacency. See Kelley Holland. 2006. "The Silent May Have Something to Say," *New York Times,* November 5: B5.

8. See, for example, Nicolaj Siggelkow. 2001. "Change in the Presence of Fit: The Rise, the Fall, and the Renaissance of Liz Claiborne." *Academy of Management Journal* 44:838–857; Jan W. Rivkin and Nicolaj Siggelkow. 2003. "Balancing Search and Stability: Interdependencies among Elements of Organizational Design." *Management Science* 49:290–311. Also, Henry Mintzberg has done a lot of work in this area.

9. For the full article and interview with Target's executives, see Ann Zimmerman. 2007. "Staying on Target," *Wall Street Journal,* May 7: B13.

10. See Michelle Conlin. 2006. "Smashing the Clock," *BusinessWeek,* December 11: 60, 62–66.

11. John Seely Brown. 1991. "Research That Reinvents the Corporation," *Harvard Business Review* (January–February): 110.

12. For more on friendships, especially among women, see Ellen Goodman and Patricia O'Brien. 2000. *I Know Just What You Mean.* New York: Simon & Schuster.

13. William Ball. 1984. *A Sense of Direction.* New York: Drama Publishers.

14. This notion of openness to failure remains one of the most common important in the creative process, yet apparently one of the most difficult for organizational members to accept. See Bernard Ghiselin. 1952. *The Creative Process.* New York: Mentor Books; Jeff Mauzy and Richard Harriman. *Creativity, Inc.* 2003. Boston: Harvard Business School Press.

15. Many of the ideas in this section stem from conversations with Jim Munger, Boise State University biologist and Associate Vice President for Academic Planning, June and August 2007.

16. See Terrence E. Brown. 2001. "Skunk Works: A Sign of Failure, A Sign of Hope?" Paper presented at the Future of Innovation Studies Conference, The Eindhoven Centre for Innovation Studies, Eindhoven University of Technology, The Netherlands, September 20–23.

17. John Seely Brown. 1998. "Seeing Differently: A Role for Pioneering Research," *Research Technology Management* 41 (3): 24–33.

Chapter 9

CREATIVITY AND INNOVATION AS COMPETITIVE ADVANTAGE: MOVING TARGET?

On the outskirts of Shanghai, 1,000 researchers are working in a state of the art Intel research facility that was built from scratch in just five months. By 2012 there could be 10,000 spread over two sites.... On the edge of Delhi, among the call centres and new shopping malls, Ranbaxy, the Indian drug company, has opened a research and development (R&D) centre with 2,000 scientists, modelled on a Bristol Myers Squibb facility in the U.S.

The Atlas of Ideas, 2007

We close the book with a question that has been underlying throughout: How are organizations, communities, and regions using the art and science of creative discipline as a competitive advantage? We'll review some of the key points that are important for leaders of organizations at any level that are building the capabilities to make them winners in the creative economy. To stay ahead, organizations and their members need to focus on the art and science of the creative discipline.

CREATIVITY AND INNOVATION ARE ESSENTIAL: ART AND DISCIPLINE

Our premise in this book is that creativity and innovation are driving competitive advantage and subsequently an organization's performance. Organizations we worked with recognize that developing new or novel, valuable ideas helps drive performance and create opportunity. Creativity and innovation as a way to create advantage appear in our case organizations in two ways.

First, creative organizations develop and market new and novel products, services, performances, and offerings in a wide sense that appeal to a market. Individuals and organizations buy and use software for decision making; customers buy tickets to enjoy theatre, or circus, or sports performances; still others want to better understand, manage, and adapt to medical conditions, and thus draw upon available information that educates them. Because customers desire—and pay for—these products or services, the organizations thrive.

Second, the organizations channel creativity into developing new and improved ways of working, including, for example, steps and tools for internal as well as external development processes, methods and approaches to managing the development process, improved contracts and working conditions for creative people, new roles within the organizations, as well as niches in different markets. This creativity appears as new business models (e.g., the circus engaging with local authorities to develop educational programs and performances, or the theatre doing performances in two different markets so it can contract actors for longer periods), in new ways of delivering their product to customers (such as the Ix for health-information delivery), in enhanced labor practices (longer contracts in the theatre, or insurance for circus artists), or in approaches to environmental scanning (such as the software company's involvement of people across the organization).

Each organization has its own way of doing it, but they all adhere to a disciplined approach of generating new ideas and finding areas to develop; testing ideas in their organizations, with partners, and in markets; and learning from results and feedback. Experiential learning not only improves their products, services, and offerings, but also results in new processes, procedures, or roles.

These processes employ a disciplined approach, but they also develop disciplinary powers, the silent yet pervasive structures that permeate how these organizations perceive and address creative work and the development of innovations. In this sense it includes and is expressed in the context—the faces, places, and traces—required for creativity and innovation. By having both the explicit approaches to disciplined creativity (3D) and the tacit contextual dimensions (the three "aces") present, the organizations advance the art and science of creativity and innovation.

The members of the creative organizations we examined acknowledge that they must continue to develop the capabilities necessary for creativity and innovation for business and economic success. Two points are important to remember. First, organizations must move far beyond "finding an edge" and must excel at execution. We'll discuss each in more depth in the following sections.

Going beyond the "Edge"

It is not enough for organizations to maintain an edge—they must go further. They are competing against many different types of groups and in many places. Across geographies and across industries, the race for creativity as a driver of innovation and entrepreneurship is on—in small and large organizations, in the public and private sectors, and in developing and developed economies. Many of the organizations, communities, and regions recognize that they are unable to operate in isolation, so they are purposefully seeking connections to spur creativity and innovation.

When A. G. Lafley became Chairman and CEO of Procter & Gamble, he identified the company's external connections as a great resource for new and profitable products and offerings. To build on this realization, he set a lofty goal: 50 percent of all P&G's innovations should come externally—whether from other companies, public or private R&D units, or wherever they could be found across a vast landscape of innovators. However, they were not intended to replace existing labs, marketing organizations, or technology development within P&G. Instead, they wanted to identify external ideas, products, and concepts that could grow and become successful by being brought through the P&G organization. Its strengths in marketing, distribution, and R&D became a platform for making the smaller firms successful and by linking them closely with P&G. In a sense, the company went beyond creating an edge—it created a new approach to business for itself. Through this purposeful and structured out-of-discipline thinking—the Connect and Develop Invention model—Procter & Gamble is developing the knowledge and skills of people, working through networks to find and select ideas and products, and developing a structure with roles and a new culture that can bring high levels of top-line growth. That is growth the company did not think would come through its previous, and the industry's traditional, innovation model based on internally focused R&D and invention, supplemented with acquisitions, alliances, and skunk works.[1]

Companies like IDEO, Google, P&G, Apple, Toyota, Nokia, and Sony, as well as smaller organizations across the globe, some of which we have introduced in this book, are developing ways to make creativity and innovation a part of their ongoing activities. Using a disciplined process and creative roles to support it, they are finding new ways to work within the organizations, build bridges to other organizations and networks, and drive a process of creativity forward. It is happening in the business world—and, as we saw, in many other sectors beyond.

Execution, Execution

Strategies vary, but are not enough. Execution will be key. To get ahead requires a disciplined approach to execute initiatives and to keep on doing it. Creative organizations learn from mistakes and successes, and continuously develop a disciplined approach to creativity and innovation. We believe a useful starting point to be the framework laid out in this book. This framework consists of two parts: three "disciplines"—the three core disciplines that organizations need to build the capacity for creativity and innovation; and a circle of three "aces," factors that can enhance, or inhibit, those creative disciplines.

Our framework is a starting point for considering elements that creative organizations pursue to enhance creativity and innovation. While we focused on a key element of the framework within each chapter, the people we interviewed frequently reminded us that talk was easy, but carrying out the activities related to a creative process or to supporting the trace elements was quite difficult. Even more, they reminded us that the pieces had to all fit together tightly—one was unlikely to succeed unless all components were integrated. To achieve this tight fit, whatever the starting point, once resources and people are allocated to upgrade creative and innovative capabilities, the development will affect other areas and processes—in your organization and among those with whom you collaborate. And just what should be your starting point? Many leaders start with what they have and are strong in. But they recognize this can be dangerous and lead to complacency. Many routinely push to change areas where the organization is weak and find ways to challenge it to be more creative. One firm in Vietnam, for instance, reorganizes its structure and rethinks and changes its product/service mix on a regular basis, almost yearly. By forcing its employees to change regularly, the senior managers instill a sense of "let's try this and if it doesn't work, we'll try something else." In a country where creativity is not encouraged in schools, such an approach in the workplace forces people to constantly rethink the way things "should" be done.

So, maintaining an edge is not enough. The other teams, organizations, communities, and regions are working hard to move their edge outbound. And they are active. Many invest in places, people and initiatives, engage private as well as public partners to develop skills, knowledge, and culture, and acquire and develop the skills and knowledge of disciplined processes and tools to measure, test, and implement what is required to ensure that creativity and innovation are at the heart of their competitive advantage. You should too.

THE CREATIVE DISCIPLINE: AT THE HEART

This book is titled *Creative Discipline* because we have found that creative organizations have discipline at the heart of what they do, and it permeates how they do things: discipline in a wide sense; discipline as an area of knowledge and competence that members of an organization need and develop over time; discipline as an openness to bring in outside ideas that members need to foster creativity; discipline as a systematic approach, or disciplined process, to generate, test, and use ideas. Together, they comprise creative discipline.

The framework's six elements are the building blocks to such a disciplined approach (see Figure 9.1). The inner triangle makes up the three core disciplines that organizations need for building creativity and innovation. Its outer circle includes factors that can enhance, or inhibit, those creative disciplines, and are the three "aces," or in our terms, the faces, places, and traces.

The disciplines and the process to grow and nurture them is as much about the formulation of a strategy as it is of execution. Organizations that excel at this, and score high on creativity and innovation, work through a combination of top-down and bottom-up processes. There are no grand strategy masters

Figure 9.1. The Creative Discipline Framework

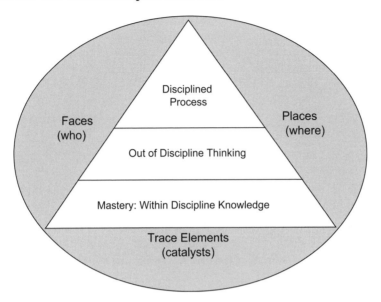

mapping out the way forward and the architecture to execute. With creative discipline, managers and employees alike take ownership to encourage creativity and innovation, and spearhead entrepreneurial ventures.

What makes this possible, and why it is also hard, are disciplined processes. These processes emerge and interact over time, creating an intermeshed system for creativity. These are not by-the-numbers descriptions of how to do things. However, they provide the guidance yet give leeway to the individuals and the groups that are working to solve problems, develop ideas into solutions, and find the work practices that are necessary to bring creative ideas to the market. At the same time they provide a platform for experiential learning, a focused process for continuous development.

The processes have performance measures. They are focused on the necessary, and avoid deflecting attention from creativity. The software company, for instance, separated logistics and project management, so that the choice would not be between deciding on the solutions and features of a product versus keeping on schedule and budget. Their measures and reporting system focus on making innovative products. The faces, the creative agents that own these processes, know this, and their measures and reporting can thus be aligned.

With all the building blocks in place and the people working hard to be creative and innovative, these organizations form a culture of experimentation and learning. This builds an organization versed in the art and science of innovation. To build it takes time to develop and requires a focused effort, combining strategy, execution, and entrepreneurship.

WHERE DO WE GO FROM HERE?

We hope that using and reinforcing the discipline(s) of this book will help your organization succeed in enhancing creativity and innovation. Innovation, and its precursor creativity, are forces that are hard to schedule, time, and operate in simple input-output models. But they can be developed and have payoffs—ideas big and small, some implementable now, some later, some which you can do on your own, others requiring partners; ideas that result in new products, services, and performances; ideas of new ways of operating or measuring what you do and how you do it.

People are the ones making creativity and innovation happen, through ideas, leadership, mentoring, bridging, and many other roles and actions. Focus on the framework, but do it through people. Adapt your approach to them and your needs.

Now Start Doing Things!

Keep four things in mind as you start working on your creative and innovative capabilities:

- *Disciplined execution is driving development.* Only through doing it, and doing it in a systematic and purposeful way, can you learn and develop the art and science required.
- *Trial, error, learning, and retrying.* Remember that the creative process is wrinkled—it follows a path that jumps, moves forward and backward, and yet in the end reaches game day or opening night and thrives.
- *Ask questions!* Read on, learn more.
- *Expect to use time and resources.* These are long processes that should be anchored at all levels of the organization. Results will come along the way, and you will benefit from day one. But only if you stay with the program will you reap the full benefit, and make it the competitive advantage others want but can't achieve because it so hard to copy.

This is where we stop and you start. Good luck and enjoy the journey!

NOTE

1. For interesting descriptions of the Procter & Gamble development, see: A. T. Kearney. 2006. *Best Innovators: A Synopsis of the Second Annual European Innovators Roundtable.* Chicago: A. T. Kearney; and Jena McGregor. 2007. "P&G Asks: What's the Big Idea?" *Business Week*, May 4. P&G ranked seventh in *Business Week*'s annual survey of the world's most innovative companies, featured in the same issue.

Index

About the Authors

NANCY K. NAPIER is professor of international business and executive director of the Centre for Creativity and Innovation at Boise State University. Her most recent book is *Managing Relationships in Transition Economies* (Praeger, 2004). Her articles have appeared in such journals as *Creativity and Innovation Management, Journal of Cross-Cultural Psychology, Academy of Management Review,* and *Journal of Management Studies.* She is also cocreator and host of "Idaho Business Matters," a weekday radio program on NPR News 91.

MIKAEL NILSSON is an advisor and researcher on strategy, technology development, and the processes of innovation and change in a broad range of industries. He is currently program manager at the Knowledge Foundation, which focuses on driving Swedish competitiveness through knowledge and competence development. He has held positions at KPMG Consulting and Linköping University and has been a visiting fellow at MIT's Sloan School of Management.